Barcode in Back

D1256483

Protecting the Public?

Protecting the Public?
Detention and release of mentally disordered offenders

Tessa Boyd-Caine

WILLAN
PUBLISHING

Published by

Willan Publishing
Culmcott House
Mill Street, Uffculme
Cullompton, Devon
EX15 3AT, UK
Tel: +44(0)1884 840337
Fax: +44(0)1884 840251
e-mail: info@willanpublishing.co.uk
website: www.willanpublishing.co.uk

Published simultaneously in the USA and Canada by

Willan Publishing
c/o ISBS, 920 NE 58th Ave, Suite 300,
Portland, Oregon 97213-3786, USA
Tel: +001(0)503 287 3093
Fax: +001(0)503 280 8832
e-mail: info@isbs.com
website: www.isbs.com

First published 2010

ISBN   978-1-84392-527-9 hardback

British Library Cataloguing-in-Publication Data

A catalogue record for this book is available from the British Library

FSC
Mixed Sources
Product group from well-managed
forests and other controlled sources

Cert no. SGS-COC-2482
www.fsc.org
© 1996 Forest Stewardship Council

Project managed by Deer Park Productions, Tavistock, Devon
Typeset by GCS, Leighton Buzzard, Bedfordshire
Printed and bound by T.J. International, Padstow, Cornwall

Contents

Acknowledgements   *vii*
Preface   *ix*

1 Executive discretion and the rule of law   **1**
Introduction   1
Executive discretion and public policy   2
Operational differences   4
Separation of powers   9
The role of forensic psychiatry   10
Risk and dangerousness   14
The changing role of victims in policy and practice   16
Political sensitivities   21

2 Care and control   **24**
Introduction   24
Restricted patients   24
On legal decision-making: the origins of a research
  culture   30
Methodology   37

3 The operation of executive discretion   **44**
Introduction   44
The restricted patient population in England and
  Wales   45
Monitoring in the restricted patient system   48
Oversight and the independence of the Tribunal   54

The decision frame of executive discretion 56
The symbolic politics of public protection 72

4 **Relationships in the system of executive discretion** **79**
Introduction 79
Rights versus control 82
Getting risk right 93
Making it legal 97
Same data, different story 101
A question of risk 102

5 **Constructing 'the public'** **105**
Introduction 105
The changing roles of victims in decision-making 108
Conceptualizing 'the public' within executive discretion 115
Responses to victim involvement 125
The relationship between patients and the public 132
Politics, policies and protection 135

6 **Human rights and the restricted patient system** **143**
Introduction 143
Safeguarding human rights 144
Constructing patients' rights 149
Practicing a rights-based approach 156
The symbolic value of human rights 163

7 **Patient rights and public protection** **170**
Control through containment 170
The patient/public divide 174
The exercise of discretion 176
Rights versus protection 179
Conclusion 181

References *183*
Index *195*

Acknowledgements

As much as it defies orthodoxy to say so, I loved doing my PhD. This was thanks largely to excellent supervision and the ongoing support of great friends, colleagues and family. I undertook my doctorate at the London School of Economics and Political Sciences (LSE) primarily for the opportunity to work with Professors Paul Rock and Jill Peay. I could not have hoped for better supervisors. Their guidance challenged my own boundaries, as well as that of the terrain I was researching. Moreover, the immense respect with which they are held in their respective areas played no small role in the access I obtained to my own field of study. I am most appreciative of their ongoing advice, support and friendship. The Crime and Deviance research seminar at the LSE was another formative environment, albeit at times intimidating. A number of the chapters in this book began as papers to that group and I acknowledge their comments and suggestions with thanks. I also acknowledge institutional support in the form of scholarships and travel funding from the Department of Sociology, LSE and the Central Research Fund of the University of London; and the facilities of the Monash Centre at Prato, which made for the most pleasurable environment in which to draft a chapter.

I am grateful to Paul, Jill, Dr Linsay McGoey and to the publishers' reviewers who generously read parts or all of the first draft of this manuscript and provided insightful comments. Throughout the PhD and writing of this book many dear friends and family provided advice and support and I thank them also: Larry Boyd, Barbara Caine, Marina Carman, Megan Clinch, Krisztina Csedo, Peter Dunn, Kim Frost, Chris Hamilton, Emma Keene, Dominic Millgate, Eva

Neitzert, Ruth Poisson, Joanne Smith, Julie Stubbs, Gabrielle Walsh and Daniel Woods.

The care of family was a constant source of reassurance as well as providing wonderful locations for respite. I thank Boyds, Caines, Duffys and Murphys in that regard. I am particularly grateful to Barbara for comments on the final draft; and for an immense proofreading effort by Peter Duffy.

Finally, this work could not have been possible without the participation of practitioners, administrators and scholars in the field: Nigel Battson, Jon Basson, Richard Charlton, Jeremy Cooper, Nihal Danis, Mark Darby, Rowena Daw, Sarah Denvir, Nigel Eastman, Kelly Foreman, Julian Gibbs, Nick Hearn, Tony Maden, Richard Mendon, Elizabeth Moody, Claire Ratcliffe, Wendy Robinson, Lucy Scott-Moncrieff, Nigel Shackleford, Penny Snow, Tim Spencer-Lane, Sandra Sullivan, Geoff Tremelling and Jacqui Woodward-Smith. I hope the book provides some small return for their generosity of time and for their insights into the care, treatment and control of mentally disordered offenders.

This book is dedicated to Louise, Vanessa and Rebecca, who provided me with an idyllic Sydney beachside setting at an important point in the writing of it.

Preface

The separation of powers between executive and judicial functions is a crucial principle of law and justice and is central to most democratic penal systems. Yet the exercise of executive discretion remains a key element of decision-making in a number of areas of public policy. These range from the release of certain categories of criminal offenders, to assessing applications from refugees and asylum seekers. Most recently, the worldwide increase in anti-terrorism laws has featured an expansion of executive power on an unprecedented scale, from the detention of suspects without charge or trial, to extending police powers of surveillance and limiting movement. Far from an obsolete process, executive discretion seems to have increasing currency. The common element in each of these areas is the exercise of executive discretion over detention as a measure to contain certain people who are deemed to threaten public safety.

Protecting the Public? analyses the use of executive discretion at the intersection of the criminal justice and mental health systems, through an empirically grounded study of restricted patients in England and Wales. Restricted patients have been convicted of a criminal offence. Instead of being given a prison sentence, they are detained in hospital under the powers of the Mental Health Act 1983. This allows them to be detained indefinitely for the purpose of compulsory treatment of their mental disorder. Once a restricted patient, they become subject to executive discretion, *via* the powers vested in the Secretary of State. Decisions about the location and level of security of their detention; any change in those conditions; leave from that detention; and discharge to the community all require an order from the Secretary of State. The presence of an independent, quasi-judicial institution is reflected in the powers of the Mental Health Tribunal. However, the Tribunal's power over restricted patients is limited to discharging a patient from hospital into the community, either subject to ongoing conditions or unconditionally. While this is an essential element of the restriction process, it usually comes after a long period of care, treatment and detention, during which time patients have been solely subject to executive discretion.

The book explores what it is about this group of offenders that renders them subject to executive discretion. Why does a cabinet minister make decisions about their discharge and not the psychiatrists or hospitals usually authorized to do so for people detained under the compulsory provisions of mental health legislation? Why not the courts, tribunals and parole boards that determine the release of other offenders? What is it about the conflation of mental illness and criminal offending that necessitates a minister making decisions about movement and discharge, rather than the institutions usually charged with such responsibility?

Underpinning these questions is the increasing dominance of the public protection agenda in various areas of public policy. The function of executive discretion is directly related to the contemporary political (and hence policy) imperative to provide the public with a measure of protection. But this agenda begs many more questions. Who do we mean by 'the public'? How are they protected through the function of executive discretion? Conversely, how is the public protection agenda reflected in the decisions made under executive authority?

I first became interested in these questions through my professional role managing the forensic jurisdiction of the Mental Health Review Tribunal of New South Wales (Australia). At that time there was considerable concern among practitioners that overly cautious decision-making by government was constraining the therapeutic progress of patients. Yet others argued that public protection was the paramount issue and all other objectives, including therapeutic, were secondary. These arguments implied that the interests of patients and of the public were opposed. As a criminologist I was sceptical of such populist assumptions, but there was very little research or analysis to inform the debate. I also became interested in why the forensic jurisdiction had retained a role for ministerial decision-making about these offender-patients, when executive discretion had been eradicated from most other areas of the criminal justice system. The dearth of research in this area led me to undertake a doctorate at the London

School of Economics. There I conducted an empirical analysis of the restricted patient system in England and Wales and undertook some comparative research on the New South Wales forensic jurisdiction. The research was conducted from 2004–2007 and I was awarded my doctorate in 2008. This book is based upon that doctoral research.

The legislative frameworks for mental health law were under review in both England and New South Wales (NSW) at the time of my research. Amendments to the laws in each jurisdiction were introduced just after the completion of my fieldwork. In the case of NSW, those amendments brought to an end the executive's discretion over forensic patients. In England and Wales, executive authority remained. There, the administration of the restricted patient system shifted from the Home Office to the newly-created Ministry of Justice in 2008, including the relocation of the Mental Health Unit to the new Ministry. The Mental Health Review Tribunal was also affected by structural changes to the administration of courts and tribunals and it became the First-tier Tribunal (Mental Health).

These changes affected some of the focal institutions discussed in this book and, consequently, the operation of the mental health system itself. But it has not changed nearly as much as was proposed. Nor has it changed to the point where it is no longer recognizable. Most importantly, the structures, processes, objectives and outcomes of the restricted patient system have remained the same. Restricted patients are still subject to executive discretion. The Secretary of State still exercises that discretion. The Tribunal still has power over the ultimate question of discharge, but not about any of the crucial steps leading to that point. The civil servants who support the executive's role continue to oversee both the patients and practitioners in the system. Above all, the justification for executive discretion remains inextricably linked with the public protection agenda. As such, this research remains a rare glimpse of how executive discretion operates and its interaction with issues of contemporary political and policy relevance.

The issues examined here relate to highly complex areas of criminal and mental health law. Yet this book is not a legal analysis. It is a sociological analysis of the exercise of executive discretion and of how the public protection agenda has come to shape elements of public policy, particularly in the criminal justice system. The questions at the centre of this analysis include what ongoing purpose does executive discretion serve? How does that purpose differ from those of other actors in the system, like practitioners or mental health tribunals? How does executive decision-making interact with these other actors, and how does that differ from the interaction between legal institutions and professional expertise? Perhaps most interestingly, how does executive discretion operate in relation to other principles such as human rights?

Chapter 1 introduces some of the key issues that are considered in this book. It begins by analysing the role of executive discretion within contemporary legal systems. It then considers the intersection between criminal justice and mental health policy, which is a central feature of the restricted patient system, and explores how forensic psychiatric practice deals with the concepts of risk and dangerousness. It concludes with a discussion of the increasingly important role of victims in legal policies and practice, as a precursor to examining their involvement in the restricted patient system.

Chapter 2 sets out the methodology underpinning this research. It begins with a discussion of scholarship on legal and discretionary decision-making, before providing a reflective account of the research process.

Chapter 3 provides an operational account of the work of the Mental Health Unit, the bureaucratic department whose function is to carry out the executive's authority in the restricted patient system. It explores the processes that relate to monitoring, supervision and decision-making about patients; and looks at the decision frame through which those decisions are made. The chapter concludes with a discussion of symbolic politics involved in the public protection agenda.

Chapter 4 examines the relationships across the restricted patient system between the Mental Health Unit, the Mental Health Tribunal, legal and clinical practitioners, and non-government organizations involved in the system. It also looks at the range of evidence upon which decisions about restricted patients are based including areas of tension such as around the role and use of psychiatric evidence.

Chapter 5 explores the ways in which the concept of 'the public' is constructed through the operation of executive discretion in the interests of public protection. It looks at the role of particular groups such as victims and the families of restricted patients, and considers the interaction between these groups and actors in the system. It also looks at where patients themselves fit within notions of public safety.

Chapter 6 examines the interaction between human rights and the restricted patient system, drawing on both the international law coming from the European Convention on Human Rights and the impact of the domestic Human Rights Act 1998. In particular, this chapter is concerned with how government policies and practices have responded to the framework of human rights in terms of the exercise of executive discretion.

Chapter 7 brings together the book's major themes of symbolic politics and the public protection agenda, in a concluding analysis of the case for executive discretion over the release of mentally disordered offenders.

Chapter 1

Executive discretion and the rule of law

Introduction

Independent decision-making is widely accepted as the backbone of criminal justice in democratic societies. That independence is based upon two fundamental elements: the rule of law, and the separation of powers between executive and judicial functions. These principles 'aim to prevent, through law, the arbitrary or tyrannical exercise of state power and to enhance thereby society's faith in government' (Manderson 2008: 222). Conversely, the appropriate and lawful exercise of the law can be assessed by reference to the independence of the decisions made. For example, one of the key distinctions between lawful and arbitrary (unlawful) detention is the independence of the authority ordering it. As the International Convention on Civil and Political Rights states:

> anyone who is deprived of his liberty by arrest or detention shall be entitled to take proceedings before a court, in order that that court may decide without delay on the lawfulness of his detention and order his release if the detention is not lawful. (article 9:4)

The European Convention on Human Rights provides similarly for the lawfulness of detention to be reviewed by a court (article 5:4), and further that a fair hearing is dependent upon an 'independent and impartial tribunal established by law' (article 6:1). Even historical alliances such as the Commonwealth of Nations have committed their members to 'fundamental political values' which include 'democracy, democratic processes and institutions which reflect national circumstances, the rule of law and the independence of the judiciary, just and honest government' (Harare Commonwealth Declaration 1991, para 9:2). Thus, the importance of judicial authority acting independently from the state is well established in international law.

Many of the roles, responsibilities and relationships between those engaged in the state and those working in the criminal justice system flow from these principles. For instance, when elected representatives of parliament form a cabinet of ministers, their role is to set broad governmental policy on issues like criminal law and justice. Ministers do not ordinarily undertake the day-to-day administrative processes or minutiae associated with these policies. That is the role of the bureaucratic departments and officials who work to support the government. Similarly, cabinet ministers with responsibility for criminal justice policy are not expected to make decisions about individual cases or offenders. That role is more commonly given to professionals and experts in the institutions of the criminal justice system such as courts, tribunals and parole boards.

Criminal justice decision-making has not always operated in this separate and independent manner. Historically in the English and common law jurisdictions, offenders were detained under the authority of the British monarch. This was originally known as 'detention at his or her majesty's pleasure' or 'at the governor's pleasure' in British colonies. Today, the monarch's power has been almost entirely subsumed within the functions of the executive branch of government, which has the responsibility for executing plans, actions and laws. Moreover, the legal authority that was once vested in the monarch or the executive branch has been further divested to independent institutions. In the criminal justice system these include the police, courts and prisons. In so far as it continues to exist, executive authority is often perceived as a formality or symbolic function, such as in cabinet ratifications of policies or programmes that have been developed by government departments.

Executive discretion and public policy

The emphasis placed upon the separation of powers has led to a common perception that executive discretion no longer has any relevance in contemporary liberal democracies. However, that perception ignores the ongoing role of executive discretion in a number of important areas of public policy, where the executive exercises direct control over processes and decisions at an individual level. For example, Australian law governing people who enter the country as refugees or seeking asylum requires an executive decision to grant an individual humanitarian or bridging visa (Australian Migration Act 1958: section 417). The problems that arise when political and legal roles are blurred in this way have been highlighted in criticisms that the system produces 'a fundamental conflict of interest between the Minister as guardian of unaccompanied children in detention centres and the Minister as the person who makes decisions about visas' (HREOC 2004: 193). The increased use of detention of refugees and asylum seekers has also been linked to inadequate protection of their human rights. Thus in the UK it has been argued that, prior to the introduction of the Human Rights Act 1998:

> officials faced few limits on their legal ability to detain asylum seekers … there was no real judicial oversight of decisions to detain asylum applicants on the basis of administrative convenience in jail or in immigration centres. Arguably more alarmingly, there was no statutory limit on how long such individuals could be held in custody. (Gibney 2004: 125)

Policies to counter terrorism have also utilized executive authority to facilitate greater control over suspects. For example, European anti-terrorism policy has 'given much greater powers to states to ensure that terrorists do not penetrate asylum systems' (Schoenholtz and Hojaiban 2008: 11). In the UK, the Anti-Terrorism, Crime and Security Act 2001 (ACSA 2001) gave authority to the Secretary of State (Home Department) to certify a non-citizen as a suspected 'international terrorist', if he or she suspected the person of being a terrorist or posing a risk to national security (ACSA 2001: part 4: 21). Subsequently, the Immigration, Asylum and Nationality Act 2006 (IANA 2006) allowed the Secretary of State to issue a certificate that an appellant was not entitled to the protection of the Refugee Convention, on national security grounds (IANA 2006: section 55).

In Australia, a key case in this respect concerned Dr Mohammed Haneef, an Indian national employed as a doctor in the state of Queensland. Dr Haneef was arrested and detained without charge (subsequently released), on suspicion that he had been involved in attempted terrorist attacks on airports in London and Glasgow in 2007. Following his release from police custody, the then Minister for Immigration exercised his executive discretion to cancel Dr Haneef's working visa, which made him vulnerable to being removed from Australia. The minister defended his decision to cancel the visa on the basis of 'reasonable suspicion', namely that 'Dr Haneef had an association with people involved in terrorism and for that reason failed to satisfy the character test in section 501 of the Migration Act 1958 (Cwth)' (Law Council of Australia 2008: 10).

The Australian government faced condemnation of these actions on two grounds. Firstly, their legality was questioned, particularly when Dr Haneef successfully challenged the visa revocation in court. Secondly, the minister's actions were strongly criticized for undermining the legitimate exercise of executive discretion. This point was emphasized in evidence to the independent inquiry that was commissioned into the matter when the government changed a short time later (Clarke 2008).

> The public's faith in the integrity of our judicial system is undermined when a Minister appears to interfere in, or arbitrarily override, the outcome of judicial proceedings in a manner inconsistent with the separation of powers. (Law Council of Australia 2008: 11)

The Haneef case was indicative of the growing tensions around the world between public safety and civil liberties. Such tensions have been heightened by the contemporary priority placed upon countering terrorism. While the government's actions in that case were flawed, they also reflected the increasing pressure upon states to act – and be seen to act – in the interests of national security. The origins of that shift are another research project entirely (see, for example, Daruwala and Boyd-Caine 2007). Moreover, some have argued that politicians have brought these pressures upon themselves in their rush to be seen as 'tough' in the face of crime and other threats to safety or public order (Sparks 2000). Be that as it may, these developments provide a starting point for this book in demonstrating the strong and growing pressure upon the executive in relation to the public protection agenda.

Operational differences

One of the interesting aspects of executive discretion is how differently it operates from traditional legal institutions. The executive is not bound by legal principles such as the rule of law or procedural fairness. Nor is it defined by the protocols of a courtroom. It may recognize these principles and processes, but the exercise of executive discretion is not constrained in these respects. Of course, the exercise of discretion itself is not unusual. On the contrary, discretion is an integral element of decision-making in many legal settings, particularly in the criminal justice system. For example, discretion is as important for the formal deliberations of a judge in a courtroom as it is for the daily tasks of court staff selecting and disseminating papers in a case (Hawkins 2003). What is exceptional is the operation of *executive* discretion; the extent that ministers have direct responsibility for individual decisions.

Examining the links between different forms of executive and discretionary authority was an underlying interest in this research. Yet from the outset of the project these parallels did not resonate with colleagues, nor were they recognized by other scholars in the field. There was little acknowledgment of the tendency towards executive authority in a number of ostensibly disparate policy arenas. Nor was there any recognition that the public protection agenda was a common element in an increasing array of detention regimes designed to control and contain particular populations.

Importantly, recognition of these links changed in the course of my research for this book. In the UK, the government began to emulate Australia's policies of detaining refugees and asylum seekers while their applications were investigated and processed. This was an issue that attracted increasing public and political attention, particularly in the campaign for the 2005 UK parliamentary election. Similarly, new measures for dealing with terrorism suspects were proposed following bomb attacks in London in July 2005. In the ensuing years there were various attempts to introduce laws enabling longer periods of detention alongside other measures such as control orders. These constrained the liberty of people who were believed to be engaged in terrorist activity but had not been convicted of any such offence. Here again, executive discretion was often key to the structures of authority that underpinned these measures; and its function was commonly to license the use of indefinite detention.

These examples illustrate recent trends towards governments giving themselves more and more powers in the interests of protecting the public from apparent threats to their safety. Most of the examples I have discussed so far have been sensitive and highly visible matters whose significant profiles derive in part from their implications for foreign policy and international relations. But they are also important indications of attempts by states to identify and control people that are deemed to be dangerous.

Within the domestic sphere, another site for the revision of mechanisms to control dangerous behaviour has been the criminal justice system. This has been particularly so in the incessant review and reform of sentencing laws (O'Malley 1999). Discussion of sentencing has long been concerned with how best to combine the objectives of punishment for a crime, prevention of future crimes and protection of the public. As early as 1948 the English Criminal Justice Act sparked debate about how best to balance the preventive and rehabilitative elements of penal policy (Advisory Council on the Treatment of Offenders 1963). So concerns about risk and dangerousness are not a new phenomenon. What has changed in recent times has been the tenor of those concerns and the extent to which they have supplanted long-standing principles of the criminal law. Prison sentences traditionally entailed detention as a means of punishment, following a conviction for an offence. The finding of guilt for an act already committed was central to determining how long a prisoner should be detained in prison. However, in recent years the punitive purpose of sentencing has been supplemented by preventive elements that are designed to prolong an individual's detention and thus forestall them committing any future harm.

In England and Wales, a raft of sentencing options have come to entail both a tariff, the period a prisoner should serve for punishment and deterrence, and a discretionary period that can be applied or avoided depending on an assessment of risk posed by the offender. One example is the option of discretionary life sentences. These may be imposed in certain cases of violent or serious offences where the offender is deemed to be mentally unstable, likely to reoffend, and to present a grave danger to the public for a long or uncertain time (Padfield, Liebling *et al.* 2003).

Such sentencing options have created a process whereby offenders can be formally classified as 'dangerous'. This is most commonly applied to people who have been convicted of sexual or violent offences and who, in the court's view, are likely to reoffend in the same way. A classification of 'dangerous' gives the court the option to apply indeterminate sentences in the interests of public protection, as Her Majesty's Prison Service explains:

> The indeterminate sentence will be given to dangerous offenders convicted of sexual or violent offences carrying a maximum penalty of 10 years' imprisonment or more. The court will set

a tariff for punishment and retribution, after which release is at the Parole Board's discretion. As with a life sentence, prisoners will stay in custody until the parole board is satisfied that it is safe to release them. After release the offender may remain on licence indefinitely but, unlike life licensees, they can apply to have their licence reviewed 10 years after release ... The extended sentence for public protection will be given to dangerous offenders convicted of sexual or violent offences that carry a maximum penalty of at least two but less than 10 years' imprisonment. The sentence will consist of two parts: a custodial period of at least 12 months and an extended licence period of up to eight years. Release is at the discretion of the Parole Board any time between the halfway point of the custodial period and the custodial end date. (Sanderson 2009)

The policy objective behind these developments has been to 'bring sentencing practices and sentencing law into line with community expectations that longer, tougher custodial sentences should be introduced for particular types of offenders, namely serious sexual and serious violent offenders' (Richardson and Freiberg 2004: 82). Their protective element is clearly geared around containment, through the prolonged incarceration of an offender. In some cases, 'the focus of dangerousness assessment and its classification became a measure of the extent to which the public needed to be protected from such offenders' (Henham 2003: 59). The added protection provided by extending someone's detention is prioritized over any harmful effect on the offender, such as a disproportionately punitive loss of liberty. But for many, the result has been a concerted shift away from traditional notions of criminal justice that once included objectives of reintegration alongside punishment.

The idea that there is a zero-sum contest between victims and offenders, causal explanation and moral responsibility, understanding and condemnation, is a key feature of the currently dominant politics of law and order ... Punitive obsessions are the undeclared projection, not the obverse, of the evils they condemn. (Reiner 2007: 19)

Yet protective sentencing policies have been widely criticized as incompatible with the central principle of proportionality, whereby gradations in punishment according to the nature of an offence underscore the preventive or deterrent objectives of detention (Ashworth 1983). Indeed some researchers have suggested that judicial discretion has been tending to 'avoid, mitigate or ameliorate' the punitive objectives of protective sentencing in the interests of preserving proportionality (*ibid*; see also Henham 2003). The capacity of protective sentencing to prevent or deter future offending has also been questioned. One study on discretionary life sentences found that they may have little effect 'on those who commit the most serious crimes for which a life sentence is likely to be imposed' (Padfield 2002). Nevertheless, they remain popular sentencing policies in light of the 'increasingly extravagant' claims by politicians to be able to protect the public through the imprisonment of risky individuals (Hope and Sparks 2000: 7). Consequently:

> a whole variety of paralegal forms of confinement are being devised ... not so much in the name of law and order, but in the name of the community that they threaten, the name of the actual or potential victims they violate. It appears that the convention of 'rule of law' must be waived for the protection of the community against a growing number of 'predators', who do not conform to either legalistic or psychiatric models of subjectivity. (Rose 2000: 334)

The purpose of this discussion has not been to analyse the changing nature of penal policy. Rather, I am interested in how those policy shifts relate to, and can help us understand, developments in other areas of the law. Nowhere are the tensions between correction and control more evident than in the management of mentally disordered offenders. Restricted patients in England and Wales are one such group. They have been convicted of a criminal offence but, instead of sentencing them to prison for punishment, the court orders their detention in hospital for compulsory treatment of their mental disorder. While the purpose of their detention is for therapeutic intervention, the decisions about their progress through the system towards release are 'restricted' to an executive order under the powers of the Secretary of State. The executive's role is expressly that of providing a measure of protection to the public. Even where an independent mental health tribunal has the power to determine the release of a restricted patient, that authority is shared with the Secretary of State.

Separation of powers

As the discussion in this chapter has illustrated, the separation of powers between judicial and political functions is not absolute. Indeed, the executive exercises its discretion in a number of important areas of law. Yet very little is known about the operation of that discretion. What is the relationship between the executive and other actors such as civil servants, practitioners or professionals? How does executive discretion interact with domestic laws and policies such as those of the criminal justice system or with international frameworks such as human rights? Perhaps most important of all, what is the role and function of executive discretion in contemporary public policy?

The exercise of executive discretion in the restricted patient system is an ideal context within which to consider these questions. It brings into stark relief the function of executive discretion. The detention of restricted patients serves two objectives. The first objective is therapeutic; a way of mandating clinical intervention with someone who is mentally unwell, to enable them eventually to live safely and well in the community. However, there is also a strong protective element. Restricted patients are generally detained within a secure psychiatric hospital following their conviction. While the system attempts to improve their mental state to a point where patients are able to live safely in the community, that process involves constant assessment and testing to ensure that the public is not exposed to any serious harm. It is in the interests of this second objective of public protection that decisions about the movement and discharge of patients are relegated to the executive's authority.

In addition, the executive has the discretion to accept or reject the recommendations of many professionals across a range of fields in the restricted patient system. These include psychiatrists and other health professionals, administrators, legal representatives and advocates. Some are accustomed to discharging patients under the civil provisions of the Mental Health Act 1983, yet have no such power in relation to restricted patients. Mental Health Tribunals, comprising a lawyer, a psychiatrist and a third member, present another important opportunity for professional knowledge in the system. Tribunals share the executive's responsibility for determining the suitability for discharge of restricted patients but they have no authority over the decisions leading up to a patient's release, such as leave entitlements or transfer to less secure facilities. The knowledge or experience the

Secretary of State brings to these issues is usually considerably less than that of members of Tribunal panels, many of whom have worked with mentally disordered offenders throughout their careers. Nonetheless, the executive's authority over restricted patients is paramount, unlike the Tribunal's; and executive decisions require the support neither of practitioners nor of the Tribunal. As a result, analysis of this system enables a rare glimpse into how the exercise of executive discretion interacts with other 'highly expert' actors.

Another important aspect of executive discretion is how it engages with other policy priorities. In this research I was most interested in the respective role of human rights. The impact of human rights on the restricted patient system has increased over recent decades, especially under the weight of case law from the European Court of Human Rights. That impact took on a domestic relevance in the UK with the introduction of the Human Rights Act 1998. Debate about public safety often juxtaposes individual rights against state responsibilities to the public, as though the two were diametrically opposed. Yet states are responsible for protecting and promoting human rights, as well as public safety. Indeed, some might argue that human rights are simply another mechanism for public protection. Thus the relationship between human rights and the public protection agenda is an important focus of this research.

Finally, the exercise of executive discretion over restricted patients is an interesting site for comparison with other jurisdictions and systems. Here, I draw particularly on the Australian example of the forensic mental health system in New South Wales (NSW). This was a useful point of reference because it had similar legal structures to the restricted patient system at the time of my research. Despite some differences in legal status, forensic patients in NSW are an equivalent population to restricted patients in England and Wales. Both populations involve offenders who have been detained indefinitely under mental health law. At the time of my research, both were also subject to executive discretion, although that ceased to be the case in NSW after the completion of this research. But the greatest benefit from comparing the two jurisdictions relates to the role of human rights, as the absence of a domestic human rights instrument in Australia brings its relative value in each system into sharp relief.

The role of forensic psychiatry

It is clear from the discussion so far that the conflation of a criminal history with mental illness is the defining aspect of restricted patients, in so far as the systemic response to them is concerned. The management of restricted patients revolves around the practice of psychiatrists under the powers of the Mental Health Act 1983. While this book is concerned with executive rather than clinical decision-making, that process is highly informed by the advice of clinicians, whose role is mandated by law. In the following discussion I explore some of the central elements of 'forensic psychiatry', psychiatric practice within the context of the criminal justice system.

The first thing to note is that forensic psychiatry is a somewhat contested concept. Some psychiatrists have argued that there is no such discipline as 'forensic psychiatry', which until recently was evidenced by the lack of any formal training or qualification in that regard (Shea 2003). That has changed, as universities and psychiatric schools increasingly cater to the needs of those practising in the criminal justice system. Others have identified forensic psychiatry through the nature of its patients (as offenders) and the importance of assessing risk of dangerousness and violence (Maden 2007). The preoccupation with risk and dangerousness may not be isolated to forensic psychiatry, but psychiatric care for mentally disordered offenders is a highly specialized area of practice involving a range of unique elements. These include the need to understand criminal as well as mental health law; an ability to work within secure settings, including prisons; the nature of the clinical and behavioural histories of the patients; and the constraints upon options for rehabilitation that are consequent on the conditions often attached to the release of offenders into the community. In this book, it is these elements of practice that I refer to as forensic psychiatry.

Some have argued that psychiatry's 'claims to scientific neutrality, objectivity and rationality' have lent an authority to the construction of mentally disordered offenders as inherently dangerous (Kendall 2005: 46). The 'claims' referred to here include offering expertise in the assessment and management of mentally disordered offenders and, perhaps most importantly, in the protection of the public from any risks these offenders might pose (*ibid*). The implication of such critiques is that the emerging specialization of forensic psychiatry has, by definition, forged the conflation of mental disorder with dangerousness and criminality.

The strongest criticisms on the subject of forensic psychiatry relate to how it is understood by other areas of practice. Psychiatrists themselves are often willing to point to the fallibility of psychiatric predictions, which are made on a population basis, when applied to the individual level. As one key scholar and practitioner in the field has commented, 'the best estimate is that two out of three predictions of long-term future violence made by psychiatrists are wrong' (Monahan quoted in Gigerenzer 2003). Yet this is rarely understood outside of psychiatric practice. In particular the law has proven itself incapable of accepting the limitations of psychiatry (Monahan and Steadman 1994). This is evidenced by legal approaches to the concept of 'dangerousness' which confound the variables on which a psychiatric prediction is based, the type of event being predicted, and the likelihood of the event actually occurring. As such, the law conflates mental disorder and dangerousness on the basis of a flawed interpretation of psychiatric evidence and clinical practice.

The process of risk assessment is a complex, lengthy process based on probabilities, not absolute numbers. Moreover, it is a process that acknowledges the social factors of an individual's situation. Yet, in the administration of the restricted patient system, there are other factors that contribute to the conflation of mental disorder and dangerousness. For example, there are political imperatives that might lead to an over-reliance on, or use of, information in unintended ways. These include the pressure on civil servants to protect their ministers from negative media attention and to maintain public confidence in a system. Representing risk assessment as a straightforward, comprehensive and accurate process serves a dual purpose in this regard. It implies that risk assessment is a formalized, clearly documented process, rather than the reality of a fluid process with constantly shifting variables. Moreover, the process of assessing risk and proposing how to manage it is different from deciding what levels of risk are acceptable. As a result, some psychiatrists have argued that their skills lie in the former and that those elected or appointed to represent the public should determine the latter (Maden 2007). Therein lies the basis for the justification of executive discretion.

This raises the question of who makes the claims about psychiatry as a definitive science? As Rose argues, psychiatry is a site of practice where 'research is under way, conflicting theories and hypotheses abound, competing programmes are suggested and occasionally implemented and failure rather than success is the norm' (Rose 2002: 5). Psychiatrists themselves are well aware of the lack of certainty surrounding effective risk management. Reviewing his own and other psychiatric practice, Monahan found a 33–50% range of accuracy for clinical (that is, non-actuarial) risk assessment (Monahan 2004: 254). Yet the law makes little allowance for such limitations. Legal and public policy are often based on the assumption that risk can be assessed accurately and managed successfully to protect the public from harm. At the same time, many psychiatrists are concerned about whether or not psychiatry is capable of meeting these expectations.

Beyond the question of whether psychiatrists *can* assess and manage risk of offenders is the equally important question of whether they *should*. As Mullen argues:

> surely it is obvious that the chances of a mentally disordered person acting violently should be carefully evaluated and every step taken to prevent such a consequence. It is, perhaps, not quite as obvious that a central, if not the primary, responsibility of a mental health professional is to the wider community rather than their patient. It is not entirely obvious how a responsibility to predict risk is to be discharged. It is certainly not obvious how a clinician should act if they do suspect their patient is more probable to act violently. And finally, it is far from obvious that we should allow concerns about the risk which some of our patients may present to others to become a major determinant of our approach to all our patients. (Mullen 2002: xv)

This discussion has important implications for our ideas about what constitutes public protection from mentally disordered offenders. As Szmuckler asks, 'the worry is that if predictions are limited (often, extremely limited) in accuracy, how do we justify the ongoing preventive detention of people who are deemed to be unacceptably risky as a result of a risk assessment' (Szmuckler 2005: 776)? What emerges is a tension between the clinical responsibility of forensic mental health professionals in the care and management of their patients and the political responsibility for controlling this population for the protection of society. Hence Rose terms these professionals 'control workers' who:

> whether they be police or psychiatrists, ... have a new administrative function – the administration of the marginalia, ensuring community protection through the identification of the riskiness of individuals, actions, forms of life and territories. (Rose 2000: 333)

Similarly, Seddon has charted the move from understanding offenders as dangerous to perceiving them in terms of risk; a framework which dissolves dangerous individuals into a combination of risk factors (Seddon 2007). Drawing parallels with Simon and Feeley's work on actuarial justice (Simon and Feeley 1995), Seddon shows how this move has underpinned a policy shift towards managing groups not individuals (Seddon 2007). The critique reminds us that institutional forces are at play even in the level of individual case decisions, such as those made about restricted patients. Yet, the manifestations of the public protection agenda sit uncomfortably with the realities of skill and resource that shape not just what mental health services can offer, but also how effective they are (Maden 2007). While actuarialism has not taken over psychiatric practice, it does influence the approach of managing offender populations systemically. In a sign of the pervasive preoccupation with risk, some officials in this research referred to police, probation and parole staff and mental health care workers as 'risk workers'.

Risk and dangerousness

If risk is an *important* concept in the management of all mentally disordered offenders (Solomon 2005), it is *definitive* for those on a restriction order. It is the risk of a patient's mental disorder, if untreated, to lead to similar behaviour in the future that justifies the order for compulsory treatment; and the potential for serious harm to the public that restricts their release to a decision by the Secretary of State or the Tribunal. Risk appears as a concrete term in legislation and policy, as though it can be clearly and unambiguously determined (Mental Health Act 1983: section 41). In forensic psychiatry, risk assessments seek to establish the factors of mental disorder that lead to a person's instability, including their likelihood to commit criminal acts. The management of risk involves assessing how best to control these factors to reduce the chance of certain behaviour being repeated. Thus clinical risk assessment depends upon an understanding of the individual's behaviour within the social factors that shape their life and the control of those factors constitutes risk management.

Consequently, risk is a concept that can be defined in numerous ways and the processes involved in assessing risk are heavily subjective. Indeed, the concept of risk has attracted a significant body of scholarship in its own right. Important to sociological conceptions of risk has been Giddens' argument that the preoccupation with risk is an inherently modern phenomenon:

> Modernity is a risk culture. I do not mean by this that social life is inherently more risky than it used to be; for most people in the developed societies that is not the case. Rather, the concept

of risk becomes fundamental to the way both law actors and technical specialists organise the social world. (Giddens 1991: 3)

The modernity thesis does not suggest that the concept of risk itself is new. For instance, Goffman's work of the 1960s recognized that risk was integral to the management practices of asylums:

Moving up and down the ward systems means, then, not only a shift in self-constructive equipment, a shift in reflected status, but also a change in the calculus of risks … appreciation that a given risk level is itself merely a social arrangement is a rarer kind of experience, and one that seems to help to disenchant the person who undergoes it. (Goffman 1961: 153)

Even earlier, the risk of contamination was an important factor in the segregation policies of late eighteenth century penal institutions (Strange and Bashford 2003). Nevertheless Giddens' point is that the priority placed upon risk is a uniquely modern feature. For instance, in mental health care the assessment and management of risk has come to shape not only the care and treatment of individuals but also the practices of whole institutions. As such, we can begin to see how whole systems have come to rest solely upon the criterion of risk (Giddens 1991; Ericson and Haggerty 1997; Rose 2000).

Alongside the sociology of risk, anthropologists have been interested in the language of risk. Douglas argues that terminology around risk predetermines that the only possibilities are negative:

Risk is unequivocally used to mean danger from future damage, caused by the opponents. How much risk is a matter for the experts, but on both sides of the debate it has to be taken for granted that the matter is ascertainable. Anyone who insists that there is a high degree of uncertainty is taken to be opting out of accountability. (Douglas 1992: 30)

Thus if public policy and perception are shaped by the risk agenda, its connotations are necessarily negative. At an individual level this can serve to undermine the interests of the mentally disordered person in question, with the demand for compulsory treatment, for example. Indeed Peay argues that the ability to provide effective intervention to offenders with mental disorder is extremely limited (Peay 1993). At a more structural level the preoccupation with risk that underpins contemporary sentencing practices has the potential to leave mentally disordered offenders 'being dealt with more harshly' (Peay 2002: 747). For Douglas, this leads to a politicization of the concept of dangerousness. However, for others, risk is already a politicized term, utilized in relation to certain populations only, and not others. Thus Rose talks about the application of risk to 'the usual suspects':

> the poor, the welfare recipients, the petty criminals, discharged psychiatric patients, street people. The logics of risk inescapably locate the careers and identities of such tainted citizens within a regime of surveillance in which they are constituted as actually or potentially 'risky' individuals. (Rose 2000:333; see also South, Smith *et al.* 2005)

Risk is a self-fulfilling concept: there can never be zero risk. For any individual subject considered to be 'risky', their actions become irrevocably associated with dangerousness. Yet, if we consider the risks associated with mentally disordered offenders, the most striking factor is the risk they pose to themselves. One inquiry found that 22% of suicides by people under mental health care in England and Wales were believed to have been preventable by care teams, with the figure even higher for those who were in-patients at the time of their suicide (Department of Health 2001). Moreover, in their key English study of homicides by people with mental illness, Taylor and Gunn found that the number of people with a mental disorder who committed homicide has remained constant since the 1970s, and the proportion of homicide offenders they represent has actually decreased (Taylor and Gunn 1999). This finding was repeated in a follow up study in New Zealand (Simpson, McKenna *et al.* 2003). Nonetheless, it is the prevention of harm to the public that categorically defines restricted patients, despite the fact that they are also members of a population for whom the greatest risk is one they pose themselves.

The changing role of victims in policy and practice

Another interesting element of decision-making in the restricted patient system is the extent to which we see the impact of key shifts that have hitherto been acknowledged only within the strictest confines of criminal justice policy. Of particular interest here is the increasing role of victims in criminal justice policies and procedures.

In the final discussion of this chapter, I examine the role that victims have come to play in criminal justice policy, as a basis for subsequent discussion about their interaction with the restricted patient system.

Historically, victims had a central role in criminal justice processes, even shouldering the financial and evidentiary responsibilities for prosecution (Shapland, Willmore et al. 1985; Bianchi 1994). Over time, the bureaucratization of responses to crime shifted the involvement of victims who were 'no longer playing a role of importance and no longer able to stop a criminal procedure by settlement without the consent of the state's prosecutors' (Bianchi 1994: 17; Rock 2004b). Since then and until very recently, victims were only included in criminal procedure as witnesses, if at all. 'Victims' interests were subsumed within the public interest, [believing] that, in the long run, the state's correctionalist policies would work to the interest of both the public and the offender' (Garland 2001: 121).

Criminological scholarship about victims' experiences dates back several decades. The notion that victims were 'the forgotten man' in criminal justice took a central focus in that initial work (Shapland, Willmore et al. 1985: 176). Yet, over the past 10–15 years, victims have assumed an increasingly important role in research and policy. It is no longer the case that victims are forgotten by criminal justice policy (Zedner 2002). In a relatively short time a veritable canon has developed on the subject of victims in the fields of criminology, sociology, social policy, law, health, psychology and geography (see for example Shapland, Willmore et al. 1985; Christie 1986; Fattah 1986; Rock 1986; Mawby and Walklate 1994; Newburn and Stanko 1994; Davies, Francis et al. 1996; Stanko 2000; Zedner 2002; Rock 2004; Walklate 2007). Moreover, at the policy level 'a concern with and for the victim of crime has become not just a symbolic reference point in government policy but the dominant one' (Walklate 2007: 7).

In this book, the interaction of victims with the restricted patient system is of interest for two reasons. Firstly, as will become clear, victims are an important element of the decision frame within which officials assess and determine applications for leave and discharge. This relates to how officials construct their idea of 'the public' and how best to protect it. Secondly, the involvement of victims in the restricted patient system indicates that the increasing priority placed upon victims has spread beyond the areas of criminal justice that have been considered to date. The analysis presented in this book makes a small contribution to the gaps in the literature between what has been observed through research to date and what is happening in the broader context of criminal justice policy.

The 'ideal victim'

One of the key themes in much of the victimological literature has been that of the 'ideal victim' (Christie 1986). Christie defined the ideal victim as constituted by his or her (relative) powerlessness. Using the example of women as victims of crime, he argued that as women gained greater economic power, they would have greater power to demand recognition as victims. However, as their power increased, their idealized victim status would diminish:

> In being an ideal victim, she (or sometimes he) must be strong enough to be listened to, or dare to talk. But she (he) must at the very same time be *weak enough not to become a threat to other important interests.* A minimum of strength is a precondition to being listened to, but sufficient strength to threaten others would not be a good base for creating the type of general and public sympathy that is associated with the status of being a victim. (Christie 1986: 21, emphasis in original)

This notion of an idealized victim type has been challenged by other work, especially regarding the utilitarian and sometimes competitive aspects of victim status. Examining the introduction of USA hate crime laws in the 1980s, Jacobs and Potter pointed to the structured hierarchies of violent offending, and by extension of victims, that were created through the introduction of these laws:

> It might be tempting to conclude that jealousies and resentments over exclusions from the hate crime laws can be avoided by drafting these laws to include all salient prejudices. While that would solve the problem of disparaging some groups' victimisations in comparison to others, it would also negate the primary purpose of the hate crime laws: to specially condemn offenders with certain prejudices and specially recognize their victims. Hate crime laws only make sense if certain bigoted offenders are condemned more forcefully and punished more severely than offenders who commit the same crimes but for nonprejudiced reasons. It is the *exclusion* that gives these laws their symbolic power and meaning. (Jacobs and Potter 1998: 133, emphasis in quotation)

In other words, the experience of having been victimized can attach a status that becomes a mark of power in the competitive landscape of identity politics. Yet as Rock notes, 'victim' is not necessarily an appealing term:

> It tends preponderantly to convey stigmatised meanings of weakness, loss and pain ... On the other hand, becoming a victim can have its rewards: sympathy; attention; being treated as blameless; the ability to bestow meaning and control on an untoward and disturbing experience; the receiving of exoneration, absolution, validation and credit, exemption from prosecution, mitigation of punishment and financial compensation. (Rock 2002: 14)

One of the problems with these idealized victim types is that they inherently obscure many of the experiences that are shared by victims and offenders alike. In particular, many offenders have experienced victimization in one form or another. There are other characteristics shared by those most likely to offend with those who have suffered the severest victimization:

> They tend to be those at the margins of groups and the feet of hierarchies: the young, male, members of minority-ethnic groups, offenders, squatters, single adults, the geographically mobile, the homeless and the residents of inner city and satellite estates. (Rock 2002: 21)

The stigmatizing effects of criminal justice

The complexities of meaning associated with victim status are deepened further by the stigma that is commonly attached to association with the criminal justice system. For example, the secondary stigma that attaches to the families of offenders has been experienced as a form of victimization (Condry 2007).

In part, the inability to reconcile the connections between victims and offenders stems from the failure to recognize processes of victimization as interactive (Rock 2002). The messages of media and political interests have also played a role in producing 'opposing distortions ... where innocent victims tend to be depicted as the very antithesis of wicked criminals' (Rock 2002: 14). The characterization of victims and offenders as dichotomously opposed leads easily to the conflating of victims' sentiments with punitiveness. Such perceptions are reinforced repeatedly by media coverage that reports crime accompanied by messages of vengeance from victims.

Yet there is significant evidence to suggest that victim concerns are often far from vengeful. Some of the earliest work on victim involvement in criminal justice found that victims were not 'particularly punitive in the sentences they wanted their offenders to receive', focusing instead on things the victim wanted directly from the offender, such as compensation (Shapland, Willmore *et al.* 1985: 177). Similarly, in restricted patient cases Rock found that victim involvement was motivated by a desire to see systemic reform rather than individuals punished (Rock 1996).

The discussion of these issues within criminological literature tends to focus on how the experience of crime can be compounded by a sense of victimization before the criminal justice system. How the presentation of this pattern impacts upon policy development is an important question.

> Criminological understanding of victims' needs is largely reliant on views expressed by victims themselves – a source that is necessarily problematic. Vocal, determined, or well-connected victims may express their needs forcibly, ironically at the expense of those whose needs are greatest but whose very vulnerability or inability to ask for help ensures their silence. (Zedner 2002: 431)

Clearly, the success of particular claims by some victims does not necessarily reflect the range and diversity of all: the loudest voice is not always the most representative. In addition, while the political priority placed upon victims may be attributable to successful lobbying, their publicly acknowledged status does not necessarily translate into systemic change or policy transformation (Zedner 2002). Policy responses do not always meet the aims and objectives of victims themselves. Moreover, the claims of victims are susceptible to being used for political purposes. Research into the experiences of victims involved with the Home Office suggested that 'victims and witnesses came ineluctably to take some part of their character from their relation to the twin imperatives of crime reduction and public confidence' (Rock 2004: 38). Indeed, victims themselves recognized that the politics of law and justice meant that the impact of their advocacy might be limited to the objectives of the government of the day (Rock 2004).

Victim surveys

One indicator of the increasing significance of victims in criminal justice policy has been the gaining popularity of victim surveys. 'If a problem of crime is to be taken "seriously", it seems that a crime survey is one of the major devices used to demonstrate the pervasiveness of an issue and to advocate for sympathetic treatment of newly identified "victims"' (Stanko 2000: 15). Surveys make little allowance for the nuances and complexities of experience in terms of victimization and offending. Their validity for determining policy directions has also been questioned. Indeed some survey responses are a direct product of the methodologies employed and therefore 'the correct political response is to disregard what is essentially unreliable evidence' (Hough and Roberts 1998: 13).

Despite these concerns, surveys have been important in shaping public perceptions of crime. They may also serve an instrumental purpose in defining social attitudes as a tangible basis for public policy. Rock has suggested that surveys influence perceptions and behaviour no matter how unrepresentative they are:

> Although public attitudes can assume many shapes, surveys do have a most important effect on political and social conduct ... Ironically, what may initially appear to be sociologically naive is actually a fairly literal and exhaustive definition of one manifestation of the phenomenon of society's attitudes. (Rock 1986: 34)

The capacity of surveys to inform public policy is a good basis for considering how certain values and expectations might be brought to bear by officials implementing executive discretion. It shows us that both the prevalence and severity of crime is increasingly understood through its effect on victims. It also shows us how the interests of victims and offenders are reinforced as oppositional by these methodologies. The question that interested me was how these shifts influenced decision-making under executive authority within the restricted patient system.

Political sensitivities

From my work in Australia I had become aware of how susceptible politicians were to the interests of victims, over and above the interests of offenders or their families. At the outset of this research there was a perception among those I spoke with in England that victims did not hold as much sway with decision-makers as I described in Australia. But, like the expanding terrain of executive discretion itself, there was a marked shift in the currency of victims in criminal justice policy during the life of my research. By the time I completed my study, criminal justice policy was characterized by slogans that talked of 'placing victims at the heart of criminal justice processes' (Home Office 2006). Attention to victim interests was increasingly at the fore of reforms and policy initiatives; and victims were attaining formal recognition as stakeholders in criminal justice processes and outcomes. This was most clearly demonstrated in the government's appointment of a leading victim advocate to the position of 'victim's champion' (Ministry of Justice 2009).

Of course, presence in a policy statement does not necessarily translate into cultural change. Nevertheless I wanted to investigate whether the currency of victims was evident in executive decision-making about restricted patients. It was no longer plausible to suggest that victims were irrelevant to the processes of forensic mental health. The key questions were: how did they interact with those processes; and to what effect? I explore these questions more fully in subsequent chapters.

The relationship between victims and the restricted patient system is not just innately interesting. It is also an important indicator of the transparency, accountability and legitimacy of the decision-making process. The exercise of executive discretion is particularly susceptible to criticisms in this regard because of common assumptions about the values of politics and the folly of public opinion. Judges are no less immune than politicians to public commentary on their work. Yet the institutions of the law maintain that their value derives in part from their independence of political processes, which in turn allows them to disregard such public scrutiny. Such notions of objectivity are highly questionable. Nonetheless there is no doubting that politicians are, by contrast, highly influenced by such pressures. The reflection of public will via the media, however fallacious, is a powerful determinant of political action; not to mention democratic processes of accountability like elections.

This book is concerned with how, increasingly, contemporary public policy draws its mandate from the perceived expression of public sentiment. As such, the state's legitimacy turns upon how effective the government can be in showing its receptiveness to that sentiment. The emphasis upon the public protection agenda in the restricted patient system is one vehicle through which to explore these processes further. The restricted patient system offers a unique environment in which to investigate not only how executive discretion operates in the interests of public protection; but also how that function serves to reinforce the executive's own legitimacy. For all the theory about the separation of powers and the rule of law, executive discretion is playing an ongoing and important role in determining matters of great public significance. We need to better understand those processes and their impacts.

Chapter 2

Care and control

Introduction

In the realm of criminal justice policy and practice, the term 'mentally disordered offender' is frequently used. It presumes some form of relationship between a person's mental state and their criminal offending or subsequent involvement in the criminal justice system. It implies also that there is not commonly a relationship between mental state and offending for other offenders. Yet closer scrutiny of this category reveals the 'plurality' of a population who are neither homogenous nor exclusive and who challenge accepted notions of illness and offending behaviour (Peay 2002: 746; see also Peay 2004). While the classification of someone as a 'mentally disordered offender' is singular in nature, it obscures the many differences among the people encompassed by the term. These include people who have been convicted of an offence and diverted to hospital prior to serving a sentence; transferred out of prison into hospital for compulsory treatment; found unfit to stand trial because of their mental disorder; acquitted on the grounds of insanity; or those who have been convicted of an offence but diverted to hospital for compulsory treatment of their mental disorder (James, Farnham *et al.* 2002).

Restricted patients

Restricted patients fall into the last category. They have been convicted of a criminal act but are detained in hospital instead of serving a prison sentence. Following a conviction, and subject to certain conditions, a court may order that a person be detained in hospital for compulsory psychiatric treatment. This means that the person is suffering from mental disorder at the time of sentencing 'such as to warrant their detention in hospital', although no causal relationship is required between their mental disorder and the offence committed (Jones 2004: 1–507). At this point, patients are known as 'hospital order' patients and their detention falls under the powers of the Mental Health Act 1983. A restriction order constitutes a further step by the court once a hospital order has been made.

> Where a hospital order is made in respect of an offender by the Crown Court, and it appears to the court, having regard to the nature of the offence, the antecedents of the offender and the risk of his committing further offences if set at large, that it is necessary for the protection of the public from serious harm so to do, the court may, subject to the provisions of this section, further order that the offender shall be subject to the special restrictions set out in this section, either without limit of time or during such period as may be specified in the order; and an order under this section shall be known as 'a restriction order'.
> (Mental Health Act 1983: section 41)

Restriction orders

In essence, restriction orders are made when the sentencing court has concerns about the level of risk the offender poses to themselves or to the public (Potts 1995). As a result, the court restricts who is able to make decisions about the patient's detention and, most importantly, their discharge. Prior to 1983, the power to discharge restricted patients was vested solely with the Secretary of State (Home Department) (under the Mental Health Act 1959). In 1981, the case of *X v UK*[1] before the European Court of Human Rights found that the lack of a mechanism of independent review for restricted patients was a breach of the European Convention on Human Rights, article 5(4). That required the lawfulness of detention on the basis of someone's unsoundness of mind to be reviewed by a court with the power to order their discharge (Jones 2004: 1–826). The ruling led to the Mental Health Review Tribunal (as it was known then) obtaining the power to order the absolute or conditional discharge of restricted patients. This reform met the requirement under human rights law that decisions to detain patients for compulsory psychiatric treatment could be reviewed independently. However, the executive retained its exclusive discretion over the steps that lead up to a decision about discharge. They include moving a patient to a new hospital; changing the level of security under which the patient is detained; permitting the patient to take leave from a secure facility, such as from a ward to the hospital grounds; and whether, when and how a patient may spend time in the community. Thus while the extension of determinative authority to the Tribunal appeared to be procedurally significant, it did little to curb the extent of executive discretion over restricted patients.

The making of a restriction order is itself a fascinating process and is illustrative of 'a long series of prior decisions or recommendations about the fate of a case' (Hawkins 2003: 196). Those decisions relate to both psychiatric and legal processes. It has been argued that mental illness is 'a metaphorical disease' (Szasz 1974: x) and that 'psychiatry is not a medical, but a moral and political, enterprise' (Szasz 1974: xiii). More importantly for my own research, Szasz contributed to a broader body of work whose project was to attribute social values to medical processes.

> The temptation to embrace all medical interventions as forms of therapy, or to reject them all as forms of social control, must be firmly resisted. It behoves us, instead, to discriminate intelligently and to describe honestly the things doctors do to cure the sick and things they do to control the deviant. (Szasz 1974: 69)

In a similar vein Goffman argued that, while the detention of people in psychiatric hospitals could be justified by those outside ('in society'), in reality the distinction between who is inside and outside was relatively arbitrary.

> Society's official view is that inmates of mental hospitals are there primarily because they are suffering from mental illness. However, in the degree that the 'mentally ill' outside hospitals numerically approach or surpass those inside hospitals, one could say that mental patients distinctively suffer not from mental illness, but from contingencies. (Goffman 1961: 126)

Goffman did not necessarily share Szasz's nihilist view that mental illness does not exist. Rather, he was interested in people who were detained because of their mental illness. Understanding detention as a result of contingencies complicated the notion of madness as an objective, diagnosable, physiological condition and situated it within broader social processes of inclusion and exclusion.

Public protection

Goffman was also interested in the question of public protection. As he saw it, 'part of the official mandate of the public mental hospital is to protect the community from the danger and nuisance of certain kinds of misconduct' (Goffman 1961: 307). For Goffman, the elements of danger and nuisance posed by people with mental disorder were key in justifying detention for the purpose of social exclusion. Goffman's work is also relevant to this study methodologically. His essays on psychiatric asylums integrated a theoretical discussion of the purpose of incarceration with his analysis of the processes and people engaged in those institutions. He examined the relationships between staff and inmates in asylums, showing how those processes produced meaning themselves, as well as being shaped by the impact of institutional imperatives and expectations upon them. Goffman found that relationships between psychiatrists and inmates were:

> doomed by the institutional context to a false and difficult relationship and are constantly funnelled into the contact that will express it: the psychiatrist must extend service civility from the stance of a server but can no more continue in that stance than the patient can accept it. (Goffman 1961: 320)

Goffman's interest in what he termed the 'governed' and the 'governors' was instrumental in turning sociological inquiry towards the interaction between all the players in institutions of incarceration, not simply the inmates. The legacy of his arguments also resonates with contemporary critiques about the randomness of the classification of mentally disordered offenders. This is one of the greatest problems inherent in the law's response to mentally disordered offenders, including whether a defendant is given a psychiatric or penal dispositional outcome. For example, studies of case law have shown that the same legal arguments have produced different outcomes for defendants (Peay 1993; Prins 1993). This creates serious challenges for managing offenders post trial. As Rock has argued, mental disorder lies on the boundary between psychiatric practice and models of punishment and the mentally disordered offender is one with whom the prison system cannot cope (Rock 1996). Yet the extremely high rates of mental illness among offender populations are consistent irrespective of where they are detained (in prison or in hospital), and regardless of whether they are formally categorized as mentally disordered (Rock 1996). As Padfield notes:

> once a person is labelled a restricted patient, he or she has different procedural rights than does the 'dangerous' person detained in prison. Yet people with similar characteristics may find themselves in one, rather than another, category. And, conversely, the people within the different categories do not necessarily share the same characteristics. (Padfield 2002: 124)

Importantly, then, the category of 'mentally disordered offender' is characterized – at least in part – by an element of arbitrariness. That is not to say that it is random. It is a classification which is produced by the application of particular systems and beliefs, not least about the law, mental health and moral responsibility. It is also a classification that is affected by particular attitudes, or what some describe as stigma or discrimination. But it is to acknowledge that the category of 'mentally disordered offender' is highly contested.

Basis of this research

The determination that someone is a mentally disordered offender, or specifically a restricted patient, is the start of a long process. This book is concerned with the end of that process: the decisions about care and control, leave and release, that lead to the eventual discharge of a restriction order. As such, my research focused on the applications and determinations about discharge from hospital, and the supervision, once in the community, of restriction order patients who were admitted to and detained in high security and other hospitals in England and Wales. There were other people who came under the purview of the restricted patient system, including prisoners on remand and those transferred from prison for psychiatric assessment and treatment. As their period within the restricted patient system was generally short-term and their discharge usually resulted in their return to prison, they did not form a central part of my study.

Executive authority in the restricted patient system is vested in the Secretary of State. In practice, decisions are carried out by the Mental Health Unit. At the time of my research the Unit was part of the Home Office; in 2007 it moved to the newly-formed Ministry of Justice. The declared mandate of the Secretary of State's authority is to provide for the protection of the public (Potts 1995). That mandate informed some of the main questions underpinning this research. How was the concept of 'the public' constructed? Was the public an all-encompassing term for anyone and everyone who might come into contact with a restricted patient? Were there particular groups who constituted the public, for instance the local communities in which patients had committed their offences or to which they were discharged? And to what extent did notions of 'the public' have an impact upon decision-making across the restricted patient system?

My interest in who constituted the public intersected with other developments in criminal justice policy also. As discussed in the previous chapter, a major factor here was the increasing importance placed upon victims. However, there had been very little research about their interaction with parallel areas such as the mental health system. I was interested in the extent to which victims were involved in the restricted patient system in England and Wales. What were the effects of victim participation on the work of practitioners such as psychiatrists and other healthcare professionals or lawyers, whose focus was upon patients? How did victim involvement influence constructions of the public within the framework of executive decision-making? What effect did those constructions have on the decisions made?

The second set of research questions related to how the Home Office had maintained executive discretion in this system, when it had been replaced by judicial and quasi-judicial structures in so many other jurisdictions. Was it a matter of public confidence? Did confidence intersect with the public protection agenda at the level of policy or individual decision-making? How did the Home Office perceive the possible impact of mistakes or embarrassments on public confidence and how did such concerns influence decision-making about individual restricted patients? Did maintaining public confidence require preventing or managing media attention, or attention from other quarters? Did it extend to protecting the reputations of the Secretary of State (Home Department) and other ministers? How did those priorities sit alongside the objectives of other actors, such as practitioners or advocates?

From the outset of this study, I sought the answers to my questions in the words and experiences of those working in the system. If we know little about the contemporary function of executive discretion, we know even less about how its processes operate on a daily basis. In part, this may be because the political sensitivities of executive decision-making can make systems highly opaque. I was concerned about the potential for high levels of mistrust and defensiveness from various actors towards my research; or poor relationships between actors that would obscure their capacity for systemic analysis. I knew that the extent to which these dynamics were present in the restricted patient system would determine the range and quality of data in my research.

Fortunately, there was a high degree of engagement between the various actors working in the restricted patient system of England and Wales. There was also a small but dynamic research culture that was recognized and valued across the system. The responsiveness and candour of those who participated in my research reflected a refreshingly open approach, from civil servants to legal and medical practitioners and non-government organizations. Not only did that attitude ease the way of my study, it was also indicative of some of the cultural aspects of the system.

On legal decision-making: the origins of a research culture

Legal decision-making processes can be both formal, such as the workings of a courtroom; and informal, for example the work of court registry staff who select and prepare particular papers for a case (Hawkins 2003). The informality of these processes does not imply an absence of rules. On the contrary:

> very often the environment of a legal decision, so far as the official is concerned, is partly made up of existing decisions which comprise a policy purporting to inform the handling of particular kinds of cases in particular ways. (Hawkins 1986: 1171)

A broad approach to the terrain of decision-making is important for enabling us to look beyond the formal institutions that are readily identifiable, to the structures that support those institutions. Research about decision-making needs to:

> get away from approaches which focus on 'criteria' or 'factors' said to have been taken into account in making a particular choice. The argument, instead, is that decisions can only be understood by reference to their broad environment, particular context, and interpretive practices: their surrounds, fields and frames. (Hawkins 2003: 189)

Beyond the specific study of legal structures and decision-making, this approach draws on the work of the phenomenologists and symbolic interactionists who redefined scholarship in the social sciences, particularly in sociology (see, for example, Kitsuse and Cicourel 1963; Douglas 1967). These analytical frameworks allowed me to move beyond the specific outcomes of decisions about applications to examine the policies, people and other elements that shaped the decisions being made. These were the factors of the 'decision frame', a 'structure of knowledge, experience, values, and meanings that the decision-maker shares with others and brings to a choice' (Hawkins 1986: 1191).

To describe executive discretion as a form of legal decision-making relies on a number of assumptions. In some jurisdictions, criminal justice officials are directly elected, such as in parts of the USA. However, for countries such as England and Australia, the very nature of a decision being made by an elected representative seems to contradict what we commonly think of as legal decision-making, such as the independent judicial or quasi-judicial structures of courts or tribunals. Additionally, the scope of executive discretion can fall well beyond the procedural constraints often applied in legal settings. Nonetheless I deem executive discretion in the restricted patient system to be a form of legal decision-making, particularly as it was bound by legislative frameworks that clearly constituted a legal decision-making environment. These included the Mental Health Act 1983 and the principles of human rights that were enshrined in both international and domestic law.

To that end, the literature on legal decision-making provided some useful tools of analysis. For instance, Hawkins' description of 'street-level bureaucrats' who exercise informal discretion in legal settings was apt for administrative tasks of many officials at the Mental Health Unit. It is a description that recognizes administrative capability but assumes no professional expertise. Of course as Loughnan reminds us, lay knowledge has a longstanding history at the intersection of criminal law and mental incapacity, and members of a jury contribute a third level of knowledge to those of the legal and medical (psychiatric) forms already embedded in criminal procedure (Loughnan 2005). The officials of the Mental Health Unit could be deemed a fourth layer of knowledge within this hierarchy. They were not employed for their expertise in forensic mental health. There was no requirement that staff had a background or training in the areas of law, criminal justice or mental health, and only one staff member participating in my research spoke of their psychology training as a motivation for this work. On the contrary, some staff members described themselves as members of the public representing the interests of the non-expert in the restricted patient system. At the same time, Unit staff had a breadth of knowledge and experience of the system that allowed them to carry responsibilities well beyond those of lay actors with no expertise.

Two previous studies had examined the restricted patient system though neither had focused on the process of decision-making under executive authority. The operations of the Mental Health Unit had been the subject of empirical research a decade earlier when Dell and Grounds examined the discharge and supervision of restricted patients (1995). Theirs was a study of the supervision of conditionally discharged restricted patients in the community. While they examined some of the issues around the process of Home Office decisions to release, they were interested primarily in the attitudes of care teams and patients towards those decisions, rather than how the Home Office arrived at them (Dell and Grounds 1995: xi). Meanwhile, Street's study of restricted patients examined how restriction orders were imposed and the behaviour of patients under supervision in the community following a conditional discharge from detention in hospital. Like Dell and Grounds' study, Street did not examine the actual process of executive discretion over restricted patients. Beyond those two studies, Peay's research on Mental Health Review Tribunals is rare within a literature that has tended to focus on civil rather than forensic mental health patients. Thus the restricted patient system provided a little-studied arena through which to consider the practice of executive discretion and its wider implications.

The practice of executive discretion

At the time of my research the Mental Health Unit had approximately 60 staff. These were mainly caseworkers whose duties revolved around matters arising in relation to the care and supervision of restricted patients. Individual staff members each had about 200 'live' files in which a decision was required on a patient matter, with the population totaling 4,771 (as at August 2005). Around one-quarter of those patients were likely to have been released on conditional discharge in the community; the rest were detained in secure hospitals.

The Unit's staff had two primary roles: dealing with the steady flow of applications for leave, transfer to a different hospital or discharge; and responding to concerns raised about the conduct of a patient.

Such concerns were generally transmitted by mental health workers in the patient's care team but they could be raised by anyone.

> The main role of the Home Office in the management of restricted patients is to protect the public from serious harm ... Our task is to scrutinise proposals relating to restricted patients ... looking for evidence of thorough risk assessment and effective risk management. We need to satisfy ourselves that any risk to the public has been properly identified and evaluated, and that sound measures have been taken to guard against any risk.
> (*Mental Health Unit Casework Guide*, March 1998, 1A.1, 2)

As this excerpt from the Unit's staff manual indicates, the purpose of the Unit's powers was expressly acknowledged in terms of protecting the public from serious harm. For the Unit's caseworkers, this provided them with a clear mandate to make decisions about restricted patients that were in the interests of public protection. In theory this related to all decisions made, but in practice the greatest caution was exercised in relation to patient access to the community. For most patients, their time on a restriction order involved a lengthy process of testing their compliance with treatment and their responsiveness to therapy, while also moving from (initially) highly secure hospital to locations with diminishing levels of security. Patient progress was also tested through occasions when they took leave from hospital and spent time in the community. These exercises were partly to prepare patients for life outside the institutional confines of a hospital; and partly to test their safety and capacity. Each of these steps in a patient's case was tracked in patient files that were maintained by the Unit. Patient files were the single most important source of information available to staff in their decision-making.

The decisions of the Mental Health Unit were what Hawkins would call 'negotiated decisions ... made in private with a low degree of visibility of process and result' (Hawkins 1986: 1170). Consequently, it was a process that was vulnerable to criticisms of being 'arbitrary, inconsistent or unfair decision-making' (Holloway and Grounds 2003). But these conditions were not unique to the restricted patient system. For example, a study of Mental Health Review Tribunal decisions in a regional secure unit questioned 'whether MHRTs act with sufficient independence to balance the rights of both the public and the detained patient, or whether they are unduly receptive to the [Responsible Medical Officer's] views' (Mohan, Murray *et al.* 1998: 63). Rules can never be exhaustive and their interpretation and application is necessarily context-specific (Bittner 1963). To assume the contrary would require extreme and impractical inflexibility. All we can do is acknowledge that decision-making takes place within social contexts, political values, available resources and competing demands upon priorities; and recognise that these factors may shape or compete with the interests of those making decisions and those affected by them.

Understanding the operational dimensions of how these processes worked in practice was a central objective of my research. Executive decision-making shared some but not all of the characteristics of other legal settings, such as regard to the rules of procedural fairness or transparency in the provision of written reasons. It also contributed new elements to the picture. For example, people interviewed in this research repeatedly returned to the idea of 'flexibility' in how they made decisions. While flexibility might accord with some notions of discretion, its meaning was not self-evident. I needed to observe decision-makers in practice and discuss these issues with them in order to engage with what this notion of flexibility meant in practice.

The concepts of the 'decision frame' (Hawkins 1986) and 'surround' (Hawkins 2003) were also helpful analytical tools for understanding the Unit's decision-making processes. These concepts describe the environment in which decision-making took place: the 'structure of knowledge, experience, values, and meanings that the decision-maker shares with others and brings to a choice' (Hawkins 1986). As Hawkins notes:

> One of the major tasks for those interested in legal decision-making is to understand why and in what circumstances decision-makers accord changing priority to competing decision frames. This is a massive task, however, because it requires close and careful investigation of the fundamental decision model employed by legal decision-makers. It means, to begin with, lengthy and detailed exploration of the jungle. (Hawkins 1986: 1242)

Examining the decision frame of executive discretion in the restricted patient system necessitated establishing which agencies and personnel were involved in the decision-making process, including those beyond the machinations of the government in parallel decision-making bodies like the Mental Health Review Tribunal and hospitals. While each of these had discrete responsibilities under the Mental Health

Act 1983, they were not necessarily complementary to each other's purpose. It was impossible to investigate the operation of executive discretion without also understanding how these different actors operated, and how they interacted with the executive.

In the end, participants in this research came from a range of institutions and perspectives across the restricted patient system. They spanned the Home Office; the Mental Health Review Tribunal; clinical practitioners, including doctors, nurses, social workers and other health professionals; legal practitioners who represented restricted patients; and non-government organizations, specifically those representing the interests of patients and victims. In using the term 'actors' to refer to these research participants collectively, it is not my intention to dehumanize them, nor to suggest that they were *performing* in any pejorative sense of the term. However, it is an acknowledgment of the very different roles that were occupied across the system. Indeed, many people I observed and interviewed represented particular perspectives, fulfilled responsibilities or adhered to policies because of their institutional or professional affiliation that they might not necessarily have maintained personally. Engaging with this wide range of actors in the system enabled the multiplicity and complexity of the system to be explored.

Beyond actors with specific roles in the system, there was the amorphous notion of 'the public'. Analyzing the ways in which 'the public' was constructed within decision-making was one of the major challenges of my research. It was equally challenging to design a starting point from which to explore this 'actor' in the system. I established a working definition by a process of exclusion. The public included anyone who was not directly or professionally associated with the restricted patient system. This excluded the Home Office, the Tribunal, healthcare professionals, lawyers and patients. It included families and friends of patients; victims; non-government organizations such as advocacy groups; and anyone else who might appear incidentally in restricted cases. At the outset, the broad scope of this definition created the conditions to allow new ideas or elements to emerge that might not otherwise have occurred to me. Subsequently, as my analysis developed, I was able to explore how decision-makers themselves understood the public in their work; and how that understanding shaped the decisions that were made in the interests of public protection.

Policy-relevant and critically engaged

While this project developed in response to the gaps in our knowledge about the interaction between public protection and executive discretion, it strove to be highly relevant to policy and practice. The notion of 'policy-relevant research' has attracted strong criticism among some criminologists. They have expressed concerns that criminology has become obsessed with evaluative research at the cost of theoretical and empirical analysis; and that over-reliance on quantitative methods has led to a renaissance of positivism, abandoning the more effective processes of social inquiry (see, for example, Hayward and Young 2004; Young 2007). Some have called for criminological research to be 'counter-hegemonic' (Hillyard 2004) and to resist the lure of evaluative research as merely administrative criminology that is inherently atheoretical (Hope 2005; Walters 2005). These critiques are underpinned by a concern that rigorous criminological research is increasingly being ignored by policy-makers, or manipulated to suit the political ends of government (Hillyard, Sim *et al.* 2004b; Hope 2005; Loader 2006).

Of course, a counter-hegemonic agenda has its own dependencies. But independent and rigorous research is vital in any context, even (and perhaps especially) if it does not meet the political objectives of the day. At the same time, policy-relevant research is not inherently conservative or uncritical. Like all bodies of literature, some policy research is poor and some is excellent, with a vast range in between. Research into the various uses of discretion in criminal justice is a good example here, encompassing a body of literature that interrogates some of the most central aspects of state power, as well as the operation of specific aspects of sentencing law, and of the daily practice of police, prison guards and other officials (see, for example, Hawkins 1992; Cunnen 2001; Padfield 2002; Gelsthorpe and Padfield 2003). Scrutiny of government policy and practice can also balance out essentialist approaches that reify 'the system' and allow flaws to continue unattended (Downes and Rock 1979).

Contributing to a 'critical narrative' of criminological inquiry does not mean criticizing everything observed in the conduct of research (Walters 2005: 7). Such an approach would assume one knew the answers in advance of the research; and that those answers all tended towards one direction. States, governments and bureaucracies have problems to resolve which are obdurate and complex. Some policies are well constructed while others are far from perfect. It is not my intention to reject or challenge what I observed on this basis. Rather, my intention is to question and probe the issues that I observed by engaging critically with the field; to interrogate the status quo; and to consider alternative possibilities and explanations for how executive discretion functions.

My pursuit of a policy-relevant analysis influenced the process of the research as much as it did the analysis and writing. I wanted my research to be of interest to policy-makers, decision-makers and practitioners working in the system, as well as to researchers and those interested by the question of public protection in general. The exceptional openness of participants in my research, and the consequent insights into the stocks of knowledge that officials brought to bear in their practical work, were important data in their own right. At the same time, research and writing are not neutral processes. They depend upon the selection of particular pieces of information and the exclusion of others. The decision to use or discard certain quotations is a good example of this selectivity. In an effort to maintain the work's relevancy for policy-makers, I presented my initial findings to those I had interviewed or observed and I incorporated their responses into my final analysis. I also sought a level of legitimacy from those in the field by maintaining contact with them and with other scholars and practitioners who might be interested in this study. My driving goal was to produce a piece of research that is as relevant for those engaged in policy and practice as it is for scholars and other readers.

Methodology

In their discussion of methodology Genders and Player note that:

> it would be a mistake to conceive of each element of the methodology as constituting a discrete area of research ... Rather, they were overlapping and complementary components which needed to be pursued and understood in relation to each other, in order to produce a coherent picture of the life of the institution. Collectively they enabled the cross-checking of information and made it possible to identify the internal consistency of particular findings which, it is hoped, will act to strengthen the validity of the final conclusions. (Genders and Player 1995: 20)

In much the same way I combined several research methods in different ways to broaden the range of data available and to strengthen

37

my analysis overall. My methodology was predominantly drawn from qualitative data elicited from documentary analysis, observation and interviews; with some quantitative data to illustrate particular trends or patterns. At some field sites I used all methods; at others only one or two, depending on the context and role of the participant or institution within the system. This approach also guarded against an over-reliance on the individual case as the primary unit of analysis, which would assume that 'a case exists as a discrete entity, and decisions are made about its fate quite independently of wider forces and constraints' (Hawkins 2003: 194).

Documentary evidence

The major source of documentary evidence came from the Unit's patient files that tracked the progress of patients through the system from the time a restriction order was made to its ultimate discharge. They were a mine of information not just for their contents but for their capacity to illustrate how policies worked in practice. Documentary evidence also came from legislation, policy and job manuals setting out the roles and operations of each agency or position involved in the system.

Documents were essential for setting a baseline in terms of certain procedures and policies, but written guidelines do not necessarily capture the nuances of how processes operate in practice. Absent from written procedure are a range of elements such as the contexts of knowledge, shared understanding, and rules that operate in working environments; the deviations from policy that are necessary to respond to unforeseen or exceptional cases; and the informal relationships established to facilitate information-sharing. To capture these aspects of decision-making, I observed how officials in the Mental Health Unit conducted their daily work, including the negotiation entailed in resolving matters as they arose or making determinations on applications. I also observed Mental Health Review Tribunal hearings; meetings between lawyers and their restricted patient clients; and the hearings of a parliamentary scrutiny committee on the Draft Mental Health Bill 2004.

Interviews

I conducted 14 interviews with Home Office staff, clinical practitioners, lawyers, and representatives of non-government organisations. Interviews were based on semi-structured questions and were recorded and transcribed. Beyond these formal interviews, there was also a wealth of information gleaned from discussions with participants as I observed them at work. These accounts by participants in their own words were crucial for my analysis of the different roles and perspectives evident throughout the system; and for their insights into how the laws and policies of the system translate into everyday practice.

In a number of chapters I draw on quantitative data to provide demographic information about restricted patients such as their flow through the system and types of decisions made. Many of these data were provided to me by the Mental Health Unit. The Unit also maintained historical data that were not easily available, for instance statistics that had been published prior to the introduction of the Mental Health Act 1983.

I was interested in the individual experiences of patients and victims, and their perspectives on decision-making in the system. At the same time I was concerned not to expose patients or victims to additional stigmatization given their involvement in the system already. I decided to incorporate their perspectives through organizations who spoke on their behalf. For example, by interviewing victim advocates, I was able to hear from people with direct experience of being victims, but whose position as spokespeople gave them some level of control over the extent to which they were personally exposed by the research.

Without exception, the participants in this research answered questions and discussed issues at length in a candid and informative manner. From civil servants to practitioners and advocates, there was an openness and supportiveness that indicated a refreshing level of transparency in terms of the processes and outcomes of the restricted patient system. In so far as this attitude facilitated excellent access to a wide range of actors in the system, it contradicted the perception that government is less interested in rigorous research than in evidence to support its own objectives (Loader 2006). In particular, the Mental Health Unit's support for this research reflected a positive engagement with other actors in the system more broadly. Pragmatically, everything I had access to during the course of the research would have been legitimately available under freedom of information applications. However, the Unit's receptiveness to my research created a far more conducive environment in which to conduct my research and enabled a level of detail that has enriched the analysis throughout this book.

Experience as an insider

From my professional background working in forensic mental health, my experience as an 'insider' was particularly useful in engaging with officials at the Mental Health Unit and the Tribunal. The Unit's work reflected the part of the system with which I was most familiar. I had a working knowledge of the tasks officials had to undertake and the challenges they faced on a daily basis. My previous work with practitioners also meant that I started from a good understanding of the range of roles and responsibilities across the system. This background knowledge and experience were essential to the rapport I was able to build with the participants in my research.

The ability to gain the confidence of one's research participants and to establish a balance between participants' demands for reciprocity and the researcher's own professional need for rapport are instrumental in the research process.

> At its most basic level the reality is that researchers involve themselves in a human situation, in which demands are made upon their personal resources, to such an extent that it is their own social skills which are in large part central to the success of the whole venture. (Genders and Player 1995: 18)

Undoubtedly, I relied upon my experience to establish my competence within the field; but the wealth of data I obtained was as much in response to my interest in hearing about participants' experiences and perspectives as it was due to any sense of shared history. Taking a collegiate approach enabled me to build rapport with participants and reduced the amount of time necessary to cover background information during interviews and observation sessions. It also established certain expectations among research participants, which did not necessarily accord with my own perspective on my role and responsibilities as a researcher. For example, in discussing a difficult issue during an observation or interview, Mental Health Unit staff sometimes asked how I might have dealt with a similar issue in my own experience. Initially, I was concerned that these exchanges conflicted with my role as a non-participant observer and I found myself uncertain about how to respond. My hesitation highlighted my own assumptions about objectivity in research. It seemed that I believed in a notion of impartiality on the part of the researcher, an ideal that had subtly and unconsciously imbued my approach to research.

Reciprocity

> Beyond reciprocity as a pattern of exchange and beyond folk beliefs about reciprocity as a fact of life, there is another element: a generalized moral norm of reciprocity which defines certain actions and obligations as repayments for benefits received. (Gouldner 1960: 170)

As I became more engaged with the research and better acquainted with my research participants, my idealised notions of objectivity became less important. As Gouldner's analysis of the 'norm of reciprocity' showed, reciprocity is a matter of courtesy and elementary civility, but it is also based on the logic of helping those whose help you want (Gouldner 1960). Resisting reciprocity would have been discourteous and might have obstructed my ability to gain the trust of my research participants. As Genders and Player put it, their participants 'made it impossible for us passively to observe what was going on. Within a short period of our arrival staff and inmates directly sought out our opinions or advice' (Genders and Player 1995: 39).

More importantly, these interactions with participants were data in themselves. Genders and Player reflect on research as an 'interactive process, in which we were both shaping and being shaped by the social environment of the study' (Genders and Player 1995: 45). That interaction offers possibilities to participants too, such as the rare chance to have a detailed discussion with someone who understands the issues that arise daily in our working lives. To avoid these interactions would have been impolite and counter-productive to the research. It would also have denied participants the opportunity to gain themselves from the interactions that occurred during the research.

Ultimately, I came to see these as innate and positive aspects of the research process. However, they also raised a range of ethical concerns that I had not anticipated at the outset of the research. Ironically, my greatest concern related to one of the best elements of the research, namely the candour of participants. I became concerned that participants, particularly those in the civil service, had been incautious in their comments. A number of issues I observed or positions that were enunciated could have formed the basis of legal challenge by patients (through their lawyers). This did not mean that what I was observing was illegal. But as will become clear, there were many aspects of the restricted patient system that were open to interpretation, and each interpretation varied depending on the standpoint of the actor in the system. The interpretation of human rights responsibilities towards a restricted patient, for example, might differ between an official at the Mental Health Unit and a lawyer representing that patient. While I had set out to conduct a detailed investigation of executive decision-making, I did not want to expose participants to criticism or worse, by virtue of my analysis.

In agreeing to participate in this research, the Home Office made very little demand of me in return. Officials reviewed all quotations from Home Office staff and requested a number of them be converted to reported, rather than quoted, speech. At the same time, however, they expressed 'absolutely no desire to shade' my meaning, leaving the ultimate decision up to me. Several of the quotations they selected had been rare insights into the thought processes of officials and I was hesitant to lose the force of these verbatim statements. My intention had always been to base my analysis on the words of participants wherever possible. At the same time, I was conscious of the expectation of reciprocity from the Home Office, given the support it had provided for my research. I did not want the primary participants in my study to feel mistreated. Whether in formal interviews or casual conversation, the spoken word is a difficult art to control and meaning may be hidden or over-stated. There is far more opportunity to be clear, subtle or succinct when writing, and that is a benefit I enjoyed but which was not available to the participants in my research.

In considering how to resolve these issues, I returned to one of the priorities that had been outlined by the Mental Health Unit when it agreed to participate in the research. The Unit had stated that my research should not undermine public confidence in the restricted patient system. At the time, I had been unsure what this actually entailed. What expectations did the Home Office have about my use of data, largely obtained from their staff? Did they expect me to be as mindful of public confidence in the system as they were required to be? How might such caution enhance or impede my analysis?

On closer reflection, I began to see that my data showed how actors throughout the system were sympathetic to each other and were willing to acknowledge the competing priorities of the system, and by extension, the tensions between them. The restricted patient system required difficult decisions to be made on a daily basis. The cases were complex; the needs of patients were great; and the expectations of the community even greater. Applications routinely involved mediation between conflicting interests. Importantly, it was the actors engaged in these processes themselves, the participants in my research, who were the first to acknowledge these tensions. They readily admitted that they were fallible; and that mistakes had been made and would be made again in the future. To that end they, like me, were simply interested in an accurate account that acknowledged the challenges of the system as well as its purpose.

Such a perspective significantly altered the meaning and potential impact of criticism. The restricted patient system specifically, and the criminal justice system broadly, had been open to scrutiny by academics and other researchers long before I conducted my research, and they continue to be so. I came to see that commentary and review of the decision-making process took place in a number of ways. The Unit itself engaged in reviews of its systems internally. It was also held accountable by external forces, including the media, families of patients, families of victims and others. The access the Unit had granted me differed little from the access it provided to care teams and hospital staff who worked in the restricted patient system. Similarly, the analysis contained in this book forms part of a much bigger picture about public policy and practice in contemporary criminal justice.

Notes

1 *X v United Kingdom* (1981) 4 EHRR 181.

Chapter 3

The operation of executive discretion

Introduction

While the Secretary of State (Home Department) was ultimately accountable under the legislative mandate of the Mental Health Act 1983, it was the civil servants of the Mental Health Unit who exercised authority over cases on a daily basis. The executive placed a high level of confidence in the operations of the Mental Health Unit. Unless a matter had been raised directly with a minister, for instance by a constituent, they became involved only in matters on request or advice from the Unit.

The number of restricted patients across England and Wales numbered just under 5,000 at the time of my research. The population had been growing steadily over the years. So too had the extent of the Mental Health Unit's responsibilities, as one official from the Mental Health Unit explained:

> Not so long back, five years ago, the great majority of significant decisions like discharge and transfer to low security were taken personally by ministers. Now they're not. Ministers have delegated most decision-making to [the Unit].

Responsibility for decisions and their outcomes was shared evenly across the restricted patient population and among the staff of the Unit. There was a clear hierarchy that was strongly adhered to, delineating the bureaucratic processes through which decisions passed. The system generated formal paper trails and narratives of accountability should they be required. In an example of a 'structural simulacrum of rational decision-making', internal processes monitored the decision-making process at every level (DiMaggio and Powell 1983). This ensured that checks and balances were built in to the exercise of discretion.

Beyond making determinations about applications, staff regarded themselves as gatekeepers in the system. They were cautious about decisions that might bring the minister or the system into disrepute. Indeed some attributed great pressure to these responsibilities. One official commented that the decision-making process was 'isolating' because of the level of responsibility that came with the political sensitivity of cases. It was also stressful for the sheer volume and spread of patients.

As such, Unit officials held dual responsibilities. On the one hand, they gave effect to the executive's discretion over restricted patients, through their administrative support to the Secretary of State. This comprised a legislative mandate that was enshrined in the legislation of the Mental Health Act 1983. On the other hand, officials bore a responsibility to ensure that the system they administered was not brought into disrepute, and by extension did not tarnish the reputation of the minister. This responsibility was much more in line with the political realities of government. These dual mandates reflected the *realpolitik* of work in the contemporary civil service; what some have described as its politicization (Public Administration Select Committee 2007). Although not necessarily complementary objectives, each element was integral to the function of the Unit.

This chapter provides a descriptive account of how applications from restricted patients for leave or discharge were determined by the civil servants who implemented the executive's discretion. How did the public protection agenda shape the decisions made under executive discretion about individual patients? Was the path to public protection clearly marked at all times, or was this complicated and difficult terrain? In particular, how was risk 'managed' by the system? The framework for decisions implied a theory of risk for decision-makers separate to the framework employed by psychiatrists engaged in patient care. How did these varying approaches interact in the operation of executive discretion?

The restricted patient population in England and Wales

There were 2,347 patients detained in hospitals on restriction orders at the time of this research. Another 1,306 patients had been conditionally discharged from hospital, but were still on restriction orders. Consequently, they were still under the supervision of the Unit, as well as of mental health teams in the community. The Unit was also responsible for just over 1,000 other people who were not subject to a restriction order but were restricted patients as a result of alternative provisions of the Mental Health Act 1983. The majority of these were prisoners who were detained in prisons or immigration centres, but who had been transferred to hospital for compulsory mental health treatment (Mental Health Act 1983: sections 47 and 48). Most of these patients would be returned to their original place of detention at the conclusion of their treatment. Other patients included sentenced prisoners with psychopathic disorder who were receiving compulsory treatment before being sent to prison (Mental Health Act 1983: section 45a).

Almost one-third (27%) of all restricted patients were on conditional release in the community. Unit statistics indicated that 1,306 restricted patients had been discharged to the community. Of these, only 250 patients had been discharged by the Mental Health Unit. The remaining 1,056 patients had been discharged by the Mental Health Review Tribunal. These figures encompassed all patients living in the community on conditional discharge at the time of the research. They ranged from people who had been released since the Tribunal first received its powers to discharge under the Mental Health Act 1983, to people who were discharged immediately prior to June 2005. They gave a clear indication of the division of labour between the Tribunal and the executive in terms of decisions to discharge. It was the Tribunal that was primarily responsible for conditionally discharging restricted patients, with the executive (through the Unit) making less than one-fifth (19%) of all decisions to discharge.

Theoretically, there were 1,159 hospitals in which patients supervised by the Unit could have been detained. This included those patients outlined above who were not necessarily on restriction orders. However, in practice the patients monitored by the Unit were concentrated in a much smaller number of hospitals at any one time. Three special hospitals, Broadmoor, Rampton and Ashworth, maintained the highest level of security. Between them, these three hospitals accounted for 713 patients or 20% of the population under the Unit's supervision. The remaining hospitals were either medium- or low-security, or were open hospitals with no capacity to secure patients on the site. Patients in these hospitals numbered 2,752. Very few restricted patients were detained in open hospitals because, it was argued, if they no longer required the security of a locked hospital then they should be discharged to the community.

Beyond the demographics of the population, the majority of the information maintained by the Mental Health Unit was broken down into 'outcomes'. This reflected a broad trend across the civil service, where performance indicators and targets had become commonplace (see, for example, Home Office 2006b). They provided a quantitative measure of performance. By definition, only certain sorts of processes could be measured in this way, such as the time it took to complete a process, or whether a decision was made accepting or rejecting an application. At the Mental Health Unit, performance indicators measured discrete, case-specific decisions about restricted patients. They revealed the administrative priorities of the Unit and were also an important tool of justification, measuring the efficiency and progress of matters.

For instance, there were extensive records about applications received and the actions taken by Unit staff in response. There were also indicators that measured the time it took the Unit to complete certain actions, such as statements for Mental Health Review Tribunal hearings or responses to correspondence from patients or members of the public. Initially, performance was measured through the number of applications received against the number where a decision had been made. However, performance was also measured by timeliness, such as whether a determination was completed within ten days, two weeks, a period of months and so on. Some performance indicators also had their own targets. Leave applications had a completion target of three weeks; discharge applications had a target of two months from the date of receipt of the request (excluding any time taken to request further information); and 95% of letters from the public were supposed to be answered within three weeks. While many of these targets accorded with broad policy across the civil service, some were set externally, such as when the minister's private office determined the timeframe for replies to parliamentary questions. The Unit consistently scored well against its performance targets. This was a source of pride to staff and aided the task of managers responsible for demonstrating that the Unit was efficient and effective.

One of the areas of formal mandate that lent itself to measurement through performance indicators was the provision of statements to Tribunal hearings on applications for discharge. The statutory rules governing Tribunal hearings required the Secretary of State to be given notice of hearings regarding restricted patients. In response, the executive was required to send any relevant information to the

Tribunal in advance of a hearing (Mental Health Review Tribunal undated). Unit staff explained that the Secretary of State's statements had evolved to cover all the reports submitted for a hearing (including, for example, reports by nurses or social workers as well as psychiatrists). This was a huge task administratively: there were 4,000 such statements made by the Secretary of State each year. Yet completing these statements was a matter of routine administration, undertaken by a relatively low tier of the bureaucratic hierarchy. These statements were so routinized that Dell and Grounds had found that they were generally discounted by Tribunals because they were little more than a summary of information already available to the Tribunal (Dell and Grounds 1995). Nonetheless they were an important aspect of the Unit's work, which was reflected in the fact that performance indicators for the preceding three years had shown that 97%–98% of statements were completed on target.

While performance indicators reflected a particular aspect of the Unit's work, they were not in themselves a definitive overview of its workload or outcomes. Equally important were the 'organizational contingencies' through which interpretation, decision and action were shaped by various processes (Kitsuse and Cicourel 1963: 8; see also Douglas 1967). These elements of context were central to understanding practice. Analyzing individual actions without examining the environment in which they were made would have told very little about the 'real character' of decision-making (Hawkins 2003: 194). Indeed, the process of setting performance indicators had structured the nature of the Unit's work along particular lines. Certain 'organizational decisions' were important as much because they could be measured via performance indicators, as because they were significant in themselves (Power 1999; Hawkins 2003). This was particularly evident in the aspects of the Unit's work that could *not* be measured via performance indicators. A prime example of this was the monitoring and supervision of restricted patients in the community.

Monitoring in the restricted patient system

Essentially, the Mental Health Unit's role was to monitor the necessity and effectiveness of restriction orders as a measure of public protection. Officials in the Unit monitored every step of a restriction order. They began when patients were first admitted to hospital and continued until the patient's absolute discharge. Conditionally discharged restricted patients in the community involved the greatest likelihood of interaction between patients and the public. As such, it was an area of work that dominated much of the attention of Unit staff, who found it particularly stressful. Yet the nature of that work also made it particularly difficult to quantify through performance indicators.

Monitoring was done on the basis of information that was received from a variety of sources and was maintained in a patient's file. The first piece of information received about a restricted patient usually contained the details of the offence and the medical reports from the court case or hospital admission during the court proceedings, including any clinical assessments of the patient's mental state at the time of the offence. Staff would analyze these details against a checklist of factors that were deemed relevant to protecting the public from serious harm. The checklist contained a range of questions intended to establish the nature of a patient's past dangerousness; whether he or she was still dangerous; and the patient's treatment plan. The list asserted a system of order on the restricted patient population as a whole, providing a basis upon which Unit staff could assess individual patients against the spectrum of behaviour they encountered. It also stipulated what information was required from staff involved in patient care and treatment, including Responsible Medical Officers in hospitals and caseworkers in the community.

The nature of the offence for which the patient had received his or her restriction order and information on any other offending history were regarded as important indicators of both the level and particularities of risks posed by a patient. For example, Unit staff were keenly attuned to any changes in a patient's behaviour that seemed to reflect or relate to the behaviour exhibited at the time of the offence. They interpreted such developments as indications of increased risk in a patient, either in terms of a likely deterioration in mental state or an increased risk of dangerousness (or both). This relationship between current behaviour and index offence constituted an internal indicator of risk; it was not necessarily valued in the expert opinions of psychiatrists or others involved in the patients' daily treatment and care. In some cases, Unit staff brought these issues to the attention of treating teams when the teams themselves had not perceived such risks. This was an important indication of how the executive's focus on public protection shaped the priority that officials placed on certain pieces of information, irrespective of the advice of professionals in that regard. In pursuing the objective of public protection, Unit officials were licensed to take an active role in every aspect of patient care and treatment, even beyond the administrative remit of bureaucratic process.

Despite the latitude afforded to officials in their role, the reports of care teams about the progress of restricted patients were considered a vital source of information for executive decision-making. Reports were provided specifically in support of any application for change in a patient's restrictions. They could also be supplied in response to a particular incident or development in a patient's progress, or on request from the Unit. Certain factors were considered routinely on receipt of care team reports, such as the extent to which previously identified risk factors were being addressed in the treatment of the patient; and whether and how these risk factors were being reduced. Additionally, if a treating team's recommendations about a patient changed, Unit staff would seek an explanation for that change. This ensured that officials were kept wholly informed about any developments or deterioration in a patient's progress.

The processes for interpreting clinical reports varied across the Unit. One official routinely cross-referenced current reports against the patient's offending history. She would then check the patient's medical history to develop a picture of his or her mental state prior to the offence. From this she would make a judgment about whether the patient's current mental condition was likely to increase or reduce their risk to themselves or to others. While the official relied on the documents available in a patient's file in order to make these assessments, it was a process she had developed entirely on her own. This was an example of how decision-makers 'are rarely, if ever, totally passive participants in the decision-making process' (Hawkins 2003: 201). In this way, the process of making a decision brought as much to its outcome as the information upon which it was based.

Certain markers of behaviour came to assume importance in the decision-making by Unit staff. The focus on a patient's index offence was one example of this. Particular attention was paid to certain types of offending, such as sex offences. That information was captured routinely in the documentation provided for care teams to complete. For example the *pro forma* on which applications for leave and discharge were made included information on the person's mental state, behaviour and treatment plan. The form also asked for information about the involvement of victims or members of the public; the patient's attitude to the victims; and whether the patient posed any risks of absconding. Thus, while it was not the role of Unit staff to contribute expert knowledge to the process, they did structure the information they received along collectively identified avenues and a common work culture based on the priorities of the Home Office.

It could be difficult for caseworkers to explain their processes to other actors in the system. One official described recent correspondence with a doctor who had been frustrated when an application to transfer his patient to another hospital was rejected. The Unit had felt that the risks to other patients would be too great. The doctor asked for a copy of the Unit's risk assessment, assuming that there was a key document or process followed in this regard. In the absence of such a format, the official had sent a copy of her file notes.

In explaining the incident, she pointed out that the Unit's risk assessments were not 'actuarial', but 'a matter of personal consideration'. Subsequently, another official did describe the risk assessments conducted by the Unit as 'fairly actuarial'. This did not reflect inconsistency across the Unit. It was evidence that staff were not engaging with the principles of actuarial risk assessment in the way that clinicians might, as a process of assessing risk through numerical scores. Rather, officials were using the term actuarial to describe the routine nature of the processes they followed. These processes and the language applied to them were indexically embedded within an organizational context of institutional priorities and policies. They were examples of the acquired knowledge of administrators who based their judgements on signs and signifiers that had become condensed and increasingly relied upon over time. Their defiance of simple description to anyone working outside the Unit did not render them meaningless or irrelevant. On the contrary, they provided the central framework within which decision-making by Unit officials took place.

The nature of the care provided to a patient and how a patient responded to treatment were also key issues that were monitored by the Mental Health Unit. This meant that Unit staff maintained an interest in those charged with patient care as well as in the patients themselves. Unit caseworkers interacted regularly with care teams in written and telephone communication, even visiting case conferences or meeting with care team members on occasion. Unit staff paid attention to any changes within care teams to ensure that familiarity with a patient's history was maintained. The Unit also monitored the level of knowledge among care team members about a patient's offending and clinical history; factors that, as we have seen, were regarded as important indicators of risk among Unit officials.

In another context, such close scrutiny of health practitioners might seem interventionist coming from the Home Office. Yet for most Unit officials, these were legitimate lines of inquiry in the interests of public protection. However, one caseworker expressed concern at this tendency to monitor care teams. In his view, much of the work of Unit caseworkers mistakenly focused too closely on the work of care teams of patients in hospital. This stemmed from the common perception among officials that only their own decision-making processes took account of the public protection agenda. The caseworker disagreed, believing that care teams shared that concern and would not make applications for conditions that exposed the public to unnecessary risk. As such, he stated, he was 'highly unlikely to mistrust' the approach taken by a patient's care team. Moreover, he felt that the emphasis on monitoring care teams and hospital patients distracted the Unit from the more important role of supervising patients in the community.

Other caseworkers were equally concerned about where the weight of the Unit's attention should lie. A number of officials shared the view that patients on conditional discharge in the community warranted greater supervision than those in hospital. Even though these patients represented only one-third of the Unit's caseload, officials felt that they posed the greatest risk to public safety because of the higher likelihood of interaction between patients and the public. Yet most officials reported that the majority of their time was spent supervising patients in hospital and, by extension, hospital care teams.

The concept of trust arose in a number of these interviews. In general, there was a high level of trust between different actors in the system and this was clearly important to their professional relationships. That level of trust translated into a remarkable degree of understanding by most actors about the work of others in the system. It was also implied in some of the slogans employed by the Home Office, such as its motto of 'working together to protect the public' (Home Office 2009).

Nevertheless there were also clear cases where participants claimed that other parts of the system undermined its overall credibility or success. For instance, a number of Unit officials mentioned leaks to the media when certain patients were going to take leave in the community. It was widely believed that leaked information could only come from people engaged in that patient's care or treatment and they were motivated by financial gain. There was a sense of inevitability in the way officials discussed these events, as something unpleasant but not disastrous. Of course, for patients these leaks constituted a serious invasion of their privacy, not to mention a potential threat to their safety while on leave. Yet for officials, the problem was more about whether such leaks damaged the reputation of the system. In that sense, public confidence in the system was closely related to the responsibilities of officials for the public protection agenda.

The value placed on systemic reputation was not unique to the restricted patient system. Discretionary Lifer Panels of the Parole Board have been found to hold similar concerns about public scrutiny of their decisions, so much so that it is a standard component of their decision frame (Padfield, Liebling *et al.* 2003). Indeed, any process that has the potential to lift a criminal sanction is particularly vulnerable in this regard.

> A successful decision outcome (the released person who readjusts to life in the community, or who successfully completes his or her period of supervision) is invisible; only failure has the potential to come to public attention. To the extent this setting makes decision-makers more cautious, its effects are unlikely to show in conventional correlational research. In analysing decision-making about the risk of offenders, one aspect to take into account is that conceptions of risk have to be understood also as about risk to the decision-makers themselves. (Hawkins 2003: 211)

In practice, these realities shaped the behaviour of those involved in the system in a variety of ways. A lawyer who acted on behalf of restricted patients commented that the restricted patient system was becoming increasingly litigious, which was evidenced by the Home Office or hospital administrators increasingly engaging lawyers to oppose applications for discharge. He stated, 'as a lawyer you screw with the system', manipulating Tribunals to get particular treatment outcomes necessary for a client. Such endeavours were unlikely to achieve a discharge, he explained, but they could be useful in achieving other outcomes. For example, a patient who remained mentally unwell would not be discharged from hospital. But by seeking an application for discharge, a lawyer could bring about a Tribunal hearing. There, the hospital would have to outline their care plan. This created an opportunity for dialogue about the patient's mental state and the options for their treatment. As this could ultimately improve the patient's experience of compulsory treatment, it was seen as a positive outcome by legal advocates.

These sorts of practices could be interpreted as manipulative; a crafty legal strategy seeking to undermine the lawful clinical process of compulsory treatment under the Mental Health Act 1983. However, it was also an important indication of the level of antagonism that was structurally inherent in the system. For legal representatives, the restricted patient system pitted individual patients detained for compulsory treatment against the powers of the state and the resources that entailed. As one caseworker acknowledged, the Mental Health Unit had the resources to commission independent reports or engage barristers if it needed them, particularly for Tribunal hearings. Meanwhile lawyers were often dependent upon the limited resources of their clients. These structural dynamics forced a level of tension between the Home Office and other actors in the system and were partly accountable for any element of mistrust.

Oversight and the independence of the Tribunal

Monitoring by Unit officials extended to the decisions of the Mental Health Review Tribunal. Tribunal decisions were routinely examined to see whether the Tribunal had acted 'unreasonably or unlawfully', or whether it seemed that the Tribunal might be trying to set a precedent that could cause problems for the executive's authority. These concerns could result in a challenge to the decisions by the Secretary of State. Alternatively, the Home Office might seek representation to appear before the Tribunal and argue against an application. As one official acknowledged, 'it's not always clear cut … and there can be issues within the interpretation there'. Nevertheless, the Home Office was willing and able to take action against the Tribunal in the event of decisions to which it was strongly opposed.

Another official explained that, as the Unit was the 'last bastion of executive interference' in decisions to detain patients for compulsory treatment, the Tribunal's power needed to be 'closely defined'. The Tribunal had the authority to discharge a patient either conditionally or unconditionally, but no further power to review or determine the nature of a patient's detention, care or treatment. Yet it was not uncommon for the Tribunal to hear matters under its 'non-statutory discretion' (Jones 2004: 3–079). In one hearing observed during this research, a patient was seeking transfer to a different hospital. The Tribunal conducted the hearing, despite having no power to make the order, on the basis that if the application was supported by the Tribunal, it might improve its chances for approval by the Mental Health Unit.

There had formerly been considerable receptiveness from the government towards such extra-statutory proceedings (see for example 1987 written statement by Douglas Hogg MP in Jones 2004: 1–826). However, by the time of this research that attitude had declined significantly. Unit staff interpreted these hearings as examples of the Tribunal stepping beyond its statutory authority; and they were willing to test the boundaries of that authority through judicial review. In one example, the Home Office had sought judicial review of a Tribunal decision to adjourn a hearing and seek further information about an assessment for transfer of a patient (2001). Since transfer decisions were beyond the Tribunal's authority, the Home Office had contested the legitimacy of the adjournment decision. The court supported the Home Office, finding that an adjournment required reasons showing a 'proper purpose' that extended beyond the Tribunal exercising non-statutory powers (Jones *op cit*).

These scenarios indicated how widely interpretation of the legal and broader responsibilities varied among different actors in the system. Moreover, assessments of an individual case were largely informed by the role of the particular actor. A caseworker described one case where the patient had committed homicide while mentally unwell, but whose disorder had cleared up fairly quickly following admission to hospital. The care team was preparing an application to the Tribunal for discharge, either conditionally or unconditionally, because the patient no longer met the criteria for detention under the Mental Health Act 1983. Unit officials were concerned about the patient's likelihood of re-offending, given the severity of his offence. On that basis they opposed his discharge, despite the fact that medical evidence indicated that he no longer met the criteria for compulsory treatment under the Act. To oppose discharge the Secretary of State was represented at the hearing, where the Tribunal granted a deferred conditional discharge. As an official explained, the Home Office had never expected the patient's detention to continue; the most it hoped for was a conditional (rather than absolute) discharge. But officials had 'pulled out all the stops' to show that they had done everything within the Secretary of State's power to protect the public. The case was a good indication of the extent to which the *perception* of the system was as important as its *outcomes*.

As we have seen, the Tribunal was responsible for four-fifths of the decisions to discharge restricted patients. This meant that when problems arose regarding patients in the community, the Tribunal was more likely to have discharged them than the Secretary of State. This was an inevitable consequence of the unequal rates of discharge between the two authorities. Yet it created an extra layer in the mistrust from Home Office officials towards the Tribunal. This was most evident in the widely held perception among officials I spoke to that the Tribunal placed the system and the public at greater than necessary risk.

This mistrust did not, however, undermine the general respect with which officials held the Tribunal. While acknowledging that the Tribunal was often depicted by politicians and in the media as making risky decisions, one senior official stated that most of its decisions were 'fine'. He went on to state that even if the Secretary of State opposed an application for discharge that was ultimately accepted by the Tribunal, in general the Home Office found Tribunal recommendations to be reasonable and defensible. In other words, any antagonism between the two authorities was a result of the structural relationship between them, rather than outright disrespect.

Monitoring the operation of care teams or the decisions of the Tribunal represented an unofficial mandate under the executive's authority. It was an exercise of executive discretion, in much the same way that the Tribunal exercised its discretion to hear matters outside its statutory authority. The Secretary of State had no formal oversight of the Tribunal. On the contrary, the independence of the Tribunal was central to its function as a parallel decision-maker to the executive. Nonetheless, the decisions of other actors were included within the remit of the Secretary of State's powers, according to how those powers were interpreted by Unit officials.

The decision frame of executive discretion

While the exercise of executive discretion took place within the bureaucratic environment of the Home Office, that 'surround' was only one part of the picture (Hawkins 2003). The subjective assessments of individual staff were also central to the process. Using their familiarity with particular cases and with their focus on public protection, Home Office caseworkers would judge the quality of the information they received about a patient. Officials were seeking to probe the quality of the information received about a restricted patient for its accuracy and comprehensiveness. They questioned a report's authors in order to elicit details that might be missing from a report, as well as to verify its contents. In many ways this process mirrored that of the examination Tribunal members might conduct of a patient's care team during a hearing. But once again, the key difference lay in the objective of each process. Where the Tribunal was assessing the lawfulness of a patient's ongoing detention within the terms of compulsory treatment, the Home Office was solely concerned with the extent to which that care and treatment provided protection for the public.

The accounts provided by Home Office staff indicated a complex set of positions from which caseworkers assessed and determined patient applications. On the one hand, Unit staff were experienced administrators operating application-driven processes within a legally enshrined setting. While the qualifications necessary for that role contrasted with the professional expertise of lawyers or psychiatrists, caseworkers were not unskilled by comparison. Indeed some had relevant qualifications in the area. One Unit member had a psychology background; several others had criminology or nursing qualifications; and staff were encouraged to undertake a diploma course in forensic psychiatry.

But for many, the most important quality caseworkers brought to their decision-making was their capacity to protect the public as members of the public themselves. One official put this in the following terms:

[MHU] caseworkers aren't lawyers and they aren't clinicians. They're sort of intelligent and educated members of the public in effect, who are looking at the information coming in and then looking at what's missing and asking questions rather than necessarily substituting their judgment for that of the care team.

Another official stated that, as a Unit caseworker, it was better to have less specialist knowledge about mental illness because it enabled staff to examine cases 'like a normal person'. They might develop an understanding of the clinical terminology 'as we go along', but they did not need a detailed understanding of mental illness in order to make determinations about risk. It was more important to assess risk by putting themselves in the place of members of the public. In that sense, the decision frame of Unit officials relied upon notions of common sense that were 'evocative of an acquiescent mass public response' (Edelman 1964: 55). These notions symbolized a certain set of assumptions: both about safety, or what constituted protection for the public; and how safety was understood across the sphere deemed to be 'the public'.

Determinations

From the discussion so far we know that 'risk' operated at a number of different levels in the restricted patient system. First and foremost, it related to the question of danger and how much the public or patients themselves were exposed to. However, risks to reputation were also important for decision-makers, the Secretary of State and ultimately the system. These risks were real, as was demonstrated by the fall of at least one Secretary of State during the period of the research. This meant that in any decision made about a restricted patient, a range of risks were held in the balance.

The most frequent aspect of decision-making at the Mental Health Unit related to applications for leave, transfer or discharge. Each of these applications brought a patient closer to the public, thereby increasing the risk to public protection. These applications were determined primarily on the basis of clinical reports from a patient's care team. Even here, the framework for these reports placed priority on protecting the public, as the 'Guidance for Responsible Medical Officers' demonstrated:

> Leave programmes should be designed and conducted in such a way as to preserve public safety, sustain public confidence in the arrangements as a whole, and respect the feelings and possible fears of victims and others who may have been affected by the offences. (Mental Health Unit, March 2005: 2 at 4)

Among participants in this research there was a perception that, since the introduction of the Mental Health Act 1983 and particularly throughout the 1990s, the focus on risk had been an increasing preoccupation. However, documentary analysis of the criteria against which applications were assessed showed little change in a decade. There were four separate documents that spanned a period of ten years, setting out the factors to take into account when considering an application. The most recent document, a revised 'Guidance to RMOs' that was issued by the Mental Health Unit in April 2005, noted no 'major changes' in content, but general improvements in the representation of a broader range of views and clearer language and layout (SI 4/05, 'Revised Guidance for RMOs: Section 17 Leave', para 2). Despite the purported shift in emphasis towards public protection, these documents indicated little change in the processes themselves.

Undoubtedly, public protection was the most important factor taken into account in determining leave applications by Unit staff. Yet it was equally clear that *how* the public protection agenda featured in these decisions was a complicated and variable factor. To a certain extent, it was a consideration in terms of the defensibility of decisions. One staff member stated that leave arrangements needed to be justifiable, 'even if the purpose is made up'. She conceded that doctors might be frustrated by this, but insisted that the Home Office could not simply grant patients 'a nice time'. Another official supported this view, stating that leave required a therapeutic basis as it was unclear whether leave for 'pleasure's sake' could be justified. The need for a clear rationale indicated a set of internal criteria for decision-making, based upon the perception of those decisions and the ability to justify them. Such processes of justification 'prevent conflicts from arising by verbally bridging the gap between action and expectation' (Scott and Lyman 1968: 46). These 'rules of bureaucracy' also 'make available accounts for actions taken towards clients – actions which, from the viewpoint of the client, are untowards' (*ibid*: 54). In other words they are integral to the maintenance of social order.

In justifying their decisions, Home Office officials had to contend with two ostensibly competing factors. On the one hand, detention under the Mental Health Act 1983 was intended to serve the social order through a therapeutic, rather than a punitive, function. On the other hand, decisions to release patients from that detention needed to fit within the policy priority placed upon public protection.

A key strategy in the release of patients was to attach a set of conditions in the interests of public safety. While there was no set template for a conditional discharge, there were a number of standard elements that might be involved. These included ongoing supervision from a psychiatrist, social worker or nurse; taking prescribed medication; and residing at a stipulated residence as approved by the care team. Conditions might also include an exclusion zone restricting the patient from coming into contact with certain areas or people; or restrictions on drug and alcohol consumption. The imposition of conditions was no guarantee that they would be adhered to. But, as I shall show in a moment, conditions were important symbols of the priority placed upon public protection, as much as they were a measure of control.

My analysis so far has sought to distinguish between the Mental Health Unit's tasks of monitoring and decision-making. Like any theoretical examination of policy and practice, such distinctions are somewhat artificial. In fact, monitoring and decision-making were integrated processes, with one often leading to the other and vice versa. This interaction can be best understood through the operation of the Secretary of State's recall powers.

Recall

> The Secretary of State may at any time during the continuance in force of a restriction order in respect of a patient who has been conditionally discharged ... by warrant recall the patient to such hospital as may be specified in the warrant. (Mental Health Act 1983: section 42)

The power to recall a patient from conditional discharge in the community was one of the most sensitive aspects of the Secretary of State's powers. The most common use of recall related to patients who had been conditionally discharged and were residing in the community. There was another, less commonly used, recall power that applied to patients on leave of absence but still formally detained in hospital. For these patients either the executive or the responsible medical officer had the power to recall them to hospital, and either one could exercise that power without the involvement of the other (Mental Health Act 1983: section 41(3)(c)(iii)). However, the power to recall conditionally discharged patients was vested solely in the executive, under the auspices of the Secretary of State.

The recall power was particularly sensitive because it was the only aspect of executive discretion wherein the responsibility for depriving someone of his or her liberty rested with the Secretary of State. Restriction order patients were generally detained under court order following a criminal conviction. Recalling a restricted patient from conditional discharge in the community meant that the deprivation of a person's liberty took place under the Secretary of State's authority alone. The significance of this was highlighted by a number of Home Office participants, particularly in relation to how they determined when to recall a patient. Conditions of discharge were one of a number of elements that came into play here.

A patient had to be referred to the Mental Health Review Tribunal to review his or her detention within one month of a recall to hospital (Mental Health Act 1983: section 75). Beyond that, the Act contained no qualification about how the power to recall should be exercised. Mental Health Unit policy required decisions to recall a patient to be reviewed and confirmed by the Secretary of State within five days of the patient being returned to hospital. But, as with all other discretionary powers, the decision to recall a patient hinged on the executive's assessment of public safety.

Despite the absence of legislative qualification, certain conditions had been established through case law. Prime among these were the Winterwerp criteria, established in a case before the European Court of Human Rights, requiring that the nature and degree of mental disorder had to meet the criteria for detention under mental health law in order to avoid arbitrary detention (*Winterwerp v Netherlands* 1979).[1] As such these criteria applied to recall decisions as well as to other forms of detention under the Mental Health Act 1983.

Case law had not always supported the Unit's practice. The Unit had not always obtained up to date medical evidence of current mental disorder prior to initiating a recall. In the case of *K* (1998)[2], the court found that 'in the absence of an emergency, a patient's leave of absence should not be revoked without up to date medical evidence to demonstrate that he or she remains mentally disordered' (Jones 2004: 1–179). From then on, in order to justify a recall, up to date medical evidence was required to confirm that a patient met the criteria for detention under the Act. Importantly, that evidence was required to confirm that a patient had a mental disorder of a nature and degree to warrant detention under the Act, but not that the patient's mental state had *deteriorated* since his or her discharge to the community. Additionally, there was no requirement that the patient's treating team support the decision to recall (*B v MHRT and SSHD* 2002[3]). Case law had also established that even when a conditionally released patient was *voluntarily* readmitted to hospital, the Secretary of State could initiate a recall, thereby rendering the patient subject to compulsory treatment once more (*Dlodlo v MHRT* 1996[4]).

The exercise of discretion over recall has attracted some strong criticism. Dell and Grounds expressed concern that some of the principles on which recall operated conflicted with key tenets of mental health law, such as that of care and treatment in the least restrictive circumstances. They found that 'people were recalled against psychiatric advice, in order to prevent the possibility of their committing further offences' (Dell and Grounds 1995: xiii). Arguably, this contravened the objective of the Mental Health Act 1983 which provided for detention in order to treat mental disorders of a predetermined severity.

Yet the Mental Health Unit perceived recall in these circumstances as a perfectly legitimate operation of executive discretion in the interests of public protection. Indeed that legitimacy had been confirmed in the case of *MM*, which was concluded shortly after the completion of this fieldwork (*MM* 2007[5]). The case revolved around a restricted patient who suffered from paranoid schizophrenia and had a history of drug abuse. He had been convicted of unlawful wounding after he attacked someone on the leg with a hammer because he believed the person was having an affair with his girlfriend. He was detained for compulsory treatment for just over one year before being discharged by the Tribunal. From the time of his original discharge he experienced multiple recalls to hospital by the Secretary of State, only to be released shortly afterwards by the Tribunal. The 'risky' behaviour that led to his being recalled was repeated drug use which was perceived as a sign of relapse (or its potential) of his mental disorder. However, he was not found to have relapsed on these occasions and so did not meet the criteria for ongoing detention and treatment under the Act.

The patient sought judicial review of two of the decisions to recall, but the claims were dismissed. *MM* appealed and the court's judgment on the appeal raised a number of interesting issues in relation to recall powers. Firstly, the court considered whether evidence of deterioration was at issue in the Secretary of State's decisions to recall. The court found that one obvious part of the purpose of treatment is 'the avoidance or minimisation of risk'. Toulson LJ commented that:

> For the Home Secretary to recall a patient ... he has to believe on reasonable grounds that something has happened or information has emerged, of sufficient significance to justify recalling the patient ... he must have up-to-date medical evidence about the patient's mental health. (*MM* 2007: 50)

This ruling was important because it went so far as to say that, although current evidence of mental state was required, the purpose of treatment could be for protective rather than therapeutic aims. In other words:

> even though *MM* was asymptomatic, and even though he was not a risk at the time of the decision to recall, his further detention was justified by reference to the fear that all that might change, and change quickly ... In essence, the Court held that detention was justified before the patient reached a detainable state in order to prevent that detainable state arising. (Pezzani 2007: 222)

The case of *MM* also had significant implications for the relationship between the Tribunal and the Secretary of State when it comes to decisions about conditional discharge, as scholars have argued.

> What is immediately striking about this case is that a series of judicial decisions by the tribunal were nullified by successive decisions by the State. The question arises as to whether the actions of the Secretary of State were an expression of anything more than disagreement with the tribunal decisions. (*ibid*)

Above all, the decision in *MM* supported the prioritization of risk and public safety within the executive's decision frame. It legitimated the exercise of executive discretion in response to a *risk* of declining mental state and consequent risks to public safety, rather than current risks.

A number of Unit caseworkers said that there had been a growing emphasis on public protection, as demonstrated by the increasing use of recall powers to return a patient in the community to hospital. Data supplied by the Mental Health Unit showed that the number of patients being recalled had steadily increased from 54 (2001–2002) to 130 (2003–2004). These figures reflected an increase from just under 5% to over 11% of the patient population on conditional discharge. While these data only covered a short period of time, they supported the assertion the recall powers were being increasingly used.

Participants from the Unit attributed this to a harsher stance being taken by the Home Office in relation to behaviour in the community. One official told me that the Mental Health Unit had become more inclined to challenge care teams who were themselves unwilling to recall conditionally discharged patients. He gave the example of a recent case he had dealt with, where a conditionally discharged patient had become unsettled after consuming alcohol. Previously, the Unit would have checked the most recent medical reports about the patient and, there being no evidence of current mental disorder, would not have taken any action. Now, however, the official had gone back through the patient's file to examine the index offence. He saw that it had occurred under similar circumstances. The official wrote to the patient's care team reminding them of the circumstances of the index offence and advising them to monitor the patient more closely in the community. His action stopped short of recall. Nonetheless it constituted an intervention in the clinical approach of the care team. That response was determined by the increased emphasis on public protection and the sentiment, expressed frequently by Home Office officials, that patients in the community presented the greatest risks to public safety. The official described his role as 'acting as a trigger' for the care team, who might not pay as much attention to matters of public risk as the Home Office did.

The recall process demonstrated the hierarchy of authority and accountability of executive decision-makers in the restricted patient system; a hierarchy that enabled Home Office staff to intervene in the ways that care teams operated. From observing recall proceedings, it was clear that these decisions required close liaison between the care team working with the patient in the community and the hospital to which the patient was to be recalled. However, it was equally clear that the actual decision to recall someone was made entirely by the Unit, regardless of whether that decision accorded with the wishes of clinicians, and sometimes in spite of submissions from lawyers acting on behalf of the patient. It was well within the authority of the Secretary of State to deprive someone of their liberty on the grounds of public safety; and officials were willing to take such extreme steps in the interests of public protection.

The operation of recall powers reflected a central tension between the objectives of executive discretion and those of clinical practitioners. The purpose of clinical intervention, *via* compulsory treatment, was to treat restricted patients so that they could return to the community safely. That objective was shared by those exercising the executive's discretion, but only in so far as it provided the best measure of public protection. Not surprisingly, this produced vastly different emphases on the decisions of government officials and those of psychiatrists. One study of the supervision of restricted patients found that the Home Office relied upon the threat of recall to obtain compliance from patients coercively (Dell and Grounds 1995). Moreover, clinical practitioners were extremely concerned that the way the Home Office exercised its recall powers 'was to impose restraints on [patients'] liberties and obstacles to their discharge which were unjustifiable' (Dell and Grounds 1995: xii). These findings resonated with risk theorists who have argued that risk is immeasurable and that, by extension, it is difficult to know what is or is not justified (see for example Giddens 1991). Recalling a patient from the community did not mean that he or she presented a clear danger to themselves or to others. Indeed, Dell and Grounds found that the high proportion of cases where recall was not justified on the basis of dangerousness meant that 'recall cannot ... be equated with failure on conditional discharge' (Dell and Grounds 1995: xii). The use of recall was as much an indication of caution about public safety as it was a comment on the dangerousness of a restricted patient.

In a demonstration of this, one official reported that he would recall a patient 'where there was evidence of risk to the public. Not because of a need for treatment in hospital.' Another Unit member pointed out that a patient could be recalled if the patient stopped attending supervision sessions, because he or she could no longer be monitored. These decisions to recall did not necessarily require the patient's mental state to have deteriorated since discharge. They were based on concern that the public *might* be exposed to risk in the event of a potential deterioration. As a senior official put it:

> we're quite clear that we do not recall just because they're misusing drugs ... We're not a crime prevention agency, we're a public protection agency. So the question then is, 'is the misuse of the drugs likely to exacerbate their condition and lead them to relapse', in which case [we recall them]. I think we're quite sensitive to that interface but it is a real issue.

Used this way, recall provisions strengthened the utility of restriction orders as a protective measure by providing a mechanism for the return to preventive detention of those patients who had already been discharged into the community.

Risk could also be associated with more common problems of case management. One official told me of a 'challenging' patient whose behaviour was attributed to a combination of mental impairment and autistic character traits. According to the official, the patient also had a very difficult mother who was a 'destructive influence' on her son's progress and rehabilitation. This meant that the patient could not be conditionally discharged to his family home and that he needed to be escorted at all times while on conditional discharge. The patient had lived in supported accommodation for a short time but the arrangement had not lasted. In the absence of existing services to provide adequate support, and no appropriate alternatives, the patient was recalled. He was not exhibiting an increased risk since his conditional discharge, nor had his mental state deteriorated. But the political imperative of public protection determined that the patient might pose an unacceptable level of risk if he remained in the community unsupervised.

Above all, the utility of recall lay in the ability to detain people who posed a risk of harm to others. Yet its effectiveness was also based on a deterrent effect of the threat of loss of liberty. Breaching conditions of discharge did not *necessarily* constitute grounds for a recall. For example, one official explained that a patient who ceased to take their medication would not necessarily be recalled; it depended on the patient's mental state without medication. In practice, a breach of conditions often led to increased monitoring of the patient, rather than recall in the first instance. Another official stated it thus:

> As I understand it, it is for example not lawful to discharge somebody subject to the condition that they don't drink alcohol, because that's a lawful thing to do. Um, we would manage that, I mean if alcohol was a factor in it you probably would have a condition in place that they abstain from alcohol or something reasonable, um, but we would fully understand that if they did start going down to the pub and getting drunk there's nothing we could do about it apart from a thorough risk assessment and determine whether this was disorder-related misbehaviour in which case we probably could recall them. That's the issue.

In one example during my research, an official was monitoring closely a conditionally discharged patient who had returned a positive drug screen for marijuana some weeks earlier. Drug screening was part of the ongoing monitoring of patients in the community and was sometimes relied upon as a form of current medical evidence if recall was being considered. In this case drug use was a known trigger of deterioration in the patient's mental state. It was believed that the patient was becoming paranoid and his girlfriend had expressed fear to his care team. As we have seen, following the case of *MM* a decline in mental state and consequent public safety risks were a legitimate bases for recall, which the official decided to initiate.

Repeatedly in these examples of recall, the political mandate for public protection dominated the executive's decision frame, over and above the opinions of medical or legal practitioners. This placed restricted patients at a disadvantage in terms of sanctions against certain forms of behaviour. For example, a person charged with using marijuana would be unlikely to receive an indefinite sentence unless it was related to some far more serious offence. Similarly, a person would not be detained under the Mental Health Act 1983 for returning a positive result after a drug test. Yet for restricted patients, the fact of being on conditional discharge and at the mercy of executive discretion rendered them vulnerable to either of these outcomes.

Undoubtedly, certain forms of drug-taking were associated with some patients' criminal histories or with concerning behaviour more generally. Yet drug use is also an aspect of everyday life for many people. Nonetheless the risks that accompanied drug taking in the restricted patient system were deemed too great to ignore. Beyond the potential for drug use to alter detrimentally a patient's mental state, there was a significant risk of reputational damage if it came to the attention of the media or Home Office critics. In that light it was clear that executive discretion would be exercised to contain whatever risks in whatever way was necessary.

The use of recall powers in this way indicated the capacity of executive discretion to license preventive detention on the grounds of public protection. While this represented active control in the restricted patient system, it was reflective of more passive attempts in other areas. For example, judicial discretion has been increasingly curtailed through guideline and minimum sentencing policies and the imposition of statutory tariffs (see for example Simon and Feeley 1995; Fennell and Yeates 2002; Hawkins 2003; Thomas 2003; Richardson and Freiberg 2004; Rose 2004). It could be argued that such attempts have reflected the interests of governments to see certain categories of offenders detained for longer periods, irrespective of how that impacts upon judicial principles such as natural justice. For the officials of the Mental Health Unit, making decisions about restricted patients on behalf of the executive, their function was to exercise that unfettered discretion in the interests of protecting the public.

Yet the public served a dual purpose here: it was both the object of that discretion and the agent of the executive's accountability. There was little scope for the appeal or review of decisions by the Secretary of State. The accountability of the system derived from the extent to which ministers were answerable to parliament and subject to public criticism and electoral favour. As such, the effectiveness of executive discretion was measured by the *absence* of incidents in which the public was put at risk, or was seen to have been so exposed. Coming full circle, the democratic accountability of ministers provided a further impetus to use the powers of preventive detention to contain any risks to the public.

Determining risk

Our job is to look at the risk management implications of any proposal like, for example that the 'Yorkshire Ripper' should be given leave, and decide proportionally whether it should happen. Now that's a sliding scale. If you're talking about a patient that nobody's ever heard of, you can be totally objective. If you're talking about the 'Yorkshire Ripper', you're not only considering whether the 'Yorkshire Ripper' is going to harm somebody when he's out on leave. You're not even talking about whether he risks being lynched when he's out on leave. You're talking about the inevitable damage to the system when the tabloids find out that he's been out on leave. When huge numbers of people thought that this monster had been detained for life, find out that he's back in the community and their faith in the ability of the State to protect them is damaged. So that is a factor. You can't ignore it. But certainly in our decision-making and in our recommendations to ministers we try and minimize that. (Interview with a senior Mental Health Unit official)

Central to the ongoing assessment of risk was the level at which such risk became unacceptable. The law set this at 'serious harm', without any further qualification. The absence of any definition prompted an interesting exchange between a member of a restricted patient care team and a caseworker from the Mental Health Unit, observed during my research. The mental health worker asked who defined the level of seriousness in relation to harm. A senior Unit official replied that there was no basis in law for the term 'serious': it relied upon interpretation by courts and clinicians; and it was for the courts to determine the appropriateness of a decision to make a restricted hospital order following a conviction. He added that 'serious' was a qualification to the notion of harm that had been pressed for by stakeholders in the mental health system, including patient groups, who had wanted to ensure that decision-makers weighed up the consequences of compulsory treatment against the loss of liberty to the patient.

The process envisaged by the Mental Health Unit in the assessment of risk to the public was set out in its Caseworker Manual:

The rationale for the existence of the Home Secretary's powers is that the control of patients who are admitted to hospital following court proceedings and who are thought to be potentially dangerous should be vested in a central authority which would have special regard to the protection of the public. In exercising these powers, therefore, the Home Secretary is responsible for protecting the public from justifiable risk. The risk is generally understood to be that of harm to the person, covering significant sexual offences as well as offences of violence and arson. It is implicit in the concept of a restriction order that the hospital authority cannot necessarily be relied upon to take the protection of the public fully into account. The Home Secretary's decisions seek to give precedence to public safety considerations while supporting the objective of rehabilitation. The Home Secretary's statutory powers are not concerned with treatment of patients. This is the responsibility of consultant psychiatrists and care should always be taken by Home Office staff not to appear to interfere in what are essentially medical issues. (*MHU Caseworker Manual*, Chapter 1, p. 2, para 1.2)

The notion of 'justifiable risk' here operated on a par with that of 'serious harm'. These concepts were written into law or policy without definition; they were presumed to be self-evident and generally understood. Home Office staff were extremely cautious about any decisions that might expose the community to risk. Systemic tensions arising from the different objectives of administrators and professionals are not new, but recent criminological analysis has been interested in these tensions as one of the factors influencing policy shifts in contemporary penal policy. For Garland, new management styles and working practices have produced an ongoing tension between 'sections of the practitioner community and political decision-makers' (2001). Decisions about leave or discharge of restricted patients provided a case in point. Officials were concerned to make sure they could account for their decisions in the face of potential public scrutiny *as well as* clinical advice, even though the wishes of the public might not coincide with the therapeutic aims of treating teams. This tension reflected a disjuncture between clinical responsibilities to patients and the objective of maintaining public confidence in the system. The Mental Health Unit occupied a space in the middle, balancing the competing demands that were made on all sides.

Inevitably, that balancing role brought the Unit's officials into the position of assessing the value of professional advice such as that received from clinicians. The excerpt from the caseworker manual above indicates that Unit officials were wary of treading into the domain of clinical or medical expertise. Yet, as I shall discuss in Chapter 4, other actors perceived this as a structural reality imposed by the system of executive discretion. One senior official explained that the origins of the Mental Health Unit's caseworker roles dated from the Mental Health Act 1959, under which the criminal justice ministry took decisions on public safety while clinical decisions were maintained by hospitals and treating teams. Another official stated that:

you have clinicians looking after [restricted patients] but there is a subset of them who present such a danger to the public that it is appropriate to have some other oversight rather than just their doctors looking after them. And that result has been given to the Home Secretary. And we exercise those powers on behalf of the Home Secretary.

Both officials drew heavily on the history of decision-making in the system, particularly under the Mental Health Act 1959, as the basis for ongoing executive discretion. As one noted:

I mean I guess it's partly a quirk of history in that, in the 1950s, it was seen very much more clearly as being a government function rather than a function for the courts and so that's the way in which it was set up. And at the same time the Home Secretary personally had all sorts of involvement in life sentences and so on, which now have been pushed back far more on to the courts, particularly with the [European Convention on Human Rights]. But you know, it has survived as a Home Secretary function ... Of course you can argue that the Home Secretary ought not to have the function and it ought to be entirely down to the courts. And some people do argue that. But actually, whatever you might think in principle about a government minister having a role, in practice the system seems to work quite well. And I would expect, speaking personally, there to be far more pressure for change if it were not working well than if it is.

Many of the Unit's processes entailed summarizing clinical information that had been provided by treating teams, emphasizing certain elements that were regarded by Home Office officials as markers of risk to public safety. For example, one patient file opened with a document setting out his 'key risk factors'. It noted the date and detail of the patient's conviction leading to the restriction order and that there were no prior convictions; the patient's diagnosis; and that the patient had a history of admissions to hospital for psychiatric care prior to the index offence, as well as a history of aggressive behaviour. The document also listed four 'early relapse indicators', relating to loss of insight into the patient's illness, non-compliance, delusional beliefs and religious mania. The document concluded with a bold caution that 'risk can be considerable if [patient] starts to relapse', and an instruction to refer the case to a senior manager in such circumstances.

> Naturally it is not possible literally to 'predict' whether someone is going to do harm in a given situation ... In assessing the proposals made to us by hospitals for the transfer or discharge of restricted patients, we look for evidence both of accurate assessment and of effective risk management. (Potts 1995: 37)

Despite these processes, the Unit went to great lengths to explain that it did not undertake its own risk assessment separate from that of clinicians, as this excerpt by a former Unit official demonstrates. Rather, Home Office staff assessed the quality of risk assessments by care teams against what the Unit knew about a patient's history. The emphasis by officials on particular types of information implied a theory that past behaviour was predictive of future risk. That theory led to the identification of tangible factors that could be relied upon during casework, such as repeated patterns of behaviour. For instance, Dell and Grounds found a bias against restricted patients who required ongoing medication, in that they were more likely to have their applications for discharge refused (Dell and Grounds 1995). The need for medication was interpreted as a particular sign of risk, despite clinicians' assertions that two-thirds of their patients would continue to comply with medication whether or not they were on a restriction order (*ibid*). Similarly, the nature of the patient's index offence was interpreted as a predictive risk factor against which current behaviour could be measured, even if the index offence had occurred many years earlier or the patient had been acutely unwell at the time. It was as though the presence of a fact, such as a patient needing medication, was itself determinative of what process should be followed. As Rose cautions, 'once it seems that today's decisions can be informed by calculations about tomorrow, we can demand that calculations about tomorrow should and must inform all decisions made today' (Rose 2002b: 214).

The reliance on particular 'facts' to inform decision-making was a bureaucratic solution to the legal and medical complexities of forensic mental health. But it was also a system as likely to succeed as any other, in the hotly contested terrain of risk assessment. There is considerable debate about models of risk assessment and even leading experts have acknowledged that there are very few effective tools or clear methods to guide risk assessment in practice (Monahan 2004). Moreover, the commercialization of these tools, particularly in psychiatric practice, has clouded claims of their effectiveness. Within such controversial terrain, the executive's choice to avoid any formal risk assessment process could be well understood. However, it was also a choice that further facilitated the free rein of executive discretion, in the Mental Health Unit's administration of public protection.

The symbolic politics of public protection

Criminal justice has long been interested in the extent of fear of crime, alongside the reduction of crime itself. As far back as the first British Crime Survey, fear of crime was acknowledged as an independent issue for policy (Home Office 1982). More recently, Reiner has argued that the expectation that crime can be solved has steadily declined to the point where the Home Office no longer has confidence in its ability to control crime (Reiner 2007). This, he proposes, explains the increasing interest in controlling the fear of crime, rather than crime itself. Similarly, Simon has remarked how policies that increase police presence on the street seek to reduce fear based on the assumption that the visibility of the police will reassure the general public of their safety as much as it will effectively counter street crime (Simon 2007). Indeed the then Home Secretary herself acknowledged that reducing fear of crime sat alongside addressing offending behaviour as key objectives of contemporary criminal justice policy ('Today' programme 2007).

As a consequence, the focus of Home Office policy has shifted towards the perception of the system, rather than its outcomes.

> Decisions are taken, policies implemented, not simply because of their potential impact but, of course, because of how they will be perceived and 'received by a particular electoral community'. They are important for what they 'say' both about political parties and about individual politicians. This has always been so. Arguably, however, it is increasingly the case that individual politicians are exploiting the capital that can be made out of 'symbolic action'. (Newburn 2002: 175)

One way to understand the underlying rationales of these policies is through the notion of symbolic politics. Writing about the symbolic uses of politics in the 1960s, Edelman pointed to a shift in American political acts at the time, away from a critical probing of the limits of the state's authority, towards 'a predilection for staying so comfortably inside the limits that the main impression conveyed is one of craftsmanship in conforming to the prevailing political climate' (1964: 105). The potential of politicians to challenge people and to develop ideas as leaders was increasingly being marginalized by attempts to be seen to be doing things that would maintain political popularity among the electorate. As Edelman propounded,

> not only does systematic research suggest that the most cherished forms of popular participation in government are largely symbolic, but also that many of the public programs universally taught and believed to benefit a mass public in fact benefit relatively small groups. (Edelman 1964: 4)

The symbolism of the act was itself an assurance of political popularity, whether or not it resulted in direct or effective action. Accounts of social behaviour have also provided some foundation for the idea that assurance or predictability are important aspects of political action.

> The general pattern of social or group behaviour which is reflected in the respective organized attitudes – the respective integrated structures of the selves – of the individuals involved, always has a wider reference, for those individuals, than that of its direct relation to them, namely a reference beyond itself to a wider social environment or context of social relationships which includes it, and of which it is only a more or less limited part. (Mead 1934: 272)

Mead's work at this time was focused on globalization processes and how individual action could be understood at a broader societal (even international) level. But his thesis of individual identity as contingent upon group or social dynamics was a significant precursor to later analyses of symbolic politics. Both his and Edelman's theses contributed to a developing body of sociological inquiry into the interaction between individual, social and political behaviour.

Building on these approaches, later work examined how knowledge compared with individual associations of morality and values in the opinions people formed about their social environment. Gardiner's empirical research found that 'whenever symbols of law enforcement and official morality were brought into survey questions, most respondents opted for public norms of morality' (Gardiner 1970: 55). His study suggested only a tangential relationship between policy and operational objectives, for example between government anti-corruption strategies and attempts by police to reduce corruption.

More recently, Newburn and Jones have argued that symbolic politics 'downplays the complexities and long-term character of effective crime control in favour of immediate gratifications of a more expressive alternative' (Newburn and Jones 2005: 73). As crime policy has become more politicized and populist, so such 'acting out' has become more of a central feature; and the coupling between symbolic politics and operational outcomes in criminal justice has become ever looser (Newburn and Jones 2005: 73; see also Oliver and Marion 2008).

In Chapter 1 I discussed how the lens of risk has come to dominate the way our 'social environment' is understood. This means that actions and consequences are understood, firstly, in terms of the chance of their occurring and, secondly, by the variable consequences of that occurrence. In the context of these social perceptions of risk, individuals expect their governments to provide a social environment in which they are protected as much as possible. Being *seen* as responsive to those expectations has become as important for political viability as *actually* responding to them. An exchange during an interview with a senior Home Office official demonstrated this extremely well.

Au: What do you say to criticisms that executive discretion is overly cautious?

Official: In terms of over-caution, well that's a political issue isn't it? What we do here is not simply detain people. It's to require that they be properly risk managed, which is not the same thing as preventative detention. It doesn't entirely answer the question. We are cautious. We're here to be cautious. And by definition if you get a very low re-offending rate then you're going to be detaining some people who are false positives. That's political ...

Au: Political in what sense?

Official: Where you draw the line. What extent of re-offending is acceptable in terms of protecting the rights of individuals.

Au: And what about detention of false positives or preventative detention?

Official: Well it is a political issue. At one extreme it makes no sense for the state to just let everybody out in the knowledge that somebody will commit a horrendous offence. At the other extreme, is it proper to deprive people of liberty on the grounds that they might re-offend? I think we've got a pretty robust structure here in that for the restricted patients the Tribunal not only can but must discharge them if it is not satisfied they are detained on medical grounds. I think that's a pretty robust safeguard for the individual. And I think it's for others to say whether it works from their perspective. But I think we've got a very good balance.

This exchange was particularly revealing of how different standpoints on the question of risk and public protection played out in the decision-making process. While practitioners were concerned about an excess of caution preventing the discharge of people who could safely be managed in the community, the executive's approach relied upon a level of caution as central to its effectiveness. Yet the acknowledgement that the appropriate level of caution was 'a political issue' was also an indication of how important it was that both the government and its officials be seen as responsive to public expectations, even as those expectations were not fixed.

The conditions attached to leave or discharge demonstrated the inextricable links between the management of public fear and safety, on the one hand, and the decisions made about the therapeutic progress of restricted patients, on the other. The main purpose of these conditions was to provide compulsory supervision of patients in the community. While this purpose operated primarily in relation to discharged patients, it was also a function of the conditions on leave. Yet the extent to which these conditions were *successful* mechanisms of control was questionable. As one official suggested, they were really 'a bit of a bluff'. A number of other officials told of cases where concerns expressed by victims had resulted in an exclusion zone being included in a patient's conditions of discharge. Exclusion zones were supposed to prevent patients from attending particular areas such as a town or suburb where their victims lived. Restricting a patient's travel gave the impression that victims were being protected from coming into contact with their offender. However, exclusion zones were not enforceable. They provided no guarantee of avoiding such a confrontation, nor would a breach of an exclusion zone necessarily have negative consequences for a patient. In a stark acknowledgment of this fact, one official described conditions of discharge as 'pretty meaningless', given how easily a patient could breach them without penalty. According to that official, exclusion zones provided a measure of deterrence for patients and were an important source of reassurance that the Home Office could offer victims. But they provided no guarantee that victims and offenders would not come across each other in the community.

Another caseworker told of a case where a patient wanted to be granted leave to visit his parents who were ill and infirm. The care team had implied that the application did not pose any problems for public protection, but the Mental Health Unit was aware that the patient's victims lived in the same town and would be opposed to the patient's leave. As one caseworker explained, the process for determining the application required a judgment on the merits of the case. The Unit wouldn't necessarily involve victims in the decision-making process; it depended on how old the index offence was, as well as the geographical areas involved. In this caseworker's view, it didn't seem reasonable to hold up a patient's rehabilitation simply because victims *might* object to a patient's leave. To test the situation, the Unit authorized the patient to visit his parents on one occasion. However, it soon became clear that the patient was travelling to see his parents regularly, irrespective of the conditions of his discharge. While this was technically a breach of the Secretary of State's order, there had been no interaction with the victims as a result. The Home Office subsequently changed the patient's conditions, permitting visits to his parents as long as he avoided the victims and locations of likely interaction such as local shops. This example illustrated the symbolic importance of conditions, both as a deterrent to certain activity by patients and as a mechanism for reassuring victims that their concerns were being taken into account in the decision-making process. However, it also demonstrated the latitude with which breaches of conditions were sometimes met. While the threat of recall was always present, it was not always invoked as an automatic response when conditions were breached. The primary utility of conditions continued to be the ability to supervise patients in the community.

In the accounts given by officials, conditions of discharge were a measure of public protection. Yet the protection that they offered was as much through the appearance or assurance of public safety, as it was a substantive measure of prevention. The effect of that protection did not only touch individual patients. It was felt also by patients' families, victims and the broader community.

Media attention was another factor in decision-making. Any public attention on a case was likely to have an impact upon the entire system and consequently the level of confidence with which the public viewed it. As a result, controlling risk in the restricted patient system was both a matter of individual patient management and of controlling damage to the public's confidence in the system as a whole. As Garland notes:

> for *political actors*, acting in the context of electoral competition, policy choices are heavily determined by the need to find popular and effective measures that will not be viewed as signs of weakness or an abandonment of the state's responsibility to the public. (Garland 2001: 111, emphasis in quotation)

Symbolic politics were an important component of the executive's mandate for public protection. In reality, Home Office staff were aware that some of the conditions they put in place for public protection had no binding power. Yet symbolically, they were an extremely important expression of 'terminology and rhetoric' (Newburn and Jones 2005: 74). Similarly, the exercise of recall provisions emerged as both a mechanism for preventive detention and a powerfully symbolic tool of deterrence.

To suggest the presence of symbolic politics in the exercise of executive discretion is not to deny the substance of the Mental Health Unit's work in protecting the public. Rather, it is to emphasize the importance of the reputation of the system on individual perceptions of safety. As Mead argued, the principles of deterrence through the standards of retribution and prevention underpin public perceptions of criminal justice (Mead 1918). While there had undoubtedly been a shift in the balance of these standards over time, their symbolic importance remained as an example of 'emotional commitment' to a symbol that was 'associated with contentment and quiescence regarding problems that would otherwise arouse concern' (Edelman 1964: 32).

Executive discretion operated within a law that enabled preventive detention on the basis of public protection. The power to recall was no empty threat. It constituted a mechanism for control through containment and expressed the Home Office's willingness to use this mechanism. Moreover, as I have shown, patient recalls had been increasing over time. It was a central part of the Home Office's 'presentation of self' as an agency preoccupied with risk prevention (Newburn 2002). Yet, at the same time, the *threat* of recall had a strongly deterrent effect that was also important. Recall was both a coercive legislative provision and an important symbol of the powers that lay in the hands of the executive. In this way, symbolic politics were useful and effective ways to meet both individual and collective expectations of social behaviour.

> On the whole ... the diverse symbolic responses to political acts and events fall into place to build a remarkably viable and functional political system. It is a system that provides for both change and stability. It involves mass audiences emotionally in politics while rendering them acquiescent to policy shifts through that very involvement. (Edelman 1964: 15)

For the decision-makers in the Mental Health Unit, a familiarity with patients' index offences and therapeutic progress, and with other people such as family members or victims, reassured them that they could anticipate the concerns arising from – as well as the risks to – the public; and that they could ease those concerns effectively. The ability to detect risks and prevent harm was complemented by the process of reassuring the public to this end. Thus the risk of danger posed by patients was seen to be manageable through containment in detention and through the exercise of recall powers. At the same time, and as importantly, the fears of the public could be managed through a symbolic politics of protection.

Notes

1 *Winterwerp v. Netherlands* 6301/73 (1979) ECHR 4.
2 *K v United Kingdom* (1998) 40 BMLR 20.
3 *B v Mental Health Review Tribunal and Secretary of State for the Home Department* [2002] EWHC Admin 1553.
4 *Dlodo v Mental Health Review Tribunal for the South Thames Region* (1996) 36 BMLR 145, CA.
5 *R (on the application of MM) v Secretary of State for the Home Dept and Five Boroughs NHS Trust* [2007] EWCA (iv 687).

Chapter 4

Relationships in the system of executive discretion

Introduction

> Discretion is one of the most contentious concepts in criminal justice and related circles because it is so important and yet so difficult to define. (Gelsthorpe and Padfield 2003: 1)

One of the striking aspects of executive discretion is how much criticism has been levelled at its very existence in criminal justice decision-making. Executive discretion over mentally disordered offenders has been widely criticized for being overly cautious (Mohan, Murray *et al.* 1998); and producing arbitrary outcomes (Prins 1993). More specifically in the restricted patient system, executive discretion has been depicted as unwilling to recognize the rights of patients until forced to do so by the European Convention on Human Rights and subsequently the Human Rights Act 1998 (Richardson 2005). The pervasiveness of this opposition underpins much of the broader critique of how mentally disordered offenders are managed by the criminal justice system. For some, the limited ability of the criminal justice system to provide effective intervention for offenders with mental disorder, and the preoccupation with risk that underpins contemporary sentencing policy, means that mentally disordered offenders are 'dealt with more harshly' than other offenders (Peay 2002: 747). Others have argued that the failure to treat and manage people with mental illness effectively in the community creates a double disadvantage for mentally disordered offenders, who are both likely to be detained preventively under the Mental Health Act 1983, and to incur a consequent propensity for double jeopardy (Hawkins 1986; Peay 1993). Finally, the failure to grant decision-making power to the Mental Health Review Tribunal in the transfer and movement of restricted patients prior to their discharge has been criticized for undermining the procedural rights of offenders that are themselves related to the fundamental right to liberty (Richardson 1999).

Elsewhere in the criminal justice system, discretion is a widely accepted phenomenon. It is seen as both an integral and necessary element of practice, from police to judges to prison guards (see, for example, Cunneen 2001; Gelsthorpe and Padfield 2003; Freiberg and Gelb 2008). So the criticisms outlined above derive not from the element of discretion *per se* but from its exercise under executive authority. These criticisms are based primarily on the fact that executive discretion operates outside the principles of independent decision-making and the rule of law, as outlined in Chapter 1. In the restricted patient system, the independence of decision-making is not just a factor for tribunals or courts (such as those engaged in judicial review). It is also a factor in the clinical decisions of psychiatrists; the case management of hospitals; and the interventions of community care teams. The capacity of these practitioners to operate independently and in the interests of the best therapeutic outcome is questionable when it is widely known that the executive may not accept their recommendations for care and treatment.

Yet the absence of detailed, empirical analysis about how executive discretion operates has left us with little capacity to evaluate these concerns. Almost the only empirical analysis available is research commissioned by governments themselves. In the UK, a key study in this regard was conducted under the auspices of the Home Office Research and Statistics Directorate (Street 1998). That study pointed to a number of systemic problems faced by various actors in the restricted patient system, including the Mental Health Unit, the Mental Health Review Tribunal and clinicians. But its overall findings endorsed the role for executive discretion purely on the basis of public protection.

Meanwhile, there has been little independent analysis of how executive discretion interacts with other roles and responsibilities, such as those engaged in the care and treatment of restricted patients. How does the exercise of executive discretion affect the daily work of practitioners in these systems? How do those involved in the system assess the operation of executive discretion? Do practitioners distinguish between the principle of independent decision-making and the way that the executive exercises its discretion, such as in cases where executive decisions contradict clinical advice? What about non-government actors? Do their attitudes towards executive discretion depend upon the position they occupy in the system, such as service delivery or advocacy? Beyond the literature critiquing it, are there opportunities or positive outcomes created by the exercise of executive discretion over restricted patients?

Prior to this research, my observations in Australia had revealed a system beset by extremely polarized views about the function of executive discretion. On the one hand, many of the clinical and legal practitioners I encountered believed that the executive should have no role at all in decisions about the care, treatment and control of forensic patients. Such opposition was only fuelled by the lack of transparency about how executive decisions were made. On the other hand, politicians, advocates and commentators believed that the nature of forensic patients was so sensitive as to warrant decision-making *exclusively* by the executive. Within such a fraught environment, there was little space for cogent debate about the serious challenges facing the system, both in terms of patient care and public safety.

These tensions also led to a number of untested assumptions about preferable alternatives to executive discretion. For example, there was a widespread presumption that courts or tribunals would be less cautious in determining applications for release than ministers. These views appealed once again to the high value placed upon the separation of powers; and to the belief that judicial effectiveness derives from political independence. Yet these assumptions are not necessarily supported by research.

The relationships between the various actors involved in the restricted patient system of England and Wales provided a strong contrast to my observations of Australia and a fascinating insight into the interaction of executive discretion with other actors in the system. There was a general level of acceptance that the executive's role was unique and important. Moreover, many of the participants in my research respected the way that officials carried out that role. There were even specific benefits in terms of the supervision and monitoring provided by the Mental Health Unit. Perhaps most surprisingly, some practitioners argued that executive discretion was a highly democratic form of decision-making, since government ministers are directly accountable to the electorate in a way that judges (at least in Australia and the United Kingdom) are not. Undoubtedly, there were frustrations on all sides, as there will be in any arena that combines such a complex mix of legal and clinical practice. However, the overall dynamics between actors in the system indicated a far more complex range of opinions about the operation and outcomes of executive discretion than has been suggested by the literature to date.

Rights versus control

The relationship between the Home Office and the Tribunal

The relationship between the Home Office Mental Health Unit and the Mental Health Review Tribunal was important in a number of ways. At a theoretical level, it demonstrated the central tension between rights and control in the management of mentally disordered offenders. Empirically, it demonstrated some of the key policy challenges to those exercising discretion within the risk-averse framework of contemporary public policy. Relationally, it provided a lens through which to view the interaction between two institutions sharing a determinative power but exercising it in completely different ways. In the following discussion I explore these issues and how they informed the decision frame of those enacting the executive's discretion at the Mental Health Unit. Specifically, how did Unit caseworkers perceive Tribunal decision-making; and what influence did those perceptions have on the exercise of executive discretion?

At the outset, I imagined that there would be a degree of similarity in the concerns of those at the Mental Health Unit and the Mental Health Review Tribunal, for example about the susceptibility of their work to public attention (Hawkins 2003; Padfield, Liebling *et al.* 2003). However, my fieldwork revealed no sense of mutual sympathy about this common preoccupation between the two organizations. On the contrary, there was a tendency to regard each other as a necessary but unfortunate element of the overall system. At best, this could be described as 'institutional inertia'; a general malaise in trying to make sense of the actions of the one as perceived by the other (Padfield 2002: 137, see also Street 1998).

Unit staff repeatedly expressed frustration at the fact that the Tribunal frequently lost the Secretary of State's statements or asked for comments on a report only days before a hearing was scheduled to be held. However, this was an equally common allegation against the Home Office itself, whose timeliness in producing reports was criticized by the Tribunal and practitioners alike. One lawyer who represented restricted patients told me that the Home Office tended to send reports late or might refuse to comment on care team reports, leading to cancelled or adjourned hearings. Tribunal staff and practitioners cited the unavailability of Home Secretary reports at the time of Tribunal hearings as a major cause of adjournments and other delays. These participants interpreted the Home Office's actions in such situations as obstructionist. There was no sympathy for the fact that, for example, the Home Office might have had insufficient time to consider the case properly. Not surprisingly, these tensions led to some bad feeling between the Tribunal Secretariat and the Mental Health Unit; and to cynicism about the efficiency of the system from practitioners.

Under the criteria for detention set out in the Mental Health Act 1983, the Tribunal was required to discharge a patient unless it was satisfied that detention was necessary for the patient's health and safety; in the interests of the patient's own safety or for the protection of others; or to ensure that a patient could be recalled to hospital for further treatment (Mental Health Act 1983: section 72; Jones 2004 1–829). Mental Health Unit staff were generally of the view that the Tribunal's objective was to protect the rights of patients. According to some officials, that objective came at the expense of public protection. For example, some Unit members claimed that the Tribunal released patients even when the risk they posed to the public was too great. Staff supported this assertion by suggesting that when something went wrong in the community it was usually the Tribunal that had conditionally discharged the patient, against the wishes of the Home Office or care team.

The construction of these episodes as things 'gone wrong' was telling in itself. In their analysis of discretionary lifer panels of the Parole Board, Padfield and Liebling observe how recalls were taken as an indication of failure by officials (Padfield and Liebling 2003). They argue that recalls were often instigated in response to drug or alcohol consumption among released prisoners, which were everyday 'problems of living' yet were interpreted as signs of failure by the authorities (2003: 104). This analysis accords with the discussion of recall in the previous chapter, where a number of incidents that had led to recall could equally have been understood as 'problems of living'. Likewise, any issue arising about a patient's behaviour in the community was problematized by virtue of the response it required from the Unit.

In many ways the perception that such incidents were indications of wrongdoing, rather than predictable episodes in the daily lives of restricted patients, reflected the way in which the division of labour played itself out ideologically and culturally in the workings of the bureaucracy. It created a logic of accountability for decisions and a mechanism for attributing blame for perceived mistakes in decision-making. Of course, there was also a sense of relief that it had not been the Secretary of State who had authorized a mistaken or problematic discharge. Notably, these events were not perceived as normal episodes in the rehabilitative process. They were continually interpreted as problematic, based on the assumption that 'the perceived costs of a wrong decision to release are less than the perceived costs of a wrong decision to deny parole' (Thomas 1986: 1275). As the Tribunal was responsible for four-fifths of the decisions to discharge restricted patients, it was far more likely to have made the decision to discharge these 'problem' patients. Thus through the process of conditional discharge the cycle of patients between hospital and the community, that might otherwise have been considered predictable, reinforced a perception among Unit staff that the Tribunal was a bad decision-maker.

The structural advantage of executive discretion

The division of decision-making between the Mental Health Unit and the Tribunal was a product of the system itself, produced by the different criteria upon which each body assessed applications for discharge from patients. The Unit automatically had 'first bite of the cherry', because it could discharge restricted patients at any time. Dell and Grounds found that consultants were 'likely to be highly selective in choosing cases to recommend to the Home Secretary, and from these the Home Office can pick the best cases for release' (Dell and Grounds 1995: xiv). Thus the Mental Health Unit's decisions to discharge were selectively applied to the 'safest' cases (Holloway and Grounds 2003). In other words, if the Unit had not already released a patient, it was inevitable that they would oppose that patient's release by the Tribunal. While this was a systemic inevitability, it still resulted in the ongoing perception that the Tribunal chose to discharge patients who, in the Unit's eyes, were too risky.

Predictably, the mistrust with which the officials viewed Tribunal decisions resulted in a belief that the Unit did a better job in its decision-making. This belief was affirmed through a number of processes of rationalization. For example, Unit staff consistently expressed the view that the Home Office had a better knowledge of individual cases than the Tribunal, because the latter only had a snapshot of patients at the specific time of each hearing. As a result of their constant supervision and monitoring of patients and their care teams, Unit caseworkers believed that they made inherently better decisions.

The attitude of Unit officials towards the Tribunal indicated a number of important points about the exercise of executive discretion. Firstly, part of the 'protection' that it offered the public was not just from restricted patients themselves, but from 'bad' decisions by other actors in the system. The Home Office took seriously its legislative responsibility for public protection. As we have already seen, that responsibility extended to maintaining public confidence in, and protecting the political sensibilities of, the system. But it also extended to *de facto* responsibility for other elements of the system, including other actors over whom the Home Office had no formal or statutory authority. This included the Tribunal, which was an independent, statutory body; and medical practitioners, who were engaged by – and answerable to – local health trusts. So how did the exercise of these informal mandates affect relationships between the Unit and other actors in the system?

The relationships between executive discretion and other actors in the system

> There is mistrust between clinicians and the Home Office, particularly with regard to clinicians mistrusting the Home Office in making decisions without clinical training. (Mental Health Unit caseworker, Home Office)

In Chapter 3 we saw the tendency of Mental Health Unit officials towards watchfulness over care teams, as well as patients. Officials were particularly cautious where staff turnover or some other factor might make care teams less than cognizant of a patient's index offence or associated risk factors. At the same time, however, Unit staff were persistently troubled by the apparent mistrust that other actors in the system showed towards the Home Office's objectives. For example, one official described a case where the routine reports about a patient's progress had not been received. The Unit investigated the matter and discovered that the care team had been 'allowing the patient to dictate his own conditions, and regarded the [Unit's] concerns as exaggerated'. This was interpreted as an indication of poor confidence in Unit caseworkers on the part of the treating team. As caseworkers had anticipated, the patient's mental state deteriorated and his parents became very concerned about him. When police were called to investigate, the patient was found to have been hoarding weapons in circumstances similar to that of the patient's index offence and he was recalled. For officials, the outcome legitimated the Home Office's insistence that the behaviour of restricted patients in the community be closely monitored. As one caseworker described it, 'the care team learnt their lesson'.

Mental Health Unit 'away days' were one attempt to address these misconceptions, by educating practitioners about the Unit's role in the system. These were held every two months and were attended by mental health professionals working with restricted patients including clinicians, social workers and Mental Health Act administrators (hospital-based staff with responsibility for ensuring that the procedural requirements of the Mental Health Act 1983 were met). Away days were an attempt to show clinical practitioners how the Unit made its decisions; to improve working relationships between Unit staff and clinicians; and to build confidence in the Unit.

For the Home Office, the test of its relationship with these stakeholders was the extent to which clinicians sought discharge of their patients *via* the Secretary of State's powers rather than those of the Tribunal. Indeed, building this relationship was so important that the Unit's management team sometimes visited the regions for which they were responsible to promote applications to the Secretary of State for the discharge of restricted patients. This practice contrasted with the view of many practitioners that the Home Office preferred the Tribunal to make decisions to discharge patients, so that it could avoid the potential damage to its reputation of a 'bad' decision. As Mohan *et al.* have suggested:

> the increasing use of [Tribunals] for the discharge of restricted hospital order patients reflects a growing conservatism at the Home Office, such that it has become preferable for possibly controversial decisions to be taken by this independent body without ministerial involvement. (Mohan *et al.* 1998: 63)

Officials contradicted this analysis, describing their promotion of applications to the Secretary of State as part of a concerted effort to shift the Home Office from being reactive to assertive. They talked about a range of other activities that were also designed to increase the rate of applications to the Secretary of State. These included devoting more time to chasing up reports for regular reviews of discharged patients and corresponding with care teams. From the Unit's perspective, these were activities that increased the capacity for input from care teams in executive decision-making. Equally, however, they could be interpreted as signs of increasing interference in clinical processes on the part of the executive.

Unit officials spoke repeatedly about how the poor perception of the executive's function led to mistrust by practitioners in the system. Yet, these officials did not perceive their own mistrust of Tribunal decision-making, or their watchfulness of clinicians, as processes that were equally likely to signal mistrust. The preoccupation with public safety clouded any insight on the part of Unit staff that their own approach might be reducing trust among different actors in the system. That view was evident from the following excerpt in the Unit's *Casework Guide*:

> We should remember that ours is the only input to decision making which is made exclusively from the perspective of public safety. We should never hesitate to press any reservations we have on that score even though the care team is reluctant to address them. They have different priorities: professional pride, pressure to take forward rehabilitation, not to allow precious beds to be clogged up by lack of progress. They have a different perspective too. They have to live with the patient in their hospital; may have come to empathise with them, and will be more readily influenced by the patient's recent good behaviour; may be less keen to provoke their reaction when confronted with things the patient would rather forget or keep under wraps; may be less likely than us to remember the full details of the offending behaviour, and to realise that any recent minor incident looks like behaviour in the run-up to the offence. So we should not hesitate to ask the uncomfortable questions, which it may not be in the immediate interest of the care team, much less that of the patient, to answer. (*Mental Health Unit Casework Guide*, March 1998, 1A.8ii)

This excerpt was fascinating for its unambiguous assumption about the various mandates in the system. The expertise of clinicians in their daily work with restricted patients is clearly acknowledged, but equally clear is the perception that such relationships inherently blur the clinical responsibility towards public protection. Only caseworkers, by virtue of their isolation from daily contact with patients, can maintain the impassioned perspective necessary to ensure public safety.

These opinions of caseworkers about care teams had a significant impact upon the Mental Health Unit's assessments. For example, Unit staff placed confidence in the information they received based on the source of the evidence, as well as the type. Several officials explained how social workers in the community tended to be more reliable than doctors in terms of risk management, because psychiatrists who worked in the community often had less experience with forensic patients than those who worked in secure hospitals. As a result, officials considered these psychiatrists to be less aware of the risks to the public and consequently exercised greater caution when assessing applications from them. These accounts pointed to how Home Office officials made judgments based upon the *source* of the information as well as its *content*, indicating the different layers of subjectivity involved in assessing evidence about detained patients (Perkins 2003). While literature from the Home Office stipulated that its role was not to substitute individual assessments for those of professionals, it was clear that some Unit staff held genuine concerns about the quality of some clinical practice, not least when they believed it was insufficiently concerned with protecting the public.

In Chapter 3 we saw how lawyers were particularly attuned to the mistrust levelled against them. One lawyer interviewed suggested that 'lawyers are seen as the second coming of Satan', and that lawyers sometimes experienced difficulties getting hospitals to refer patients to them. Only enlightened advocates or hospital staff would recommend lawyers who acted in patients' interests. Otherwise, hospitals routinely recommended lawyers from firms who generally worked for the government. Such assertions might sound conspiratorial. However, they were also an indication of how entrenched were the various perspectives of those in the system. Caseworkers carrying out the executive's discretion perceived their role as central to the functioning of the overall system; maintaining its integrity and effectiveness, which they measured in terms of public perception. By contrast, lawyers acting on behalf of patients perceived themselves to be pitted against the executive and, to some extent, the system itself.

It was the perception of Unit officials that other actors doubted caseworkers solely because they were responsible for implementing the executive's function. Yet the adversarial structure of the system inevitably produced levels of mistrust between all actors. Predictably, the bureaucratic caution towards any application that brought a patient closer to the public also undermined relationships between administrators and clinicians. Highly qualified and experienced care teams might well bristle at the perception of interference by administrators who are not even clinically trained. Equally, legal interventions in the case management of patients were likely to challenge the boundaries of hospital or executive authority in an effort to make even small gains towards their clients' liberty. What was fascinating was that, notwithstanding these elements of mistrust, there was a broadly tolerant and accepting attitude from each perspective in the system towards the others.

From the other side: attitudes towards executive discretion

One of the most surprising findings of this research was that the function of executive discretion was fairly widely accepted by legal and clinical practitioners and by non-government organizations associated with the restricted patient system. In many ways this followed from the recognized divisions of labour discussed above. But it also flew in the face of the presumptions contained in much of the literature, about the detrimental effects of executive discretion and about opposition to it by others involved in the system.

One lawyer who worked in a practice with a large client base of restricted patients described the Home Office's role as one of 'public guardianship'. He stated that, 'the Home Office has a role in relation to protecting the public. I think that we would really accept that.' This acceptance of the Home Office's function in public protection spanned other practitioners also. Indeed, this lawyer's reference to 'we' indicated his perception that this was a view shared by other legal practitioners.

This is not to suggest that executive discretion was completely uncontested. It was *how* that discretion operated, rather than its mere presence, that caused concern among participants in this research. The most common issue cited here was about the balance between public protection and patient rights. The same lawyer went on to explain this in the following way:

> I think [the Home Office] are entitled to have a view. I mean, is this chap going to go and get unwell and do things to other people? You know, are people waiting at a bus stop safe, and this sort of thing? But OK, they express their views, and the court in effect made another decision.

This statement implied that the Secretary of State was unable to strike a balance between patient therapy and public safety because of the executive's preoccupation with public protection. Many of the practitioners interviewed in this research echoed similar sentiments. Across practitioners and advocates alike there was consensus that the Mental Health Unit's role related entirely to the public protection agenda. As we have seen, this objective justified the Unit's role in decision-making, including its interventionist approach to other actors in the system. By contrast, for practitioners and non-government organizations, this priority on public safety was precisely the reason why they felt that the Home Office should not be the sole decision-maker over leave and discharge. In their eyes, that mandate undermined the executive's ability to strike the right balance between public protection and the most appropriate treatment for a restricted patient. As a result, the decisions of the Mental Health Unit were believed to be overly cautious. The implication that this could be avoided by allowing tribunals or other authorities to have determinative authority was implied by some, but was not routinely articulated.

Another lawyer involved in law reform discussed the process of Home Office officials making decisions without professional training in forensic mental health. He supported the view, canvassed previously by Mental Health Unit staff, that Unit caseworkers added value to the system through their familiarity with specific cases, as well as with the workings of the system as a whole.

> They do have a considerable amount of expertise in mental health. And having worked with them in the field, they do know what they're talking about. While they don't have a good expertise in terms of clinical evidence or judgment, I think nevertheless they have built up a lot of casework knowledge which is very useful to have really.

He went on to say that even though the Unit might seek to promote transparency, the nature of the system pitted practitioners, and particularly lawyers, against the Home Office. By this rationale, there would always be conflict over particular cases. It was a structural inevitability of the adversarial system; mirroring the inherent tension between the Home Office and the Tribunal discussed earlier.

Dell and Grounds' study a decade earlier found that Unit caseworkers' supervision of patients in the community was generally considered useful by clinical practitioners, particularly in terms of the department's support of their work and the ability to discuss anxieties clinicians had about particular cases with Unit staff (Dell and Ground 1995). In my own research there was some indication by practitioners that they appreciated the supervision offered by Unit staff. But the most common reaction to the operation of executive discretion was that it was overly cautious and detrimentally so. For example, one senior psychiatrist assessed the decisions of the Mental Health Unit as operating 'with not much discretion'. He went on to explain this in the following terms:

You'd expect that if the Home Office in their comprehensive way exercised discretion, that it might be prepared not infrequently to authorize the discharge of restricted patients itself. That would be a natural consequence of properly exercising discretion. If you never exercise that power, by definition almost you're not exercising discretion. And then there are more minor ways in which discretion is heavily biased in one particular direction and I suppose what it feels more like is that there are tensions between forces, and one force is the Home Office pulling in one direction, and the other force is to some extent [Resident Medical Officers], tribunals, certainly lawyers, pulling in the opposite direction. So it feels like a sort of um, an equilibrium, if you like, achieved between forces rather than the Home Office balancing matters and exercising its discretion.

When I put that opinion to a Home Office official, his response reflected the frustration that came from dealing with numerous different perspectives on the same issue. He said:

What discretion are we talking about here? The 1983 Act does, oddly, give to the Home Secretary power to discharge a patient in his own right. That, it seems to me, is a logical nonsense. How is the Home Secretary going to take a clinical decision? The real question is what the Home Secretary's attitude is to applications for discharge from the RMO [Resident Medical Officer]. And we spend a huge amount of effort talking to doctors, trying to persuade them that the Home Secretary is the primary discharge avenue. We just can't say enough, 'look if you think that this patient should be discharged, ask us'. We might say no, but in most cases we'll probably say yes and we will have saved you and the patient and the tribunal system and the taxpayer a huge amount of effort. We're working quite hard to try and claw back the balance on discharges. So I get a bit cross with people who say we don't do discharges. We don't go out of our way looking for people to discharge. And we don't

> proactively take unilateral decisions to discharge patients and I think we'd be bonkers to do so. But we move heaven and earth to try and persuade RMOs to come to us and ask for discharge … and most of them won't.

This response demonstrated a gulf between how the Home Office constituted the operation of executive discretion and what practitioners expected from it. For the psychiatrist, the possibility offered by executive discretion was a positive one in terms of decisions to discharge. The fewer patients the Secretary of State discharged, particularly in those cases where discharge was supported by the clinical evidence of care teams, the less the executive could be said to be exercising its discretion. Whereas for the official, decisions not to discharge indicated the operation of discretion in the interests of public protection, from which the executive's mandate derived.

Those engaged in lobbying, advocacy and law reform were also largely sympathetic to the Home Office's role in the restricted patient system. One interviewee who represented a mental health charity acknowledged that the public protection agenda was central to current government policy. But she, too, claimed that the tensions within that agenda prevented the executive from acting in the best interests overall, including for patients. She attributed this in part to the influence of factors outside the government and the system's control. For example, heightened media attention to individual cases was itself driven by the intense competition between news agencies, whereby major dailies needed to maintain and increase sales through sensational stories such as those about dangerous mentally disordered offenders. In essence, she was talking about negotiated order; the bargains struck between the many interests that might be engaged in an active process (Strauss 1963). As a result, she maintained, there was no problem with the Home Office having a role protecting the public; the problem lay in how politicized those issues had become. That level of politicization was reflected in the way that the reputation of the system was prized over and above the individual rights of patients to be discharged. Her comments spoke to an essential difference in the view of executive decision-makers, on the one hand, and practitioners and advocates on the other, about how the executive exercised its discretion. That difference, of course, turned on the question of risk.

Getting risk right

> If the assessment of risk were to provide the basis for compulsory measures it would be incumbent on society to 'get it right'. If there is not a real probability of risk, but rather an attributed perception of it which prompts intervention, then the moral arguments favouring it are altogether less compelling. Moreover, if there were no real probability of danger then we would be infringing the liberty of a few, without any concomitant increase in the well-being of the many (except perhaps by falsely reducing their fear). (Peay 1989: 207)

Risk has always been important to psychiatric practice. Throughout my research, practitioners consistently recognized risk to be a major factor in the decisions made about care, treatment and discharge of patients. The unanimity of that view threw some doubt on the perception of officials that the executive was the only actor concerned with public protection. But it also reinforced the idea that the problem was not whether to assess risk, but how.

Risk assessment is most reliable when it relates to population estimates: the likelihood of certain forms of behaviour appearing among a particular population who share similar characteristics. In forensic mental health, those characteristics might be described by variables such as drug-taking, violent behaviour or criminal offending. Even when a variable such as violence can be isolated, its correlation or causality to certain behaviour is not necessarily clear. For this reason, best practice models have advocated an interactional approach to violence risk assessment, acknowledging that 'the same variable could be a positive risk factor for violence in one group, unrelated to violence in another group, and a protective factor against violence in a third group' (Monahan, Steadman *et al.* 2001: 90).

In other words, a risk assessment is not a clear prediction of future behaviour. Nor can it be the sole basis for determinations about the safety or otherwise of a proposal for patient leave, transfer or discharge. Risk assessments do not translate easily into neat policy statements or facts on which to base individual decisions. Consequently, the most contentious issue among different actors in the system was how to assess risk and what weight to place upon those assessments in the decision-making process. It was a question that spoke directly to the issue of roles and responsibilities within the system. It was also reflective of broader debates about the utility of 'expert' evidence and its place within decision-making.

The role of psychiatric evidence in the decision-making process

Psychiatrists interviewed during the course of this research tended to perceive their function as one of advising on the possible risks in relation to a patient and proposing plans to manage those risks. However, they routinely drew the line at determining the level of risk to which the public could reasonably be exposed. The following comment from a psychiatrist reflects many of the views expressed by clinical practitioners during this research:

> The question for us, and the question for society, is how much will you tolerate? ... We're not prepared to take risks. We're a risk averse society. Maybe that's right but whether it's right or wrong I can debate as an individual member of this society, which I am, I can debate it as a doctor who's involved in risk management. But at the end of the day as an employee I have to then go along the line that's been adopted at the moment. And I'm not sure that I know the answer and it would be arrogant to believe I do.

Most of the psychiatrists interviewed perceived the identification and management of risks as a job for them and their care team colleagues. But, they argued, the question of how much risk the public should reasonably be exposed to was essentially a political question best answered by elected representatives, not by psychiatrists.

A number of psychiatrists felt that expectations upon psychiatry already exceeded the limits of their clinical capability. The law was an example repeatedly offered in this respect, as the following anecdote from a psychiatrist illustrated.

> [Then Chief Justice] Lord Woolf gave the opening address in 2001 to the [Royal College of Psychiatrists] annual conference ... And he gave a wonderful ... demolition of the White Paper for the Mental Health Bill, on a civil rights basis, and the audience could have hugged him, and at the end, he said, 'of course when it comes to risk, we very much rely on you'. And there was stunned silence. Now Lord Woolf was, I think, a very liberal Lord Chief Justice, rather sensible, balanced, often outspoken, and yet even he felt unskilled when it came to mental disorder, and assumed that we were more skilled than we actually are.

Concern at the over-reliance on medical expertise was echoed by many clinicians in this research. They understood that their expertise was leaned on as a crutch by others who felt uncomfortable with certain decisions they had to make, such as whether a court should grant bail to an accused who showed signs of serious mental disorder. Nevertheless, psychiatrists argued, discomfort at having to make a difficult decision did not make that decision someone else's responsibility, least of all psychiatrists. It was a decision to be made by a judge in a court, or a minister exercising their executive discretion. As far as psychiatrists I spoke with were concerned, all that they could do was provide information that might usefully contribute to the process.

Even then, psychiatrists did not believe that risk assessment was the only form of information upon which decisions to discharge should be based. Many of those I spoke with expressed the view that the balance in the courts had shifted too far in favour of clinical evidence, which was privileged over other forms of knowledge. These psychiatrists clearly believed that they could provide useful information for court proceedings. Yet they appeared also to feel that the extent to which that information was relied upon was too great. As one stated, 'I think there's quite a strong risk of courts if you like paying too much attention to what psychiatrists and psychologists who are prepared to go into court say.'

No participants in this research denied the importance of risk in decision-making about restricted patients. But the debate continually returned to the question of who should make the decision about acceptable levels of risk, and how they should make it. As one psychiatrist stated, doctors could not take responsibility for setting the acceptable level of risk because it was not their role to protect the public. While public protection was an aspect of clinical decision-making, the priority for psychiatrists was the care and treatment of their patients. That was why the decision about acceptable levels of risk properly rested with a legal authority, either under executive discretion or through an institution like a court or tribunal.

This clinician was also insightful about the relationship between clinical practice, executive discretion and public expectations. He argued that psychiatrists had not accepted and responded adequately to the community's concerns about the dangerousness of some patients. He discussed a recent case where a restricted patient had killed a police officer while living in the community on conditional discharge. Upon investigation it was discovered that the patient had been stockpiling his medication and was not being monitored by his health service. The psychiatrist spoke of his 'amazement' at this incident in a system which, he thought, 'had moved away from the circumstances where this could happen after Clunis'.

'Clunis' referred to a high profile case from 1992 where Christopher Clunis had killed Jonathan Zito. Mr Clunis suffered from paranoid schizophrenia and had a history of extensive mental health treatment with very little continuity of care or routine follow up. Mr Zito's homicide came shortly after Mr Clunis had engaged in a couple of less serious but potentially very dangerous acts which, it was believed in hindsight, ought to have signalled the decline of his mental state. As I shall discuss further in Chapter 5, Mr Zito's widow went on to establish a victim organisation, The Zito Trust, and became an influential figure in the public discourse about victims' rights, compulsory treatment and community care.

For the psychiatrist, speaking about these issues some 13 years after the Clunis case, the fact that a homicide could occur in similar circumstances beggared belief. He had thought that the lack of caution and insight attributed to the care of Mr Clunis was 'no longer representative of the services and how the system operated. But here it happened again.' In his view, the government's staunch defence of executive discretion was partly in response to the failure by psychiatrists to take seriously the level of community concerns about such cases. It was also in that context, he contended, that psychiatrists were under increasing pressure to manage dangerous behaviour. In his view, doctors needed to win back the public's confidence in the system. But, he asserted, the way to do so was by meeting public concerns by adequately managing patients in the community. It was not by exaggerating arguments about the functionality of psychiatric expertise or the political nature of decisions about public protection.

It is rare to suspend our instinctive or natural attitudes; to stand back and reflect on our practices (Shultz 1967). This provides one explanation for why many practitioners had given little thought to the principle of executive discretion, rather than how it operated in practice. Many participants were surprised when I asked them about the value or legitimacy of the role, as though they had never considered it before. One psychiatrist was telling in his response, stating, 'in the sort of democracies we live in it's probably difficult to envisage a system which didn't involve political involvement'. His comment could be taken as a pragmatic response to the realities of the system in which he worked. While practitioners might be interested in attempts to improve the day-to-day mechanisms of the system, they had little time to consider its underlying structures.

Yet for another psychiatrist, this was typical of a level of complacency among many of his colleagues. This psychiatrist had experience working in forensic mental health systems in a number of different jurisdictions. This had given him a certain distance and a novel perspective on the restricted patient system, where he found the operation of executive discretion to be 'better in theory but worse in practice' than comparable jurisdictions. He attributed this, in part, to the acquiescence of English psychiatrists who simply accepted the role of the executive without really challenging its processes or outcomes.

Making it legal

The general acceptance of the executive's function was shared equally by psychiatric and legal practitioners in this research. Undoubtedly, some lawyers had a principled objection to executive discretion *per se*. However, most acknowledged that the executive had a legitimate role in providing public protection. Thus legal practitioners rarely criticized the *fact* that Unit staff assessed expert clinical reports and risk assessments.

Instead, they levelled their concerns at the cautiousness and slowness of decision-making by officials exercising the executive's discretion. In the view of several lawyers, the problem lay in the conflation of probabilities of risk on a population basis, with the desire to predict and prevent individual behaviour. This led to overly cautious decision-making because, according to practitioners, the Mental Health Unit was looking for minimal or zero risk before it determined that a patient could spend time in the community. Yet as we have seen, the very nature of risk assessment meant that as soon as a risk factor was identified, there would be a chance – no matter how small – of the dangerous behaviour occurring. An assessment of zero risk was a literal impossibility.

This produced a 'catch 22' scenario. Applications seeking to move a patient to less secure conditions were required to produce an assessment of the risks posed by that patient. That evidence then provided the justification to reject an application, should the Unit so determine. This was summed up in the words of one legal practitioner who stated, 'my understanding of the Home Office's position is that they want to be absolutely sure that it's safe to move somebody on before they move on. And you can't ever be absolutely sure.' For her, the worst effect of the Home Office's approach was not upon applications for discharge, because these applications had a second port of call in the form of the Tribunal. The more serious problem was the inability to achieve patient progress from more to less secure settings in preparation for release. The over caution of officials demonstrated their failure to grasp the difference between risk assessment and risk management; the fact of risks alone was enough to deny a patient's application, regardless of how well the care team had prepared for such possible eventualities.

A number of other participants shared this belief that the political imperative to prevent risk ignored the reality that risk assessment was an inexact science, nor could it predict an individual's behaviour. Officials, it was suggested, assumed that risk assessments could be easily obtained; should be comprehensive and accurate; and that a positive assessment establishing the presence of risk was grounds for refusing less restrictive conditions of detention or discharge. Some practitioners perceived this failure to appreciate the complexities of risk assessment as a consequence of non-expert decision-makers in the Mental Health Unit, as the following comments by a lawyer indicated:

> They're civil servants, they have no medical qualification whatsoever, and it is always going to be the case that if you get enough reports which express perfectly valid hesitations and reservations and things that you need to look out for and so on and so forth, it is the work of but a moment to extract these and say 'well that's gotta be sorted out before the person moves on'.

Lawyers claimed that there were a number of approaches adopted by the Mental Health Unit in order to stall the progress of patients through the system. For example, Unit officials would expect unanimous support across the system before they would authorize changes to a patient's security status or place of detention. One legal practitioner put it in the following terms:

> The Home Office say 'that everyone's got to agree before we're going to agree. We're not going to agree to it unless everyone else agrees.' And there's always somebody not agreeing. And it can take years. ... Broadmoor are saying, you know, in 2000, this person's ready to move, and in 2005 there they still are. ... whatever the Home Office may say about the public interest ... the law relating to detention and transfer and so on and so

forth is perfectly clear: people should be treated in the least restrictive alternative possible; people should only be detained in the interests of their own health and safety or the protection of others.

This comment indicated the difficulty of obtaining support from all parties prior to an application seeking a change in conditions of detention. As a result, patients could be detained in excessive levels of security.

Others spoke of cases where a clinical team and independent experts had all supported an application, but the Unit officials had refused to make a determination because there was a Tribunal review coming up. In fact many of the practitioners I spoke with recounted cases where the Home Office had avoided making a determination in a case if the Tribunal could do so instead. As another lawyer said of the Home Office, 'they're unwilling to discharge on their own. My view certainly is that they prefer to cover themselves with the Tribunal doing it.' The following account illustrated this further:

I had a case last week where there'd been some administrative problems with the client who's been on overnight leave for some time, and the Tribunal was going to convene and I phoned the Home Office and said 'well, why don't you just discharge him?' 'Oh well, there's a Tribunal coming up isn't there?' I said 'well look, you know, you could read this recommendation for leave, you haven't objected, you haven't put in statements in relation to these extra reports at all. Why don't you just discharge him?' 'Well, you know, we've had problems finding the file.' You know, you get the feeling that the Home Office doesn't like to discharge if it doesn't have to.

Participants repeatedly cited examples where the Secretary of State appeared unwilling to discharge a patient if a Tribunal had been convened for the same matter. Consequently, the attempts by some to reform the Unit's practice in this area were simply motivated by a desire to improve the speed and turn-around of applications as much as by any underlying opposition to executive discretion.

At least one practitioner suggested that the Mental Health Unit was using the Mental Health Act 1983 as a policy of containment. He described a conference at which a Home Office official had:

let slip [words to the effect of] ... 'well, I don't know what all this business is about using mental health law because very soon we won't need to use mental health law'. Now of course what she didn't seem to realise as she was saying it was that the implication was that if you did need to use it, you'd use it. Which I thought was quite interesting because I thought that was quite clear that she was saying 'well of course we'll use mental health law for public protection even when there's no benefit for the individual' ...

This anecdote spoke to the concerns expressed by a number of practitioners, that the principles of mental health law were deemed less important than ensuring the prevention of risk and the protection of the public. Practitioners did not oppose the executive's concern for public protection. But they wanted it to be done appropriately and proportionately. This was the crux of the criticisms by many people I spoke to, that the assessment of individual risks became the basis on which to deny patients' progress through the system. Regardless of the intended aims of the Unit's policies and processes, their effect was sometimes to stall patients who would otherwise have made progress towards the discharge of their restriction order. Over time, practitioners argued, this had caused the system to slow and patient numbers were burgeoning as more patients entered the system but the rate of discharge remained constant.

Delays in patients moving through and out of the system also led to a pattern of institutionalization for restricted patients who had been detained for very long periods of time. One participant talked about the problems facing aged restricted patients, for whom the world outside the hospital had changed significantly since they were first detained. In the time taken to move some patients through the system to the point where they could be released, they had become institutionalized and alienated, such that the most likely risks now related to their incapacity to function in the modern world outside the hospital.

The relationships between different actors across the restricted patient system reflected the complexities of managing people with mental disorder who were assessed as posing particular risks to the public. The level of that challenge had led the Mental Health Unit to define its role completely and uniquely in relation to protecting the public. Other actors in the system acknowledged the importance of public protection, and most agreed that it was a political objective best met by the executive rather than professionals. But they did not agree that the public protection was paramount to all other considerations. In particular, they claimed that this prioritization prevented patients from being detained in the least restrictive conditions necessary, while simultaneously blocking beds from other patients who had greater need for them. The Mental Health Unit was familiar with these criticisms and staunchly defended its processes in response. One of the key indicators it relied upon as evidence of its effectiveness was data on the reconviction rates of restricted patients.

Same data, different story

> The hue and cry over those patients incarcerated for many years who, in effect, would not have re-offended pales into insignificance in relation to public and political outrage regarding a released patient who does re-offend. (Mason and Mercer 1999: 103; see also Padfield, Liebling *et al.* 2003; Wood 1993)

Reconviction data provided a source of 'institutional legitimacy' to the processes of the Mental Health Unit (DiMaggio and Powell 1983). In the restricted patient population, less than 8% of patients had been convicted of a standard offence within two years of their discharge and less than 1% had been convicted of a grave offence within the same timeframe (Ly and Howard 2004). Home Office officials argued that this comparatively low recidivism rate demonstrated the success of its operations in protecting the public. Yet psychiatry, like statistics, has a well-documented literature showing that certain data can be used to support a number of different positions (Monahan, Steadman *et al.* 2001). These same data on the reconviction rates of restricted patients were used by both sides of the debate about whether executive discretion was overly cautious.

Practitioners were keenly aware of the political imperative for the executive to meet, and *be seen* to meet, the public's expectations about safety. One lawyer I interviewed stated:

> I think you do have to take on board that this is a serious public concern and no matter what we say about the best way to deal with people who are a danger to others, the public are always going to take this 'lock 'em up' attitude and the government have got to respond to that to some extent.

Nevertheless, practitioners argued that the reconviction data cited by the Unit was evidence that their decision-making was unnecessarily cautious, as the following comments by a lawyer indicate:

The overall recidivism rate is extraordinarily low, I mean it's something like three per cent over five years or something. ... it seems to me that what that must mean is that many people are being kept in who don't need to be. ... And you know the Home Office no doubt would say, 'well, you know, we're not making mistakes because very few people get out and re-offend', but they are making mistakes but they're just making an invisible mistake where people aren't getting out who could safely be let out. And if one accepts that people are in hospital for treatment rather than punishment then that's an error.

I interviewed another clinician with experience managing secure hospital units in the UK and overseas. He agreed that low recidivisim rates indicated an overly cautious policy on release.

Our patients generally get out after four to six years. We have a zero re-offending rate, which I think is dreadful. It means we are being too conservative. I would like to have a five to ten per cent re-offending rate, which would be one-fifth of the general re-offending rate.

For these practitioners, reoffending rates that were significantly lower than those of comparative populations were proof positive that the system was overly cautious. Moreover, some practitioners perceived re-offending as a natural event in a patient's rehabilitation, not something that should be viewed as a failure. However, the sensitivity of reputational damage in the system made it impossible for officials to share this interpretation of the reconviction data. They were yet another matter of interpretation and contestation, depending on one's perspective across the system.

A question of risk

The attitude towards executive discretion actors across the restricted patient system was far more nuanced and complex than the literature credits. It was not the case that executive discretion was an uncontested area. It was criticized for the *way* it was exercised, rather than the mere fact of its existence. The single most important point of debate was the approach to assessing risk and determining acceptable levels of public safety.

Both the Tribunal and clinical practitioners considered the matter of public protection in all applications for discharge of restricted patients. Indeed, the Tribunal was legislatively *required* to take account of risk to the public by the Mental Health Act 1983 (section 73(1)(a)). Despite this, officials in the Mental Health Unit repeatedly explained that theirs was the only agency that placed importance on the protection of the public.

It was one thing to suggest that the Tribunal did not place equal weight as the Unit on the question of public protection. It was quite another to argue that the Tribunal did not consider public protection at all. Additionally, interviews with practitioners revealed a high level of regard for the question of risk and a perception that it was central to a patient's overall care and management.

At the same time, clinicians and practitioners repeatedly claimed that the priority attached to controlling dangerousness ran counter to the intentions of the Mental Health Act 1983 and the mental health system itself. While they acknowledged the importance of public protection, practitioners believed that the way Unit staff undertook their deliberations undermined the therapeutic responsibilities of the mental health system. These included ensuring that patients were detained in the least restrictive circumstances, with appropriate treatment, and providing opportunities for rehabilitation in the community.

Indeed, some clinicians suggested that the Unit over-emphasized the risks that restricted patients posed to the public in order to justify their rejection of a discharge application. One psychiatrist interpreted this as the executive failing to exercise its discretion. That statement struck at the essence of the tension between the function of executive discretion, as embodied by the work of the Mental Health Unit, and the therapeutic objective of other actors in the restricted patient system. As long as restricted patients were understood primarily in terms of their risk to the public, their individual needs would always be secondary. And as long as public protection was constructed in opposition to individual patient needs, there could be no compromise between the two objectives. So long as the executive authority was implemented by the Mental Health Unit, that dichotomous relationship would continue to see leave and discharge applications rejected in the interests of public protection.

Yet the approach of the Mental Health Unit was firmly grounded in the powers of executive discretion that were enshrined in mental health law; the same legislation that set out the therapeutic objectives of compulsory treatment. It was in recognition of the high degree of public interest in this area, and because the tenor, scope and scale of that interest might shift over time, that the Secretary of State had been given decision-making authority in the first instance. So the system itself produced this intractable impasse between the core objectives of care and control; and it did so expressly for the purpose of protecting the public. This raises the central question of who and what constituted 'the public'; a question considered in the next chapter.

Chapter 5

Constructing 'the public'

Introduction

While the ways in which public opinion and public interest are constituted have attracted extensive sociological analysis, there is little empirical evidence about how these concepts operate in policy and practice. As we have seen in the restricted patient system, the centrality of public protection to the executive's mandate was rarely contested. However, there was an implied consensus about how 'the public' was constructed that was by no means self-evident. Interviews and observation presented the opportunity to examine how the public was conceptualized by decision-makers and how those conceptions affected their decision-making. The research also enabled me to investigate different constructions of the public across the system, from government officials to practitioners, non-government organizations and individuals personally involved in restricted patient matters.

Certain groups and experiences emerged as central to how 'the public' was conceived by actors in the restricted patient system. In particular, the experiences of victims and the families of restricted patients took on great significance, particularly for Unit caseworkers. Yet not everyone shared that conception of the public. Some disputed the legitimacy of victim involvement. Others asserted that patients should be actively involved in the public protection agenda, rather than its object. In this chapter I explore the various constructions of the public in the restricted patient system; the tensions that emerged between them; and how they informed the approach to protection that was taken by the executive.

Defining the public interest

> Those features of the world outside which have to do with the behaviour of other human beings, in so far as that behaviour crosses ours, is dependent upon us, or is interesting to us, we call roughly public affairs. The pictures inside the heads of these human beings, the pictures of themselves, of others, of their needs, purposes, and relationships, are their public opinions. Those pictures which are acted upon by groups of people, or by individuals acting in the name of groups, are Public Opinion with capital letters. (Lippmann 1922: 18)

The relationship between formal political structures and the everyday world in which they operate is crucial to understanding how key concepts are constructed. For Lippmann, bureaucratic decisions were based on 'pictures' of the world that were drawn from experience and opinion. They depicted 'a social environment, where there are innumerable large and small corporations, and institutions, voluntary and semi-voluntary associations, national, provincial, urban and neighbourhood groupings, which often as not make the decision that the political body registers' (Lippmann 1922: 14).

Others have talked about this as a 'reference phenomenon'. De Sola Pool and Shulman analysed the 'fantasies' of journalists and those in the media to examine how their perceptions of the public shaped the content of their journalism. They found that journalists tested the consequences of their actions 'by fantasy reference to people's expected reactions' (de Sola Pool and Shulman 1959: 156). Yet the process was not simply one of imagination: 'it involved adopting dissonance reduction strategies to sustain an established mental picture of the world' (de Sola Pool and Shulman 1959: *ibid*). It also relied upon the corroboration of colleagues with whom that picture was discussed. Colleagues gave their approval, objectivity and solidity to what would otherwise have been individualistic and subjectivist constructions.

From the rule of law, we often expect legal decision-making to operate in certain institutions like courts, parole boards or tribunals, based upon clearly defined systems and principles. Equally, we imagine bureaucratic processes to be based upon coherent, rational policies informing how decisions are made. But these elements are not always present, and even where they exist, they are only part of the picture. The work of Lippmann, de Sola Pool and Shulman and others shows us how decision-making is also informed by a range of 'mental pictures' that enable policy and procedure to be applied on the basis of common sense judgments or past experience. This is part of the 'common sense outlook'; a description of 'the normal, ordinary, traditionally sanctioned world-view ... that is faithful to facts of observation even though we have no data that would satisfy the canons of scientific demonstration to support this description' (Bittner 1963).

Legitimacy is another essential element of decision-making processes, as Thomas has explained:

> The problem of justice follows logically from the symbolism of formal rationality in decision-making, when it is expected that decisions in individual cases will be grounded in general rules faithfully applied to specific cases. From this perspective ... a basic difference in the decision frames of legal institutions is the extent to which the decision-making process is governed by the need to avoid threats to legitimacy. (Thomas 1986: 1284)

Legitimacy is as vital to the decision frames of governments and the bureaucracies that support them as it is for legal institutions and their officers. At its core, the function of the civil service is to act in the interests of the public. Yet the actions of the civil service are also in response to the political and public dynamics of the day (Rock 1986 and 2004; Stenson and Edwards 2004). These dynamics merge and intersect to form the 'interpretive practices' of decision-makers (Hawkins 2003: 189). Key among these interpretive practices are the indicators that determine legitimacy.

Invariably, actors in the restricted patient system constructed mental pictures that set out a particular view of the world and simultaneously legitimized their role and actions in that system. Through these interpretive practices it was possible to see some of the differences between approaches, priorities and objectives between the different actors in the system. For example, we have seen how the priority the Home Office placed on protecting the public distinguished it from the priorities of other decision-makers in the restricted patient system; and was perceived by the Home Office as a unique component of its own decision frame. Yet concern for protecting the public was also a feature of decision-making by the Mental Health Review Tribunal; and was a consideration that informed the recommendations of clinical and legal practitioners in applications about restricted patients. In other words, the protection of the public was accepted within the mandates of many actors in the restricted patient system, despite variations in how the notion of the public was constituted.

One of the key distinctions between how different actors approached the notion of the public stemmed from whether they worked within the criminal justice or mental health systems. For instance, executive discretion was exercised within the framework of legal principles like the rule of law and natural justice by virtue of it residing within the bureaucratic surrounds of the Home Office. These principles were all aspects of the criminal justice decision frame and were central to the operations of the Home Office at the time. (Subsequent restructuring saw many of these aspects of criminal justice relocated to the newly created Department of Justice.)

However, these legal principles contrasted strongly with those of the health system, which operated on the basis of individual patient need and professional judgment. In the health system, the doctor-patient relationship was primary and was sustained through fundamental health care principles such as the confidentiality of patient information. Patient progress was perceived in terms of the individual, with only passing reference – if at all – to the interests of other parties such as the patient's family, victims or local communities. These core systemic differences informed how each actor responded to the notion of public interest, as well as to the application of that interest in particular patient cases. As such, notions of the public were constructed differently according to those operating within the criminal justice framework or as health practitioners. One area where this was most evident was in relation to victim involvement in the restricted patient system.

The changing role of victims in decision-making

Since the 1990s at least, criminal justice policy-makers have been increasingly engaging with victims of crime as key stakeholders. The period encompassing this research was characterized by a particular fervour in victim-focused policy announcements, media releases and other events designed to show the increasing amounts of attention being paid by the British government towards victims of crime. The Home Office presented the strongest front in this regard. Policy statements revealed objectives of 'reforming the justice system so that the needs and rights of victims and witnesses are placed at the heart of what we do' and the phrase 'your rights as a victim' littered Home Office press releases and publications (Home Office undated).

In a characteristic statement of New Labour's policy in relation to victims, the government announced that it was:

> rebalancing the criminal justice system in a way that gives the law-abiding public much greater involvement in the criminal justice services they receive. That starts with ensuring *the needs of victims must be at the heart of what the criminal justice system does.* (Home Office 2006, emphasis in original)

On one reading, such statements were an attempt to make amends for the claims by victims that they had been 'forgotten' by the criminal justice system (Shapland, Willmore *et al.* 1985). Indeed, attention to victim-related concerns and a focus on victims in policy were being reflected at the highest levels of government, not only within the Home Office. However, it was unclear to what extent these slogans reflected novel approaches in the work of the Home Office, or whether they were in fact simply a rebranding of old policies using new slogans. As Walklate notes, 'a concern with and for the victim of crime has become not just a symbolic reference point in government policy but the dominant one' (Walklate 2007: 7). Alongside initiatives in policy and public engagement, it was plausible that victim involvement in the restricted patient system was another element of symbolic politics playing out through the public protection agenda.

Some organizations opposed the change in policy direction that was implied by these statements. The UK human rights organization Liberty argued that the notion of 'rebalancing' implied a position against the presumption of innocence, prioritizing the interests of victims at the expense of offenders' rights (Chakrabarty 2007). As we have seen, the construction of victims and offenders as dichotomous categories has been widely criticized (see for example Von Hentig 1940; Davies, Francis *et al.* 1996; Zedner 2002; Stubbs and Tolmie 2005; Walklate 2007). Nevertheless, idealized conceptions of victims and offenders still abound, not least in policy statements designed to appeal to popular conceptions of justice (Christie 1986).

Other criticisms focused on the potential for such statements to remain empty promises to victims. In particular, there was concern about potentially compromising the role of the civil service. While the relationship between policy and politics is often tenuous, empty policies promised to constituencies like victims fuelled warnings that 'the old version of the "public service bargain" in which there was an implicit division of responsibility between ministers and civil servants has become confused' (Public Administration Select Committee 2007).

Through these developments, there remained very little empirical evidence of how victims felt about the people who victimized them, or about the systems (criminal justice and otherwise) with which they came into contact as a result of that victimization. There was even less evidence on which to base an analysis of how policies and policy-makers worked with the concept of victimization or its representation in lived experience.

Victim 'peace of mind'

For Mental Health Unit caseworkers, the notion of a victim's 'peace of mind' was central to their decisions about what information should be provided to victims. But it was also linked directly to public levels of confidence in the system, as the following comment from an official indicated.

> In fact the answer is usually that there is actually nothing or very little explicitly in place for the protection of the victim. What is much more important is for the victim to have access to understanding of how the system works and the fact that the person has been discharged from hospital ... because he's somebody who's been undergoing intensive therapy and will not be doing that sort of thing in the future and you can be reassured that he's receiving psychiatric care in the community which means that he's most unlikely to revert to that pattern of behaviour and if he does he'll be whipped back into hospital. Most victims I think are fairly reassured when they realize that that is what the system is for and how it operates and that there are safeguards ... The difficulty in the past has been [that] they're told absolutely nothing [because of] medical confidentiality. 'Once a monster always a monster', so that's that. That sort of pattern of thinking is not addressed by [refusing] to give any information.

Of course, the restricted patient population included some people who had committed horrific offences. There were also patients for whom a history of mental health treatment and supervision had neither prevented nor anticipated the severity of the crimes they came to commit later (see, for example, the triple homicide by Jason Mitchell in Blom-Cooper, Grounds et al. 1996). But beyond these specific cases, there was a widespread view among Unit caseworkers that victims often opposed discharge of a patient because they did not understand how far a patient had improved as a result of their compulsory treatment. Thus opposition to discharge could be alleviated, officials argued, through the provision of information about the patient's progress.

By contrast, clinicians were extremely troubled by the assertion that individual patient information should be released to members of the public, irrespective of their interest in the patient. As one clinician said:

> I start from the position that these are patients. And I think that's something that other agencies don't understand. … That police officers can't understand why a doctor would want to resist giving information about a patient, forgetting that if they went to their GP and the GP told lots of other people that they have a sexually transmitted disease, they might be a bit upset about it. But they can't somehow see that mental health care is as intimate as that and almost more intimate on occasion. So I start from the position that, well, if you're in the mental health system you're part of the medical system and therefore you have a right to medical confidentiality.

The weight of public policy went against this position. Increasingly, victims were able to gain access to information about offenders, such as when they were seeking or granted parole. Pressure mounted on parallel systems that were seen to be out of kilter with this growing recognition that victims had a legitimate claim to certain information (Rock 2004). The management of restricted patients was not exempt from this, as the following comments by a Unit official indicate.

> Historically [victims] were just completely bounced by the medical establishment. They said if somebody was a patient then information about them was medical in-confidence and that was that, which came to the crudest contrast when you've got a prisoner transferred to hospital where the victim might have been kept quite well informed by the Probation Service until they went to hospital and then they were told they could know nothing. That sort of case quite often ended up with the victim coming to us either directly or through a minister and [the Home Office] having to decide what [the victim] could reasonably be told, which meant generally [whether] somebody's still detained; they were or were not being considered for transfer to another facility or discharge; that they had been moved; and

whether they were in the victim's [geographical] area. Um, nobody's going to give addresses in this context, but the fact of somebody's detention and rough geographical location so that people can know whether their offender's in the area of not. And in the long run, details of discharge, whether there was anything in place to protect the individual victim's family ... .

Thus the contact between victims and the Mental Health Unit had slowly increased over time, as the provisions of the criminal justice system in relation to offenders were extended to restricted patients. Officials began to release what they regarded as 'basic information' to victims. Basic information was described by caseworkers as anything that ranged from 'the fact of a person being detained to their treatment'. In the words of officials, this was not about victims having a role in decision-making. Rather, 'the issue is victims' access to information'.

Victim contact with decision makers

The parameters of victim contact were not always clear. One official explained that caseworkers needed to know what contact there had been with victims and what the victim's views were on each particular case in order to determine what information was appropriate for them to access. However, the Mental Health Unit did not have the resources or expertise to take on this level of interaction with all victims. A number of officials also questioned whether it was in the victim's best interests to be contacted in the first place, which is a question I shall return to shortly.

As far as Unit staff were concerned, these measures simply brought the provision of information to victims of restricted patients in line with victims of other offenders. However, other actors resisted the assumption that policy in the restricted patient system should be on a par with criminal justice policy. In particular, the Mental Health Review Tribunal resisted moves towards victim participation in the restricted patient system. Initially, it refused to provide information about hearings to victims or to accept their submissions as evidence in its hearings. Even if there had been principled support for victim involvement, there were procedural challenges in adapting the processes for victim involvement in court or parole board hearings to those of the Tribunal's hearings for restricted patients. Tribunal hearings commonly took place in hospitals and were closed to the public unless specifically ordered otherwise. This had made it easy

Constructing 'the public'

for the Tribunal to exclude the public, including victims, from its processes in the past.

Proportionality of victim interests

Eventually case law placed an onus on decision-makers to take into account the proportionality of the chance of harm in sharing the information requested by victims as against the harm caused by not sharing it. Grudgingly, the Tribunal began to shift its policy on victim involvement in restricted patient cases. After some years the Mental Health Unit sought legal advice on victim access to information about restricted patients. Officials explained that the advice had supported the existing practices of the Unit, indicating that victims had legitimate expectations of access to information 'for peace of mind', as long as that information did not infringe on medical confidentiality. This was subsequently formalized in legislation through the Domestic Violence Crime and Victims Act 2004 (DVCVA 2004) which enabled victims to make submissions to any relevant determinative authorities in all offender cases, including restricted patients (DVCVA 2004: section 37). That legislation, which applied to the Tribunal as well as the executive, required victims to be notified about a patient's conditions of discharge; details of any conditions relating to contact with the victim or family; notification of any set date on which a restriction order was to cease; and 'to provide that person with such other information as the board considers appropriate in all the circumstances of the case' (DVCVA 2004: section 38). These responsibilities to victims of restricted patients were assumed by the Probation Service. Interestingly, in another indication of the increasing priority placed upon victims within mental health law, the Mental Health Act 2007 further extended the right to information about mentally disordered offenders to victims of non-restricted patients.

The difference in approach to victim involvement between the Home Office and the Tribunal was interesting because it spoke to their contrasting approaches to the role and relevance of the public in the processes of the restricted patient system. Despite case law requiring the Tribunal to consider the provision of information to victims, it continued to refuse them the right to attend or speak at Tribunal hearings until a policy change in 2005. In a view typical of Tribunal members observed during the course of this research, one member questioned the relevance of victim submissions. By contrast, caseworkers at the Mental Health Unit regarded their contact with victims as a significant opportunity for hearing first-

113

hand from the public. That perspective enabled caseworkers to lay claim to representing the public in their decisions, thereby adapting the various permutations and combinations of public opinion to a smaller, manageable model (Lippmann 1922).

In theory, providing victims with certain sorts of information seemed to resolve any systemic inconsistencies in victim-related policy. In practice, however, it raised as many questions as it answered. How did one determine the boundaries of medical confidence? For example, providing the location of a patient's detention might seem unrelated to the information about their diagnosis or treatment. Yet, as certain hospitals specialized in particular conditions, even stating a patient's location of detention could unintentionally reveal information that should have been medical-in-confidence. As one official explained:

> the difficulty is that you're getting into areas of patient confidentiality. Leave, for example, is regarded as part of a patient's rehabilitation. And there are arguments that if you started getting victims involved in leave decisions, where do you draw the line between the doctor saying 'this is for rehabilitation' and the victim saying 'well we want to know anyway'. And so we get around that at the moment by taking it upon ourselves to look at the victim issues and have exclusion zones or whatever.

As this example demonstrated, staff tried to put themselves in the position of a victim, imagining what information the Unit had access to that could alleviate the victim's concerns. In practice, the staff of the Unit assumed a role as representative of both the executive and the public at the same time. This enabled them to carry out the dual function of determining what information victims would want to have access to and providing it accordingly. While these practices might seem like an extension of the official mandate of the Unit, in fact there was no standardized method of communication between victims and those exercising the executive's discretion in the restricted system. The Probation Service had been given the responsibility for liaising with victims of restricted patients, but that was only just being introduced at the time of this research. Beyond that, Unit caseworkers relied upon individual and direct contact with victims for their information.

In some ways these social processes of the Mental Health Unit were nothing more than 'organized forms of group or social activity

– forms so organized that the individual members of society can act adequately and socially by taking the attitudes of others toward these activities' (Mead 1934: 261). But they were also indicative of the mental pictures civil servants constructed for themselves in order to understand the public protection agenda. Civil servants do not serve a representative function. It is ministers who are directly elected and civil servants are one step removed from that representation, functioning at the direction of their ministers rather than the electorate itself. Yet there is an inherent contradiction in the *realpolitik* of the civil service, as its responsibilities are not simply to the government of the day, but 'should include responsibility to Parliament, and to the constitution' (Public Administration Select Committee 2007: 3). In that sense civil servants have to mediate between several and sometimes competing demands upon them, including the expectations of the political executive and the public; and the restraint required by limited resources. Inevitably, the pressure of those demands led to particular processes of rationalization among caseworkers about how to balance the policy and political priorities of the restricted patient system.

Conceptualizing 'the public' within executive discretion

From the perspective of Unit officials, there was an anonymous body of people who could at any time be exposed to risk by coming into contact with a restricted patient. To that extent, anyone and everyone was encompassed within the protection being offered to 'the general public'. Yet there were ways of breaking down this construction, for instance on the basis of likelihood of coming into contact with patients by members of the communities in which restricted patients lived or visited. Such reductive strategies signified the way in which 'the bureaucracies of the criminal justice system have had to become more responsive, more attuned to the interests of individual consumers and stakeholders, and less assured in their definition of what constitutes the public interest' (Garland 2001: 117).

The media

The media provided an important conduit for information about the public. Claiming that something is 'in the public interest' is a common strategy exercised by media organizations who are seeking information and applying pressure to those unwilling to provide it

(Ardron 2007). Undoubtedly, the media were important elements of the 'surrounds' within which the Mental Health Unit made decisions about restricted patients (Hawkins 2003). As one official commented, 'we all know that the tabloids go berserk and print complete rubbish on occasion. But they do have a useful role to play in keeping the public interest in mind and whether risk management is working.' Just as public polling on the criminal justice system and projected voting behaviour fed into how officials analyzed public opinion, equally newspaper and other media reports about restricted patients provided a tangible expression of opinion that was taken to reflect the public generally.

Of course, media interest in the restricted patient system also played into the Unit's mandate to protecting the political interests of the system and, ultimately, of the minister. As far as Unit officials were concerned, the sensitivity of media interest in a restricted patient depended upon where the authority lay for the patient's current situation. One caseworker explained that, in an incident with a patient on leave from a hospital, there would be different political sensibilities at stake depending on whether that leave had been authorized by the hospital's Resident Medical Officer or under the authority of the Home Secretary. These were similar to the issues discussed in previous chapters in terms of patients who had been discharged by order of the Secretary of State or the Tribunal. Unit staff were keen to avoid decisions coming under the glare of publicity, knowing that any negative press about an individual restricted patient could yield trouble for the entire system. One official said:

> It's high profile when it goes wrong. [If] somebody has been subject to mental health treatment and has ... disengaged with that treatment or requires mental health treatment and their need hasn't been identified, and they go and commit an offence, particularly if they commit a murder, then it's high profile.

There were also routine forms of contact between the Mental Health Unit and members of the public that contributed to the construction of the public in particular ways. One example was the correspondence sent either to a minister or to the Unit directly. Responding to public correspondence was prioritized within the Unit as a measure of how the executive was fulfilling its formal role of providing public protection. Public correspondence could also lead to questions being raised on behalf of constituents in parliament. Processes of correspondence between the public and the Unit were measured by performance indicators and each had a target timeframe for completion. Public correspondence was also a useful indication of the sorts of issues that might harm the reputation of, and hence the public's confidence in, 'the system'. As such, correspondence was not simply interpreted as the expression of an individual. It spoke to the far wider issue of legitimacy in the eyes of the public.

Thus, while official conceptions of the public could encompass anyone and everyone, they also broke down into examples of interaction on an individual basis. 'The public' defined broadly did not mean everyone at the same time. Moreover, it was highly informed by the mental pictures developed by those making decisions in the interests of public protection. For caseworkers at the Mental Health Unit, these mental pictures contrived to construct the public according to two specific categories of people. These were the families and the victims of restricted patients.

The families and the victims of restricted patients

The more there is informed public debate, the more [that] reasonable people understand the purpose of the system is to manage risk and not to punish, the better it runs too. I mean I've really been quite taken by the extent to which some quite well known victims whose families have suffered some pretty horrendous offences actually take on board very well the implications of managing people in hospital rather than in prison. They just want to know. The more debate there is the more people understand how the system operates. And when it goes wrong, the better the quality of decision-making. But it is a balance. Whenever you take a decision ... you balance the potential benefits to one side against the potential harm to the other. (Interview with Mental Health Unit official)

In recent decades a body of literature has developed around what is sometimes referred to as secondary victimization, namely the alienation victims have felt from the processes of the criminal justice system (Mawby and Walklate 1994; Rock 2002). Perhaps less remarked has been the striking similarity between these accounts of the experiences of victims in the criminal justice system, with those of offenders and their families. Indeed, families of prisoners have made those comparisons themselves, in terms of feeling victimized by criminal justice and social systems (Condry 2007). It should come as no surprise, therefore, that the experience of secondary victimization 'by the system' has also been shared by compulsory mental health patients. Mental health service users and their families have described themselves as 'survivors', either in relation to the mental health system or to the stigma that is associated with it; and, in some cases, have referred to themselves as victims (see, for example, Tait and Lester 2005; Thornicroft 2006; Nacro 2007).

These accounts are important because they illustrate how terms like 'patient', 'victim' and 'offender' often belie the complexities of relationship, interaction and history that constitute the lived experiences of criminal offending. In the restricted patient system, these complexities were further heightened by the intersection of criminal justice and mental health. The impact of mental disorder on the lives of many restricted patients, and on their offences, meant that a large proportion of victims were also family members or carers of those patients. Indeed mentally disordered offenders were more likely to have killed family members or acquaintances than other offenders (Department of Health 2001). As such, the already-contested boundaries between offenders, their families and their victims, were even more blurred within the restricted patient population.

From the outset of this research it was clear that victims were extremely important to how staff of the Mental Health Unit constructed their notion of the public, in terms of the executive mandate to protect the public. Victims had a strong effect upon the 'surround' of Home Office decision-making (Hawkins 2003). Anecdotes routinely referred to victims individually or as a population within the system. When I asked for examples to illustrate a general point being made, or for descriptions of the most difficult issues staff had to deal with, the responses invariably involved victims.

Yet the matters relating to victims that were observed during fieldwork illustrated the level of complexity in the connections between patients, their families and victims. Often caseworkers would receive correspondence by relatives who were concerned by a restricted patient's ongoing detention, or that the patient was receiving appropriate care and treatment, while simultaneously expressing anxiety about the risks to their own safety should the patient be discharged. On one occasion an official was considering a compassionate leave application for a patient to return home to visit a sick relative. The index offence had been committed against another family member and the victim still lived in the family home. The official was sympathetic to the sensitivities of the situation for the victim if the patient returned home on leave and asked the Probation Service to make contact with the victim about the application. At the same time, however, the official was conscious that other family members were extremely keen that the patient should be able to join the family at this time. In this case the official looked for a compromise between the interests of the patient and other family members and respect for the victim's sense of security. The official proposed that the victim be absent from the home during the patient's visit, which would allow the Unit to approve the leave without offending its responsibilities (as it saw them) to victims.

Unit staff routinely reflected on how much it was reasonable for victims to 'dictate the process'. In another example, a caseworker described a leave application that was strongly opposed by someone associated with the victims in the case: the current partner of the restricted patient's ex-wife. The patient had been married at the time of the offence and had two children. His ex-wife had a new partner who claimed he was concerned about the risks posed to his stepchildren by having contact with their father. The stepfather had contacted numerous authorities seeking information about the patient's current status and care plan. The Mental Health Unit took a dim view of his behaviour, which they regarded as unwarranted interference, particularly because the children's mother had not raised similar concerns. As one official explained, the stepfather appeared to be 'obsessed' with the patient. The father did not live in the same area as his family and visits to his daughters were only permitted under supervision. The Unit was planning to approve the leave, but to include conditions reinforcing the supervision orders of the Family Court. In the words of one official, the purpose of these conditions would be to 'safeguard us to an extent from any future enquiries from family members', referring to the man's family and in particular his ex-wife's new partner. Thus, for the Unit, the risks involved in this case were more about vexatious action on behalf of a victim than about safety concerns posed by the patient. The conditions of a discharge would serve a symbolic purpose in reinforcing existing measures in place to protect the public. But they would also counter the possible actions of an overly zealous victim or associate.

Victim status

I have argued that the terms 'victim' and 'offender' suggest simple, discrete categories that were far more complicated in reality. While these complexities were part of the daily work of Unit officials, they were also difficult to acknowledge in the face of very powerful messages about victim status (see Rock 2000). Sometimes it seemed as though officials were only able to define 'the public' in terms of those people who had been victimized by restricted patients. The symbolic politics of criminal justice generally, and of the restricted patient system specifically, turned on the representation of victims and offenders as distinct, disparate categories. This informed the narrative from Unit staff who talked about putting themselves 'in other people's places' in order to understand the issues of public safety. Officials did not talk about imagining themselves as restricted patients or their families. They routinely invoked images of people fearful of an offender returning to their area. Thus, while the exclusively oppositional relationship between victims and offenders was a construct of certain powerful messages, it was also an indication of the political impact of those messages and their effect on the policies and practices of the bureaucracy.

How, then, did victims articulate their own interests in the restricted patient system? The most significant expression in this regard came from The Zito Trust. While there were other victim groups active in policy and public discourse at the time, The Zito Trust was the only charity that specifically represented victims of mentally disordered offenders. The Trust featured prominently in the accounts by both government and non-government participants involved in this research. Additionally it was known for *not* haranguing people, which was a strategy that undoubtedly improved its political effectiveness compared with other, more aggressive victim groups. The Zito Trust described its work in the following terms.

> We respond to primary and secondary victims of mentally disordered offenders, to carers of mentally disordered offenders, to those who feel they may be at risk of becoming a victim, and to people who have concerns about service provision in the community or at work. In some cases of homicide we have actively helped the families of both the victim and the offender. Families on both sides are victims, in our view. (The Zito Trust 2006)

In this description, The Zito Trust provides a nuanced account of the lived experiences of victims, particularly in terms of their support for offenders. Yet such nuance was missing in many of the descriptions about The Trust particularly by media agencies, whose descriptions ranged from victim organization to mental health charity (see, for example, BBC 2006). Similarly, The Zito Trust's stated objective of improved healthcare for mentally disordered offenders was notably absent from the messages about a victim focus that were conveyed by the government, demonstrating once again that 'victims and witnesses came ineluctably to take some part of their character from their relation to the twin imperatives of crime reduction and public confidence' (Rock 2004: 38).

Earlier in this chapter, I discussed how the release of patient information emerged informally in Mental Health Unit practice, in response to the perceived imbalance between victims who could obtain information about offenders in prison and victims of restricted patients who had no such access.

> The matter was particularly harrowing for an anomalous and distressed group of secondary victims, represented by such organizations as Justice for Victims and The Zito Trust. And there was the question of consistency: it was, thought Home Office Ministers, indefensible, intellectually as well as politically, to treat patients differently from other sentenced prisoners and, they protested, 'our commitment to the rights of victims and protection of public is a matter of public record'. (Rock 2004: 163–5)

The idea that not releasing information about restricted patients was 'indefensible' indicated a further *realpolitik* of the policy environment in which executive discretion over restricted patients was exercised. Withholding such information was entirely defensible for the same reasons it had always been withheld, on the basis of patient confidentiality. But that framed the issue in medical terms, whereas victim groups and the Home Office framed it in terms of justice. Public pressure, encapsulated in the specific interests of victims, made it virtually impossible to continue to exempt restricted patients from policies that applied to offenders generally.

The shift towards providing information to victims of restricted patients, informally at first, then *via* formal policy and statute, reflected the political effectiveness of victim advocates like The Zito Trust. Members of another lobby group, the Mental Health Alliance, spoke with some chagrin about that success, which they felt they were not able to emulate themselves. One example mentioned by a number of different participants was a meeting convened by the Department of Health following the report of the Joint Scrutiny Committee on the draft Mental Health Bill 2004. While The Zito Trust had been invited, the Alliance had not. Likewise, a Home Office official spoke of a (separate) meeting on the needs of victims that had been organized by The Zito Trust and a member of the Metropolitan Police. It was attended by all the ministers of the Home Office and by the Minister for Health, who was responsible for the review of the Mental Health Act 1983 under way at the time. In the official's view the meeting had been 'quite a coup', demonstrating the significant political influence of The Zito Trust.

Another indication of the gap between the intentions of victims and how they were portrayed related to the continuing representation of victims as vengeful. Vitriolic sentiments are often attributed to victims and their advocates (Stanko 2000; Zedner 2002) and quotations from victims such as 'nobody worries about the victims at all these days' are routinely used to embellish media reports of 'scandalous' decisions to release restricted patients (Johnston 2005). Indeed, the broader return to vengeance in popular discourse and policy has been attributed to the political value of being seen to be victim-friendly, at the expense of traditional principles of criminal justice (see, for example, Garland 2001; Downes and Morgan 2002). Yet the extent to which these sentiments accurately reflect the interests of victims has been challenged (Rock 2004) and evidence from the British Crime Survey suggests that victims are no more punitive than anyone else (Hough and Roberts 1998; Reiner 2007).

The Zito Trust did not actively propound vengeful sentiments. Its policy platform focused upon systemic reform to improve healthcare for patients as the best prevention of harm. In fact one clinician interviewed suggested that the vengeance towards offenders that was often attributed to victims was actually propagated by the government, as it sought a mandate to impose greater restrictions on offenders and others deemed dangerous. He stated that victim sentiments were 'used by government' for political mileage, when in fact victims almost always wanted treatment to make the patient better. Similarly, Rock has argued that while victims sought to assert their agenda in addition to those already in New Labour's policy framework, the government response was simply to subsume victim interests within 'frames that actually served other policies and politics' (Rock 2004: 39). Once again, the ideal types of victims and offenders obscured the character of victims and their objectives for policy reform. The legacy of such typification could be seen in the earlier notion of 'rebalancing' criminal justice, as though the system comprised individual, categorical interests spaced along a continuum, rather than the deeply complex lives of victims, offenders and their families.

Of course, the Mental Health Unit did receive vitriolic or vengeful messages from victims on occasion. One official showed me a letter from the father of a homicide victim. He complained about the range of therapies offered to 'prisoners' when, in his view, there was an absence of support for victims. He returned to the idea repeatedly put forward by some elements of the media, that offenders receive better treatment than victims. For officials, these letters often required an individual response to the victim and sometimes involved follow up with a patient or their care team. But they were simply one aspect of the complex terrain of interests and anxieties expressed by victims about the care and management of restricted patients. A senior official explained this range of interests expressed by victims and how staff responded to them.

> This is a value judgment that we always have to make in the [Unit]. There are victims of offences who share the common version of justice, which is that justice is about ensuring your offender gets strung up. If the primary motive is revenge then it's obviously not particularly helpful to anybody handing out too much information. The great majority of victims are concerned to know why it's not going to happen to them again, which is a legitimate expectation. It's that balance between revenge and proper concern for self-protection. Much easier to say than it is to put in place. But the great majority of victims only want to know what seems to us entirely reasonable. Is the person going to continue their detention? If they're not, are they going to be living next door? If they are going to be close at hand, what is in place to ensure [their safety]?

Another official explained that, for victims from the patient's family, the Mental Health Unit would usually be in contact with them routinely *via* correspondence from caseworkers. By contrast, this official commented, it was sometimes more difficult to contact and interact with victims who were not family members. This was particularly so for cases that pre-dated the Domestic Violence (Crime and Victims) Act 2004 when victim-specific data had not been routinely collected. Interestingly, this caseworker also commented that for victims who were less well known to a caseworker, it could be difficult to gauge how much contact to have with the victim; 'how to assess their feelings'. As a result, victims were not routinely contacted in cases that predated the current policies about access to information.

This example illustrated how a familiarity with victims led Mental Health Unit staff to anticipate what interests a victim might have in a specific case and act according to that perception, rather than enabling victims to be involved in the process in the way they might want themselves. Handing over responsibility for victims of restricted patients to the Probation Service's Victims Liaison Officers (VLOs) had been an important objective of the Domestic Violence (Crime and Victims) Act 2004 in this regard, creating a mechanism for consistent procedures in the handling of victim-related issues by officials trained for that purpose. Clarifying the objective of victim interaction was also a key aspect of this policy and was set out by the National Probation Service in the following terms.

> It is important to recognise that the victim is not being canvassed to consent to temporary or final release/discharge of an offender/patient but that they are being given an opportunity to comment on, and contribute to, the conditions under which the release/discharge might take place. (Draft 10 New Legislation: Guidance on working with victims of mentally disordered patients)

That policy also set out minimum standards in terms of the contact required between officials and victims of restricted patients.

> The plan of victim contact *must*, as a minimum, agree to inform the victim of the offender's hospitalisation and agree and record whether this should be with or without the offender/patient's agreement. The plan needs to record the agreement that the victim will have a contact point, usually the VLO. The plan *must* also include arrangements to inform the VLO of the Key Stages in the patient's progress through treatment and of any plans to discharge the patient. Agreement *must* also be reached as to how and by whom, appropriate cases will be referred to [Multi Agency Public Protection Arrangements]. Difficulties in agreeing such a plan *must* be referred to the appropriate Victims Manager and to the London Probation Mental Health Advisor. (*ibid*, emphasis in original)

The discussion so far has shown how victims shifted from the periphery to the centre of conceptions of the public whose protection was provided for by executive discretion. Victims' rights to information about restricted patients moved first from an informal but accepted practice to a matter of policy, before eventually being enshrined in law. Subsequent amendment ensured that the law applied to the Tribunal also. As one Mental Health Unit official described it, victim involvement was 'not the sort of "big bang" and suddenly the world has changed. But it's having an effect on changing the culture so that victims are more to the fore.' So what effect did the shifting emphasis on victims have across the culture of the restricted patient system more broadly?

Responses to victim involvement

While the Home Office had clearly stated its intention to award greater prominence to the interests of victims, this approach was not shared by the mandates and division of labour accorded to other actors in the restricted patient system. Very few of the practitioners in this research had direct experience of victims and both clinical and legal practitioners expressed concerns about the effect of victim involvement on the system. In a number of interviews, my questions about victim involvement seemed to prompt the first serious consideration of the matter by the research participant. This lack of insight into the growing significance of victims in the system was typical across a range of actors, from members of care teams to lawyers, representatives of mental health charities and civil society organizations engaged in law reform.

To a certain extent it was predictable that clinicians would have had little contact with victims. Remarkably, however, solicitors also conveyed little awareness of victim involvement in the system. Most commonly, they expressed doubts about whether victim statements were relevant to decisions about leave or discharge, particularly when the offence had often occurred many years previously. One comment typical of lawyers' responses was that victim statements 'shouldn't affect the outcome of a decision. But because they shouldn't, I wonder why they're doing it at all.' Others made comments about victim statements to the effect of 'I don't see where it has a role within the statutory criteria'. This reaction was somewhat surprising given the parallels between legal practice in the restricted patient system and legal practice in the criminal justice system, where victim involvement in criminal proceedings was well established.

Resistance to victim involvement

The resistance to victim involvement reinforced a key distinction between the approach of various actors in terms of whether they thought of restricted patients foremost as patients or as offenders. The fact that some practitioners had not anticipated how victim policies in criminal justice would spill over into the restricted patient system was a further indication of how extensively the framework of mental health care – rather than offender management – informed their institutional view.

One of the claims upon which The Zito Trust based its advocacy for victim involvement in Tribunal hearings was that victims often had important information about a patient that could be of benefit to their care team. Lawyers concurred with this sentiment, but felt that such information should be obtained initially, when the patient first entered the system, when the experience was fresh in everyone's mind and when it would have the greatest impact on the patient's treatment plan. One practitioner suggested that it might be useful for care teams to hear from victims when a patient was first admitted because:

> for treatment purposes it would obviously be extremely helpful for the treating team to really understand the dynamics of what was going on. Because it may well be that the only side they get is the patient's side and he might not have a very good recollection of it or be able to express it very well.

Legal practitioners said it was important for leave and discharge planning to know the status and interests of victims at the very outset. But this was motivated as much by attempts to speed up the process of discharge as it was by any principled support for victim involvement. One lawyer described a number of cases that had been held up unduly because all the discharge preparation had taken place, over a period of time and including referrals and assessments, only to be rejected by the Home Office because of the presence of victims in the vicinity of the proposed area. In such a case, it was vital for both the lawyer and the treating team to be aware of any victim involvement from the outset of the restriction order. But lawyers clearly saw that process to be relevant only when a restriction order was first made. They could not see the purpose or benefit of victim involvement continuing throughout the process of care, treatment and ultimate discharge of restricted patients.

Practitioner responses to the idea of victim involvement also strayed into personal beliefs about what was in the best interests of victims. Many participants questioned whether involvement by victims in decisions about leave or discharge was productive for the victim's own recovery after the offence. Lawyers argued that the most important time for formal intervention by a victim or their family was after the court had made a restriction order. In their view, such intervention should include an explanation about the restricted patient system and what would happen to the patient going through it. The following excerpt from one interview with a lawyer was typical of responses on this issue.

> If the last time that the patient was seen by the victim or the victim's family, they were sort of highly dangerous and extremely mad and very frightening ... that's the image that remains with them ... to do work at the very, very beginning to explain what's happened to that person, where they've gone, what they're going to have to go through, not in any way that breaches confidentiality but just in a way that explains the process, might be useful.

To some extent this reflected a sanguine view of the effects of therapeutic intervention. However, it was supported anecdotally by a number of clinicians. In one example, a patient had attacked police in their station during a period of severe mental illness many years earlier. The patient was now much better and had repeatedly sought leave to test his readiness for discharge into the community. Every leave application had been rejected by the Secretary of State in the face of strong opposition from the victims in the case, who were the officers at the police station where the index offence had taken place. As the practitioner explained:

> we ended up having a sort of conciliation meeting between the police officers and the patient, with the social worker from our service ... And as far as I could see, it completely defused the situation because they saw this 'monster' who'd gone down in the annals of their police station as being the most violent man for twenty years, as a sweet young kid actually, who's very well now and has a rather nice demeanour. So it can be ... in a sense that was pragmatic. The legal response would be to say to the Home Office 'you have absolutely no right to do this' and so on. The pragmatic response, which I said to the patient, was 'look, you're going to have to live in this area. You're probably better off pragmatically meeting them.' And that was the right thing to do, I think.

In this case, engaging in communication with the victims had a positive effect on the progress of the case, for all involved. As victims of the patient, the police had maintained an impression of the patient that was decades old. Far from assuming that the patient had been successfully treated, they believed he was still severely dangerous. In the end, contact with the patient enabled the victims to understand the level and effects of the treatment that had occurred as a result of the restriction order, thereby allaying their fears about his release and ending their opposition to the patient's discharge.

A number of clinicians expressed sympathy for the experiences of victims. However, they were also troubled by continuing victim involvement in restricted patient cases. One psychiatrist stated:

> I suppose that I would accept that a victim probably has a right to know that somebody has been released, because of the argument they might meet somebody. Whether it's good for them to know that the person's been released is another matter. It might actually make them fearful when they need absolutely not to be fearful.

Limiting victim involvement

A number of participants in this research shared the idea that limiting victim involvement was 'in their best interests'. This reinforced an idea, well established in the literature, that victims have always been exposed to the views of others who believe they know best (Rock 2008). Such approaches have been widely criticized as paternalistic and as tantamount to secondary victimization in their systemic responses that undermine victims' primary objectives (see, for example, Newburn and Merry 1990). Criminal justice practitioners and victim advocates have long argued that it is best to provide victims with a choice rather than to determine what is in their best interests (Maguire and Kynch 2000). Yet these debates did not register in the rationales with which practitioners in the restricted patient system viewed victim involvement.

Another area where victim involvement was virtually untested was in the proceedings of the Mental Health Review Tribunal. As described earlier, the Tribunal had moved grudgingly towards accepting victim involvement. Some Tribunal members were less than sympathetic to the expectations of victims, particularly in relation to conditional discharge. Following one Tribunal hearing, a panel member commented that victims who did not like patients returning to their local area should move themselves, since patients often had no choice about where they were required to live under a conditional discharge order. Nevertheless, the Tribunal's policy change did force upon members a greater openness to victims' perspectives. This was evident in the comment of another Tribunal member who observed, 'you're so focused on the patient, yet when it's violence within families you forget the family are the victims'.

Most people I spoke to were unaware of the newly introduced Tribunal procedures relating to victim statements. Even practitioners who were aware of their existence were unfamiliar with their detail. As I probed this further during interviews, they began to give greater consideration to the effect that this policy might have on the system. Generally, they said that they felt both that victims should not influence Tribunal decisions and that the new policy would have no substantial effect anyway. As one lawyer put it:

> ... the fact is the law is quite clear: Tribunals don't operate in accordance with common law developments, they operate in accordance with statutory criteria. ... And I mean, it just doesn't have a role. If I was faced with a situation where suddenly I saw a victim statement before the Tribunal, I would immediately, unless it met one of those exceptions, seek to have it put aside. And certainly if I thought in any way it was involved in swaying the Tribunal in its decision, then I think it would be a matter for judicial challenge.

This participant went on to say that, while he agreed wholeheartedly with providing support for victims, this did not imply that weight should be given to victims' statements when making decisions about restricted patients. Interestingly, the Tribunal's new policy did not stipulate what weight was to be placed upon victims' submissions. Indeed, lawyers participating in this research consistently stated that victim statements should have no bearing on decision-making about restricted patients. Ironically, the procedural code of the Mental Health Review Tribunal had long provided a discretionary power to hear 'any other person who, in the opinion of the Tribunal, should have an opportunity of being heard' (Mental Health Review Tribunal Rule 7). Thus the potential for victims to be involved in Tribunal proceedings was not entirely new.

This discomfort at the idea of victim submissions reflected how accustomed legal practitioners working in the mental health system were to operating without formalized victim participation.

It was an observation that echoed those of legal practitioners elsewhere, such as when the UK government had consulted on the question of whether the families of victims of murder and manslaughter should be able to make personal statements in court at the point of sentencing (Department of Constitutional Affairs 2006). At that time 'the judiciary and legal profession expressed concerns about whether introducing an oral statement would be an effective and appropriate way to improve the experience of relatives of victims' (*ibid*: 2).

Yet criminal justice processes had formalized victim participation, through measures such as Victim Personal Statements, where a record from victims was included in the official papers of a case file, which might come before police, prosecution and defence lawyers and courts (Home Office 2001). Thus they were an accepted part of procedure in parallel legal systems. Nevertheless, their effectiveness was still debated (see, for example, Morgan and Sanders 1999). As my research was completed before there was any evidence of how the Tribunal's victim policy was implemented, it was impossible to estimate what affect it would have upon Tribunal decision-making or the restricted patient system more generally.

Punitive effects of victim participation?

Practitioner resistance to victim participation was frequently based upon the perception that victim involvement could induce punitiveness towards patients on the part of decision-makers. In part, this was an acknowledgement of the high public profile and media attention that particular cases attracted; and the disrepute they brought upon the system as a whole. Indeed, despite The Zito Trust articulating its objectives as systemic reform rather than vengeance on patients, it had been criticized on that very same basis.

> In spite of its best endeavours to be as sensitive to the needs of people with a mental illness as to those who have died at the hands of a very few of them, in practice it may have served most prominently to highlight the killings and a drive to more restrictive care. (Taylor and Gunn 1999: 9)

Having seen how carefully officials sought to protect the reputation of the system, practitioners held justifiable concerns that increased attention to victims would result in a greater stigmatization of restricted patients. Thus, while The Zito Trust did not necessarily advance a punitive agenda, its work was seen by some to feed the symbolic politics fuelling the prioritisation of control over care.

The Trust's agenda was constructed as much as anything else out of the fears and projections that were commonly held about mentally disordered offenders. Elsewhere I have discussed how these fears existed despite evidence that people with mental illness pose a greater risk to themselves than to others (Taylor and Gunn 1999). Indeed, the disparity between fear of mentally disordered offenders and risk from them is akin to the disparity between fear of crime and risk of victimization across criminal justice more broadly. As we know, fear of crime often does not accord with risk of criminal victimization (Stanko 2000). Yet fear of crime continues, seemingly unabated, and draws increasing resources in the form of policies directed at its reduction.

The increasingly prominent focus on victims in policy statements took place against this backdrop of mounting fear of crime victimization and increasing policies to address it. Yet practitioners continued to resist any greater role for victims in the restricted patient system. As one caseworker acknowledged, doctors could be 'resistant' to the Unit's concerns about the interests of victims. She said that care team members often saw victims as irrelevant or unimportant and they implied that it was unreasonable for the Unit to raise victim-related issues when assessing patient applications. But, for caseworkers, victim concerns went directly to the question of risk and public protection.

One official remarked that where an application did make reference to victims, it was often because the Mental Health Unit had already highlighted their relevance to the care team. For example, a Home Secretary's statement to the Tribunal might note that 'discharge should not be ordered until or unless consideration of the victims takes place'. In other words clinicians were less likely to pay attention to victims if they hadn't been prompted by officials to do so.

Another caseworker explained this in terms of the structures involved in decision-making for medical practice. She described the medical tendency to respond to matters 'immediately' as a function of how doctors, in particular, worked. In her experience, doctors were often so focused on treating the mental illness that they didn't think about the offence at all. As a result, clinical assessments of risk were often based on current indications of mental illness, behaviour and the patients' security needs; while ignoring the index offence, the victims, or the patients' interaction with family or other avenues of support. By contrast, the Mental Health Unit encouraged practitioners to think in advance and with a broader perspective, so that provision could be made for any extenuating circumstances in each case prior to an application for discharge.

On the one hand, these findings lent support to the perception held among Unit staff that other actors in the system paid insufficient attention to protecting the public. If 'the public' were constructed through specific groups like victims, then the lack of reference to them in applications by treating teams suggested a failure to consider the public's protection. On the other hand, beyond Unit officials, many of those working in the restricted patient system did not consider victims to be the embodiment of 'the public'. Thus the suggestion that public protection was being compromised was harder to sustain. The failure of legal and clinical practitioners to recognize the symbolic value of victims might have been naïve but it was not, in itself, evidence that practitioners were unconcerned about public protection.

The relationship between patients and the public

So far, family members have featured as a complex but somewhat peripheral constituency within the various constructions of 'the public'. Family relationships were acknowledged as one of the factors affecting victims of restricted patients. At the same time, family members were frequently absent from the ideal victim types constructed by popular and media accounts. This raises the question of where patients were situated on the spectrum of constructions about the public.

There is a growing body of literature indicating that mental health patients are particularly vulnerable to certain forms of victimization. Colombo investigated the victimization of mental health service users in terms of non-criminal acts such as harassment or exploitation by family members, and in terms of criminal offences including repeat victimization (Colombo 2007). He found that patients were subject to the same risks of crime and victimization as the general population (see also Wolpert and Wolpert 1976). He found that their mental illness rendered them particularly vulnerable to certain forms of victimization. Moreover, they were susceptible to systemic failures to take their victimization seriously, because of their underlying status as mentally disordered (*ibid*). These findings further undermine the popular misconception that mental health service users are particularly risky individuals. Nevertheless, Colombo argues, because society is less able to acknowledge and absorb the risks *to* patients than it is the risks *from* patients, the public protection agenda is aimed at protecting 'innocent us' against dehumanized, risky others (Colombo 2007).

Fears of restricted patients

Research has also pointed to the specific fears that restricted patients have of crime and victimization because of their patient status. For example, sensationalist media representations of 'crazed offenders' have been implicated in a preoccupation with the fear of violence when restricted patients in a medium security unit were on leave in the community (Ardron 2007). In that study, a number of patients had experienced hospitals cancelling their leave in anticipation of adverse publicity (Ardron 2007). Unit officials told similar stories of measures taken in the interests of protecting patients from victims who routinely staged protests during patient visits in the community. In these circumstances, an official explained, the decision to permit leave was made with regard to the risk of the patient being exposed to harm as much as it was to the damage in public confidence that could be caused by any adverse attention to the case.

Another Mental Health Unit staff member told of a case where a hospital had sought escorted leave for a patient convicted of murder. The proposed leave was to be spent in a place far from the geographical region in which the victim's family lived. Yet the minister had been unwilling to approve the leave because the victims had threatened media attention if the patient was let out of hospital. Unit staff met with the care team to assess the patient's progress for themselves. They then resubmitted the recommendation to the minister including details of how far the distance was from the location of the proposed leave to the victim's family. That distance reduced the likelihood of media attention on the case, thereby removing the cause for the minister's concern. In this way, staff had sought to placate concerned victims while simultaneously supporting a recommendation for patient leave. Importantly, they had managed the risk of media attention to the individual patient as well as to the system as a whole.

Public protection

As we have seen, the priority placed upon public protection by the Unit generally operated at the exclusion of patients' interests. Only one official described patient welfare as integral, rather than incidental, to the process of decision-making about leave or release.

133

For this caseworker, improved mental health among the patient population was the best mechanism for public protection. Thus she approached applications to progress patients through the system as opportunities to reduce risks to public safety. Yet for the majority of her colleagues, the interests of the public were diametrically opposed to those of patients. Given that binary construction, there was very little capacity within the Unit's decision frame to consider patients as members of the public.

By contrast, the construction of patients as outside 'the public' was strongly contested by practitioners. One lawyer stated: 'I understand [the Home Office's] position, which is protecting the public, but actually the concept of the public that they ought to be addressing includes the patient, who's a member of the public'. She referred to the Home Office's then tagline 'to build a safe, just and tolerant society for everyone in the UK' as evidence of this. She argued that this meant 'justice for all, not just justice for some', and that the Home Office had a role to treat all people fairly, not to divide them into categories and treat them accordingly. Essentially, her view reflected that of many practitioners who argued that patients should not be seen in terms of risk alone. Whether it was from their risks of self-harm, or the negative attention from media and elements of the community, practitioners perceived patient vulnerabilities and their need for protection as relevant factors in decision-making.

There were other warnings against constructing offenders in opposition to the public. The report of the Joint Scrutiny Committee on the Draft Mental Health Bill noted that 'it should not be overlooked that prison staff and fellow prisoners are members of the public' (2004: vol 1, para 272). However, that perspective appeared irreconcilable with the political symbolism of patients as dangerous people needing to be subjected to enhanced powers of control. Likewise, idealized notions of victims of crime had come to define 'the public' and, in doing so, operated at the exclusion of the interests of offenders or the mentally ill. Sociologically, such constructions are well understood as central to the political process:

> politics is interesting when there is a fight, or as we say, an issue. And in order to make politics popular, issues have to be found, even when in truth and justice, there are none – none in the sense that the differences of judgment, or principle, or fact, do not call for the enlistment of pugnacity. (Lippmann 1922: 106)

As long as the symbolic politics of the restricted patient system turned upon the assumption that victims and offenders were mutually exclusive categories, there was very little scope to include patients within the broader agenda of public protection.

Politics, policies and protection

> There is a description of some aspect of the world which is convincing because it agrees with familiar ideas. But as the ideology deals with an unseen future, as well as with a tangible present, it soon crosses imperceptibly the frontier of verification. In describing the present you are more or less tied down to common experience. In describing what nobody has experienced you are bound to let go … The formula works when the public fiction enmeshes itself with a private urgency. But once enmeshed, in the heat of battle, the original self and the original stereotype which affected the junction may be wholly lost to sight. (Lippmann 1922: 109)

These social 'rules' operate at every level to determine which issues capture the public imagination and which do not. Civil servants, like others, are subject to these rules, both as members of the communities which they serve, and as individuals responsible for mediating between the 'public fictions' of the community and the (often-limited) capabilities of government to respond. On top of the service they owe their communities, and the 'impartial' duties they owe as policymakers, civil servants are answerable to their ministers. Here lies the greatest capacity for blurring the roles between policy and politics. The actions of civil servants are often determined by how the demands of the public determine the legitimacy of politicians (specifically cabinet ministers) striving to respond. In truth, the messy realities of government require integration at least, and often something far more akin to mutual dependency between policy and politics.

While officials in the civil service have always been responsible for protecting their ministers from embarrassment, the criminal justice system comes under particularly intense media scrutiny on a daily basis for decisions that might lead to a public outcry or calls for ministerial action. Earlier in this chapter, I discussed the concerns voiced by some that these processes were leading to an increasingly politicized civil service. Yet such shifts are also attributed to the changing expectations of the community. One psychiatrist interviewed for this research argued that the role of the caseworkers giving effect to executive discretion was to represent the community interest. This could be interpreted as support for Mental Health Unit caseworkers' own perceptions that their role entailed a direct reflection of the interests of the lay public. Yet, in this psychiatrist's view, civil servants acting in the community's interests simply mirrored the work of care teams acting in their patients' interests. Consequently, the Mental Health Unit was in a position to give voice to the community's concerns, while still providing a layer between government action and that of individuals (such as victims).

Demands of the public

The shift towards greater receptiveness by Unit officials to the demands of the public was, in all likelihood, unavoidable. The high profile of serious and violent offenders was consequential on the role of Mental Health Unit staff in protecting the Home Secretary. They were keenly aware of the damage to the reputation of the system, and implicitly to the Home Office, that could arise from negative media attention. Thus they were sensitive to any case that might attract public attention, even if it fell outside the realm of concern for safety. They would routinely refer such cases to ministers for a final determination.

Certain areas that were considered to be the most difficult or sensitive required that those who took decisions about them had the highest authority. These were generally described by Home Office staff as the cases that involved a high degree of risk, difficult victim issues, or 'really nasty stuff'. Such a characterization implied greater levels of risk than usual. But who was it that was exposed to risk more than usual? What set these determinations apart from the plethora of decisions that were constantly being made on the basis of public protection?

Some matters were sent for ministerial approval as standard practice. One official explained that a matter would go back to a minister if it had had previous ministerial involvement. Sometimes ministers had directed that applications in particular cases should come directly to the minister for determination. These included cases where the patient or the victim was distinguished by a particularly high profile, or where the victims were members of the minister's constituency. Ministers were also sent cases where the patient's lawyer was engaging in greater than usual activity. This implied to Mental

Health Unit officials that judicial review was being considered, thus more attention was paid to the file.

Diplomatic relations

A second area that was considered to be particularly salient touched on matters involving diplomatic relations. One brief being prepared for the minister during the period of this research related to a woman who had killed her husband because she thought he was going to take her baby daughter back to his home country of Pakistan. Initially perceived as delusional, caseworkers had come to believe that the woman's fear might have been justified, on the basis of her husband's concern about her mental illness. This was another example of how a caseworker's familiarity with a case developed confidence in their own ability to determine applications. The case was notable because of the widespread support the patient had received from her local community. Her parents were involved as they looked after their grandchild while the patient (its mother) was detained. The patient's social worker had made contact with the family and with networks in the community including the family's mosque. The Mental Health Unit was now considering her application for leave for a home visit. However, the case was perceived as being particularly sensitive because of the involvement of the Pakistani community. The decision was referred to the minister to warn him of the possible public attention that might arise from the case.

These examples indicated how the formal mandate to protect the public was mirrored by an informal mandate to protect the system from reputational damage and, more specifically, to protect the minister. The particular sensitivities in decision-making about restricted patients spoke to the highly charged nature of contemporary politics regarding mental health and criminal justice. Yet these were not novel factors for the civil service.

> Administrative agencies are to be understood as economic and political instruments of the parties they regulate and benefit, not of a reified 'society', 'general will', or 'public interest'. At the same time they perform this instrumental function, they perform an equally important expressive function for the polity as a whole: to create and sustain an impression that induces acquiescence of the public in the face of private tactics that might otherwise be expected to produce resentment, protest and resistance. (Edelman 1964: 56)

Adverse media publicity

The official view of the Unit was that the potential for adverse media publicity could irritate staff and the system, but would not directly influence the decisions that were made. One official commented that 'our concern is the credibility of the system, not how it would embarrass an individual minister'. Yet he went on to acknowledge that the two tended to be pretty hard to separate, as both were central to 'the credibility of the system'. How a decision might affect public confidence in the system necessarily had to take account of the potential for political fallout. As I have shown, staff identified some matters as warranting ministerial determination because of their political sensitivity, not necessarily because of the particular risks they presented to the public. In some cases it was a risk *from* the public: for example, the volume or kind of public attention that certain patients attracted. Consequently, these were decisions that exposed the system, and ultimately the minister, to reputational damage; rather than the more personal dangers one might envisage from a dangerous offender.

Despite the concerns expressed by practitioners and scholars about excessive caution, matters were not always determined on the basis of minimizing public attention. One of the most high profile matters to emerge during my research related to Peter Sutcliffe. Mr Sutcliffe was a restricted patient who had been convicted of the murder of 13 women from 1975–1980. Dubbed the 'Yorkshire Ripper' in media and public accounts, he was one of the most notorious restricted patients at the time of my research and was subjected to persistent media attention throughout the history of his criminal trial and subsequent detention (see, for example, BBC 2001). Although a sentenced prisoner, he had been transferred to Broadmoor Hospital in 1984. Transferred prisoners were usually returned to prison. However, because of the particularly long period of Mr Sutcliffe's detention in hospital, he remained under the discretion of the Mental Health Unit.

A particular matter that arose during the period of my research centred on whether to grant leave for Mr Sutcliffe to visit the site where his father's ashes had recently been scattered. The index offence had been of great public interest and the patient and his victims remained extremely prominent. This meant that any application for leave in the community warranted direct ministerial authority over the decision. Ultimately, the decision was made to allow him to visit the grave, having been denied the opportunity to attend the funeral. The decision was attacked publicly for being insensitive to his victims, who maintained that he should never be released. The Home Office defended the decision on the grounds that this would give him 'closure' (Jay and agencies 2005; Johnston 2005). Unit officials I spoke with confirmed media reports that the decision had been made by one Home Secretary and subsequently reaffirmed after a new minister was appointed to the portfolio. Officials were not surprised that the matter had attracted such attention. As one Unit official commented, 'it's not the obvious knee-jerk, you know, public-pleasing line to take'. Nevertheless they had decided to approve the leave anyway because, in the words of the then Home Secretary David Blunkett, 'it was the right and proper thing to do' (Jay and agencies 2005). Another official concurred:

> And you saw that the Yorkshire Ripper did indeed have leave and it did get all over the tabloids. And the Home Office took a hell of a beating. But it was the right decision, in my opinion. And quite a courageous decision taken personally by a Home Secretary who was not renowned for a human rights-friendly face. But it was the right decision, in my opinion.

In another case referred to the minister, the patient had been convicted of the murder of one woman and had seriously injured another woman who had come to the aid of the first victim. The offender was a foreign national and a repatriation request had been successfully negotiated with the diplomatic mission of the patient's country of origin. He was also a Muslim and was reported to have been holding a copy of the Koran during the attack. The offence had received considerable media attention when it was committed. Additionally, the BBC had been making a documentary in the police station at the time that the accused was charged. Interestingly in this case, victim interests were not prioritized when considering the patient's discharge. The murder victim's family lived in Eastern Europe and it was believed, although not known for sure, that there was no family in the UK. The victim's family were known to have opposed the mental health disposal of the case, believing that the offender should have received the death penalty (despite there being no such punishment available in the UK). While the police and Crown Prosecution Service had had contact with the family, the Mental Health Unit had had none since the restriction order was imposed. The ability of the victim's family to attract public attention was regarded as limited because they were outside the UK. Meanwhile the second victim (who had survived the attack) took a sympathetic approach to the offender, having stated in court and to local media that she believed the offender should receive appropriate treatment. The case was referred to the minister because of the history of media interest at the time of the offence. The referral included a proposed media strategy outlining 'lines to take', should there be further media interest in the case. These revolved around maintaining the confidentiality of the patient's whereabouts unless 'pressed', including the details of the hospital at which the patient was currently detained and the country of proposed repatriation.

These two examples indicated a spectrum of cases where the Mental Health Unit had anticipated public and media interest but approved applications anyway. The first case had resulted in considerable criticism of the Secretary of State, though no media attention had eventuated in the second case. Notably, and contrary to the perceptions of some practitioners, the Home Office did not oppose leave or discharge merely because of the risk of negative public attention. At the same time, both cases indicated that potential media attention had a direct effect upon the decisions made. In the Sutcliffe case, the patient had been denied the initial opportunity to attend his father's funeral on the grounds that the public outcry would have been too great. Officials were constantly seeking to find a balance between how much public pressure the system could withstand in approving applications for leave or discharge. Where a decision was likely to attract media attention, a strategy for dealing with potential media attention would be devised as part of the decision-making process. In addition to actually planning for potential media attention, these precautions offered reassurance to the minister that any such attention would be responded to strategically, thereby safeguarding the reputation of the system.

Behind the scenes of individual case decisions, a broader part of the Unit's 'risk management' strategy utilized the established relationship between the Home Office and the media. As was common practice throughout the civil service, the Home Office had developed networks with the police and media, including a dedicated Press Office. These strategies did not necessarily make the media biddable, nor were they designed to do so. However, relationships between the civil service and the media were well developed, reflecting in part the mutual dependency between the media's reliance on information from government sources and the government's reliance on the media for delivering its policy and other messages to the public. Such relationships were unique to government actors in the system, providing a stark contrast to the way the media treated patients themselves or those advocating on their behalf (Colombo 2007). They were also a clear expression of how important the management of media interest and public attention on the restricted patient system was to the public protection agenda.

When Mental Health Unit officials talked about 'the public', they implied a reference to 'anyone and everyone'. These were unidentified members of the general public whose ongoing anonymity indicated the success of decisions for leave and discharge. They would often be identified only in the event of a problem arising, for example, a member of the community making a complaint to police about the behaviour of a patient during leave from hospital. It was this construction which served to legitimize the status of Unit staff as lay workers in the system, because it allowed them to claim their representativeness of the general public. This broad construction of the public also encompassed the 'voting public', to whom the executive was democratically and ultimately accountable.

However, there were also particular constituencies who took the focus of the executive's preoccupation with the public. These constituencies rested upon the many applications where people outside the restricted patient system had become involved in a decision, beyond clinicians, lawyers and care teams. This was the public as represented by victims and their families and by the families of patients. They were members of the public by virtue of the fact that they were neither professionals nor practitioners working in the system. Yet they had a direct interest in that system, usually motivated by the one case with which they were personally involved. They were the interested parties who were routinely cited by Unit staff when I questioned them about how the public affected Unit decision-making.

These particular constructions of the public spoke to the formal mandate of the officials in protecting the public from risks posed by restricted patients. They were constructions that rested on idealized conceptions of victims and offenders as opposing forces, obscuring the realities of many victims who were also family members of patients, or for whom effective care and treatment were their primary concern in relation to a patient. These constructions embodied the external focus of the official mandate for public protection. Consequently, the public protection agenda and the therapeutic progress of patients were not always complementary objectives of the restricted patient system.

The third aspect of the public protection agenda was to protect the political sensibilities of the system, and ultimately the minister, from negative attention. While this aspect was rarely articulated, it was a central function of the civil service in the restricted patient system. It led to a consideration of media attention as an inseparable component of the public's interest. The likelihood of media attention did not necessarily preclude decisions in a patient's interests, in much the same way that active victims did not necessarily determine the outcome of applications for leave or discharge in a particular case. Nevertheless, both the role of victims and the potential for media attention were important elements of the Mental Health Unit's decision frame, through which the public was constructed in particular ways. Those elements proved to be integral not just to how discretion was exercised, but also to the ways in which it was constrained.

Chapter 6

Human rights and the restricted patient system

Introduction

The executive's role in the restricted patient system was legislatively mandated on the basis of protecting the public. Yet, as we have seen, the choice to prioritize public protection over all other objectives in the system was the result of both implicit assumptions and explicit policies of those exercising the executive's discretion. Above all, the executive's approach to the restricted patient system was based upon the presumption that preventing risk to the public could be 'grounded in notions of social protection and medical paternalism' (Richardson 2007: 76). The belief that other actors in the system did not share this concern for public protection only strengthened the priority that executive decision-makers put upon it.

Yet there was one framework that was deemed, at least in law, to be paramount to all others. This was the framework of human rights. It had emerged in the first instance through international law, predominantly in the form of the European Convention on Human Rights (Peay 2002; Richardson 2005; Robinson and Scott-Moncrieff 2005). The Convention had played a significant role in (re)shaping legislation and processes in the interests of the human rights of restricted patients. Indeed the origins of the Mental Health Act 1983 lay in case law from the European Court of Human Rights, as a result of which the Tribunal was given determinative powers over the conditional or absolute discharge of patients. Of course, the mere presence of procedural safeguards does not offset concerns about the human rights of people who are detained indefinitely, such as restricted patients. Procedural fairness is no substitute for substantive fairness. Moreover, the paramountcy of human rights seemed to be undermined by the persistent priority placed upon public protection within the executive's decision frame. This chapter explores how the values of human rights operated alongside the objective of public protection; and how different actors in the system related to these ostensibly competing frameworks.

Safeguarding human rights

Systemically, the major protection for the human rights of restricted patients derived from the institutional role of the Mental Health Review Tribunal. Under the Mental Health Act 1959, the Mental Health Review Tribunal had no authority to discharge restricted patients; the executive had sole discretion over their supervision and release. In 1979, the Dutch case of *Winterwerp* before the European Court of Human Rights established a need for objective medical evidence of mental disorder of a sufficient nature or degree, and its continued existence, to justify deprivation of liberty *via* detention under mental health law (*Winterwerp v Netherlands* 1979)[1]. Two years later in the same court, the case of X *v* UK (1981)[2] established that the English restricted patient system contravened article 5 of the European Convention on Human Rights (ECHR) which requires that 'the lawfulness of ... detention be decided [speedily] by a court' (ECHR, article 5: 4). It became necessary to have a judicial body not just reviewing the basis for detention, but also with the power to discharge in the event that the grounds for that detention were no longer satisfied (Jones 2004). The new Mental Health Act 1983 addressed these inconsistencies by granting the Tribunal the right to discharge restricted patients, alongside the Secretary of State. This was a right the Tribunal already had in relation to civil patients.

Under the new legislation, applications for conditional or absolute discharge by a restricted patient could be submitted to the Tribunal, in addition to the Secretary of State (Mental Health Act 1983: section 73). Restricted patients were able to apply to the Tribunal once they had been detained on a hospital order for six months, and at yearly intervals thereafter (Mental Health Act 1983: section 70). The Secretary of State also had the power, indeed was required in some cases, to refer matters to the Tribunal. For instance, the executive was required to refer patients to the Tribunal if they had not been reviewed within the previous three years. While this requirement highlighted the importance of the Tribunal's role in reviewing whether patients still met the conditions for detention under the Act, the statutory timeframe allowed for a relatively long period in detention, should that detention prove to have been unjustified. The Tribunal was also mandated to review decisions by the Secretary of State to recall patients who had been conditionally discharged, within one month of their return to hospital (Mental Health Act 1983: section 75(1)).

Pre-Mental Health Act

Prior to the Mental Health Act 1983, law reformers were not necessarily concerned about human rights *per se*. Rather, there had been mounting unease at the absence of safeguards for patients and it was believed that the new Act would improve this situation through independent Tribunal decision-making. However, as practice under the 1983 Act developed, scholars began to view the protections offered by the Tribunal as inadequate. Two concerns were principal in these critiques. The first was the burden of proof required to demonstrate that a patient was not detained lawfully. In order to be discharged, patients had the extremely difficult task of showing that they were no longer suffering from a mental disorder warranting compulsory treatment in hospital; in other words, proving a negative (Eastman and Peay 1999). Following case law, this problem was addressed by reversing the burden of proof so that hospitals had to prove that a patient met the criteria for ongoing detention, rather than patients having to prove the converse.

The second key criticism about the Tribunal's effectiveness as a safeguard was its lack of power to move patients through the system towards release, including *via* transfer to other hospitals. Notably, in much of the relevant scholarship the system prior to 1983 is generally described as one of indefinite detention, initially at Her Majesty's pleasure, and subsequently at the government's discretion (Verdun-Jones 1989; Richardson 1993, 2005). By contrast, analysis of the changes brought in with the 1983 Act often presumes that indefinite detention under executive discretion was no longer a feature of the system, now that the Tribunal had the power to discharge. Throughout the literature the Tribunal is consistently presented as a more appropriate body than the executive to be making these decisions; and as the major safeguard for patients (see, for example, Holloway and Grounds 2003; Richardson 2005; South, Smith *et al.* 2005). This is despite the fact that the Tribunal's powers over restricted patients remained limited to decisions about conditional or absolute discharge.

It was given no powers over detention, leave or other aspects of the restriction order process, which remained entirely in the hands of the Secretary of State. Thus, ten years after the 1983 Act was introduced, Richardson warned that while the acquisition of the Tribunal's power to discharge was 'without a doubt … of immense formal significance … its significance in practice should not be overestimated' (Richardson 1993: 285; see also Richardson and Thorold 1999).

The right to discharge

One of the key ways in which the Tribunal's effectiveness as a safeguard for patients' rights could be assessed is through the number of patients being discharged under its authority. As we have seen, the conservatism inherent in executive decision-making gave rise to concerns that patients were being detained longer than was necessary or reasonable under the criteria of the Mental Health Act 1983. It was presumed that a quasi-judicial process like the Tribunal, where the rights of patients were in greater balance with public safety concerns, would facilitate the release of patients who might otherwise have been detained solely on the basis of protecting the public.

In terms of the measurable effects of the Mental Health Act 1983, there was a marked shift in the process of release after the Tribunal was granted decision-making authority over discharge applications. Home Office data show that the Tribunal is now responsible for making almost 90% of release orders (Johnson and Taylor 2002). However, these figures can be deceptive, for they do not reflect an *increase* in the *rate* of patients being discharged. The following Home Office data on decisions to discharge indicate how this shift occurred (Tables 6.1 and 6.2).

The base population in these data comprise detained restricted patients, thereby excluding patients who were already on conditional discharge and residing in the community. Nonetheless, these data suggest that patients released as a percentage of the detained restricted patient population fluctuated at around 10% in the 10 years preceding and immediately following the introduction of the Mental Health Act 1983. In the decade following 1994, that percentage was approximately the same and sometimes slightly less. As one Mental Health Unit official interviewed noted, while the 1983 Act produced a dramatic shift in the figures on *who* was discharging restricted patients, there was no change in the proportion of restricted patients who were discharged every year. In other words, once the Tribunal had the power to discharge restricted patients it became responsible for far more discharge orders than the Secretary of State. Yet there was no increase in real terms to the number of discharges being approved.

Table 6.1 Restricted patients discharged (d/c) by Home Secretary or MHRT, 1975–1984* (Mental Health Unit undated)

	1975	1976	1977	1978	1979	1980	1981	1982	1983	1984
TOTAL detained	2018	2017	1930	1912	1884	1864	1812	1816	1780	1708
D/c to the community	N (%*)									
Home Secretary	171	136	152	142	147	151	146	128	100	63
	(10)	(8)	(9)	(8)	(9)	(10)	(9)	(8)	(8)	(6)
Tribunal	–	–	–	–	–	–	–	–	5	110
									(0)	(6)
TOTAL discharge	199	160	176	162	172	180	171	148	150	208
	(10)	(8)	(9)	(8)	(9)	(10)	(9)	(8)	(8)	(12)

Table 6.2 Restricted patients discharged (d/c) by Home Secretary or MHRT, 1994–2003* (Ly and Howard 2004)

	1994	1995	1996	1997	1998	1999	2000	2001	2002	2003
TOTAL detained	2288	2478	2549	2650	2749	2842	2858	2969	2989	3118
D/c to the community	N (%*)									
Home Secretary	43	24	35	29	34	34	23	27	24	32
	(2)	(1)	(1)	(1)	(1)	(1)	(1)	(1)	(1)	(1)
Tribunal	147	140	136	163	173	162	212	196	223	263
	(6)	(6)	(5)	(6)	(6)	(6)	(7)	(7)	(7)	(8)
TOTAL discharge	211	178	181	197	213	205	242	236	269	217
	(9)	(7)	(7)	(7)	(8)	(7)	(8)	(8)	(9)	(7)

*All figures rounded to the nearest whole percentage point.

Conservatism in decision making

In previous chapters I showed how Home Office officials perceived the Tribunal as incautious in its discharge decisions, because of the number of recalls and other 'problems' encountered in relation to patients the Tribunal had discharged to the community. This was despite the fact that the Tribunal was legislatively required to have regard for the safety of patients and the public (Mental Health Act 1983: section 72(1)(a)(ii)). It was also in contradiction of the Home Office's own data here. These data support the growing body of literature suggesting that conservatism in decisions about release is not limited to executive decision-making, but is evident in judicial and quasi-judicial processes also. In particular, a number of studies have shown that Tribunal panels often seek to justify decisions *not* to release patients (see, for example, Peay 1989; Holloway and Grounds 2003; Perkins 2003). This is despite a presumption in the relevant laws that patients should be released unless there is evidence of serious risk of harm. The Mental Health Act 1983 was one such law, stipulating that the Tribunal should direct a discharge on receipt of an application from a patient, unless certain criteria were not met. As a study of the Mental Health Review Tribunal's hearings for civil patients found, there was:

> a recognition that the Mental Health Act 1983 gave tribunal members the freedom to take risky decisions. In the observed tribunals, however, the risks of 'getting it wrong' seemed so great that members appeared to gather evidence to justify not discharging rather than actively pursuing the possibility of discharge. (Perkins 2003: 109, see also Holloway and Grounds 2003)

The problem, as Perkins found, was that Tribunals did not discharge patients who no longer met the criteria for detention under the Act, for the same reason that ministers exercised over-caution in restricted patient cases because of a concern about risk to the public.

The idea that this concern played a dominant role in Tribunal decision-making was supported by a number of practitioners in my research. One lawyer who represented restricted patients at Tribunal hearings commented:

> [T]here is real caution in the way Tribunals operate. In restricted cases they are, I mean they're judges or recorders who sit on Tribunals. And they're not trying to find all the arguments they can to release somebody. Some judges and some Tribunals are very cautious. And sometimes they're right to be, on the facts. But it's not a, it doesn't operate as a court, from that point of view.

Such cautious decision-making has also been observed in other quasi-judicial decision-making bodies such as the Parole Board. As Padfield *et al.* note:

> we were struck by the cautiousness of the decision-making ... The Parole Board's responsibility to 'protect the public' too easily swamps the rights of the individual prisoner, whereas it is part of their 'core function' to test whether the prison and probation services are respecting the rights of the prisoner. (Padfield *et al.* 2003: 114)

Given the general preoccupation with risk aversion in public policy (Hope and Sparks 2000), it is not surprising that panels of the Mental Health Review Tribunal or Parole Board should err on the side of caution in their decision-making. One is much more likely to be criticized for being too liberal than for being too cautious (Mason and Mercer 1999). Such scrutiny is one important factor in the conservatism of Tribunal decision-making.

However, this leaves a number of important questions unanswered. The first is to what extent such caution is in keeping with the intention of the law? The Mental Health Act 1983, like the mental health laws of many other jurisdictions, emphasized a presumption to discharge patients unless there was a risk of serious harm to the patient or to others. This implied a very different process to that observed at the Mental Health Review Tribunal, where evidence of risk was sought to justify rejections of discharge applications. The second question is, to what extent the Tribunal provided an effective safeguard for patients? That question informs the rest of the discussion in this chapter.

Constructing patients' rights

In Chapter 5 I discussed how the mental images of executive decision-makers pitted restricted patients against the public, as though the two were distinctly dichotomous groups. That discussion laid an important basis for the central issues in the current chapter. If the executive defined its mandate entirely in terms of the public protection and at the exclusion of patients, where did the Home Office's responsibility to patients lie?

To a certain extent, the Mental Health Act 1983 provided some of the context in which officials perceived their responsibilities to restricted patients. At one of the 'away days' when care teams visited the Mental Health Unit, a Unit caseworker explained that the Unit did not consider restricted patients to be different from civil mental health patients (non-offenders detained for compulsory treatment under the Act). The Mental Health Unit, he continued, was concerned with the preservation of compulsory treatment in hospital rather than punishment of mentally disordered offenders in prison. The alternative to the existing system would be that mentally disordered offenders went to prison. In fact, he argued, caseworkers were trying to preserve the intention of the Mental Health Act 1983 by diverting people from punishment to treatment in spite of their conviction. In that way, the Unit believed that the system ultimately served a better purpose in terms of upholding the human rights of people with mental disorder. At the same time, according to this official, it ensured a good system for public protection.

Mental Health Unit caseworkers spoke frequently of 'weighing up' the implications of information coming from care teams about individual patients with the needs of the public in terms of its own safety. In principle, this meant that the therapeutic needs of patients were *balanced* with the interests of the public in the decision-making process. Yet, as I have shown, the public protection agenda was paramount for those operating the executive's discretion, including the therapeutic progress of patients. Thus in practice, the notion of balance belied a distinction between the theory that underpinned the exercise of discretion and the way decisions were made in practice.

Distinction between theory and practice

The distinction between theory and practice in relation to the human rights of patients proved to be one of the few areas where the views of Mental Health Unit officials varied. While staff were consistent in citing the Home Office's responsibility for public protection, there was far more variance in how they considered the executive's responsibility to patients. For example, one official stated boldly that he had no duty of care to patients when determining their applications. The Home Office's only duty was to public protection. In his view, responsibility for patients lay entirely with clinical care teams. Indeed this caseworker had a policy of explaining Home Office responsibilities in these terms so that patients would not be confused about the executive's role in the system.

Other officials took a different view. As one senior official put it, the Home Office's interest was to get patients through the system efficiently and effectively. He argued that the Home Office was so successful in that regard that it frequently won court cases challenging a human rights principle because it ran a better system through its decision-making, monitoring and supervision. When I asked him whether the Home Office had a responsibility for or to restricted patients, he replied: 'Yes … but it's not explicit. The whole system, as we keep saying, is a balance. Because the Tribunal is there to protect the patient's rights, we can be that much more focused with the risk.'

Yet another caseworker described her approach as 'holistic', wherein patients were 'part of the process'. In her view, public protection was best served by ensuring that restricted patients were well supervised. That perspective was evident in the concerns of other Home Office staff, in cases where an application for leave might expose a patient to negative public or media attention. Staff were particularly sensitive to cases where victims or other members of the community were vociferous in their opposition to a patient obtaining leave or discharge, especially if they perceived such opposition as jeopardising a patient's safety in the community or their chances for making progress through the system. Clearly, the interests of patients were a high priority within the decision frame of some Home Office staff, if not all. As with constructions of the public, the way in which patients were conceived was not simply a matter of legal interpretation. It was also dependent upon interpretive processes that varied between officials. While Home Office policy clearly revolved around the protection of the public, it left space for officials to exercise their discretion in how they applied it, particularly in terms of striking the balance between patients' rights and public protection.

Legal and procedural obligations

How, then, did these bureaucratic priorities accord with the legal and procedural obligations under human rights law? For one senior official, these issues were not new: the restricted patient system had always rested upon a balance between the rights of the patient and the protection of the public. He suggested that the question really came down to where the balance was struck and by which actor within the system:

> Under the [Mental Health Act 1959] as you know, all the decisions about the discharge of restricted patients were before the Home Secretary. The [1983] Act changed that dramatically

by giving it to Tribunals. And in terms of the proportion of restricted patients who got their discharge every year, absolutely nothing changed, and in terms of the rate they went on to commit serious offences, absolutely nothing changed. So what we've got now is a rather more expensive and human rights-oriented structure which is using the same balance of individual rights with public protection that we used to do back under the 1959 Act ... and getting the same result ... Everybody in the system is doing that balance of the proportionality of infringing the individual rights against the likely harm to others if you don't do it right. And we are on one extreme of the spectrum: our primary concern is risk. The Tribunal is at the other: their primary concern is human rights. But everybody is operating the same balance.

This perspective on the balance within the system was reflected repeatedly in the comments of Mental Health Unit officials. They did not draw on case law or statute to support that perspective. Their analysis was simply a product of how they, on behalf of the executive, perceived the different roles and responsibilities across the system. Most of all, it was a perspective informed by the political priority placed on public protection. In the words of one official interviewed, everything the Home Office did in the restricted patient system was 'human rights-oriented'. Although critics might challenge that assertion, the comment was illustrative of a rationale within the Home Office that accepted the existence of human rights, yet attributed the responsibility for their protection elsewhere.

According to one official, the effect of the European Convention on Human Rights was deemed to have been 'absolutely fundamental' on the system. Yet, when pressed, that effect was reduced to the fact of the 1983 Act that gave the Tribunal the responsibility to protect the human rights of restricted patients. In other words, the mere fact that the Mental Health Act 1983 was introduced as a result of human rights case law automatically made the system operating under that legislation human rights compliant. This view signified a proceduralist assumption about what human rights protection entailed and how it was best ensured.

Human rights principles

The application of human rights principles caused some problems for the exercise of discretion. One official said that European case law had fettered the discretion of the Home Office to maintain public protection. In particular, some officials were concerned that the responsibilities towards patients' rights might conflict with public protection. One example given was the need for up-to-date medical evidence before initiating a recall, discussed in Chapter 3.

> I guess the most extreme example of that is in how we use our recall power. [The case of] *K v The UK* says you can never be recalled, except in emergency, without medical opinion that the individual is mentally disordered. Which is reasonable enough but operationally it can be quite difficult. And I can think of at least one case where somebody was not recalled because of explicit evidence from his Resident Medical Officer that he was not mentally ill at the time, who subsequently went on to kill. So the [European Convention on Human Rights] has quite a real impact on what we do. And it fetters our discretion to operate in a preventative fashion, and quite rightly so, but sometimes at a cost.

This comment indicated that, as much as officials understood the principles that underpinned human rights standards *in theory*, these principles posed significant challenges to the Unit's role in practice. It also implied that not only were patients' rights beyond the scope of public protection, but they might even lead to jeopardising public safety directly.

This brought the matter right back to the question of how officials balanced protecting the public with the protection of patients' rights as required by human rights law. Consistently, when speaking with Mental Health Unit caseworkers, they explained this balance through the existence of the Tribunal. The balancing process did not take place in the decisions made by the Unit. Rather, it was achieved systemically, by the complementarity of the executive's function to provide public protection with the Tribunal's function to protect patients' rights. One official put it in the following terms:

> The only question the Home Secretary cares about is whether the patient is dangerous. *In extremis*. And obviously in considering any proposal for discharge, we are going to be looking at the criteria for detention. But the Tribunal exists and because the Tribunal exists with its powers, Article 5 is not breached so we can afford to be cautious. What that means in practice – and what a lot of people don't understand – is that it is not just

two parties to a question having an argument, with the Tribunal being more likely to support the patient and the Home Secretary being more likely to support detention. The Tribunal is applying the criteria and what it needs from the Home Secretary is not to be told how to assess the criteria, it's to be told why the Home Secretary hasn't used his own power to discharge. So what the Home Secretary's involvement in any Tribunal hearing should be is to explain to the Tribunal why he has not discharged, what he thinks the risks are and what he would need to be satisfied before he did. So it's not the same decision. His decision is whether it's safe to discharge. The Tribunal's decision is whether it's appropriate to detain. The two are not the same.

Once again, this conception constructed human rights entirely within a procedural framework. In the perceptions of many government officials, the rights of restricted patients were guaranteed simply by the existence of the Tribunal with its authority to discharge. Notwithstanding the questionable capacity of procedure alone as a human rights protection, this conception flew in the face of evidence about how those procedures were operating. For instance, the effectiveness of the Tribunal as a procedural safeguard was undermined by the extensive delays in its hearings. One study had found that 'less than 8% of patients had tribunals within the first three months of recall; 33% waited four or five months; 51% waited between six months and a year, and three waited for over a year' (Dell and Grounds 1995: xiii). These data, they argued, rendered the compulsory tribunal review following a recall 'a totally inadequate safeguard' (*ibid*).

> This is a matter which warrants urgent attention. The Home Secretary's authority to recall is an immensely powerful weapon, giving him unfettered discretion to remove people from the community and to detain them in hospital. Those who advise him are instructed to err on the side of caution, and they administer the system on the understanding that a tribunal will soon meet to review the need for the patient's detention. In practice, however, this safeguard is a chimera since people can be detained for an unlimited length of time, waiting for a tribunal to convene. The situation is clearly unacceptable. (Dell and Grounds 1995: xiii)

Indeed Home Office research had added further support to the body of work criticizing the Tribunal's reviews of recall decisions (Street 1998).

Within a framework that emphasized procedural safeguards, delays in Tribunal hearings were a serious impediment to the protection of patients' rights. Clearly, the Home Office was not accountable for the operations of the Tribunal. Indeed, the Tribunal, the Home Office and the Department of Health were all autonomous agencies who would not usually take kindly to interference in their operations and duties. As we have seen, while the Mental Health Unit may not have interfered in Tribunal processes directly, officials did monitor Tribunal decisions with a view to curbing the Tribunal's attempts to operate outside its strictly legislated mandate. On that basis alone, Unit officials should have been aware of these systemic problems in Tribunal procedure. Moreover, these problems had been published in Home Office research. Nevertheless the Home Office continued to construct the protection of patients' human rights entirely on the basis of the Tribunal's existence as an authority for discharge.

Human rights of restricted patients

In some respects, the idea that the Secretary of State has no direct responsibility for the human rights of patients is highly questionable. The government is subject to the European Convention on Human Rights and its own Human Rights Act 1998, regardless of any legislative authority extended to the Tribunal under the Mental Health Act 1983. Human rights law places the obligation to protect and promote human rights on all state parties. On that basis, it could be argued, the executive had a direct responsibility for restricted patients, irrespective of any other actors in the system. But beyond human rights law, the rights of patients were also enshrined in mental health law, as we have seen, *via* the incorporation of the *Winterwerp* criteria in the Mental Health Act 1983, requiring that 'for the detention of a person of unsound mind to be lawful the mental disorder from which the patient is suffering must be of a kind or degree warranting compulsory confinement' (Jones 2004: para 1–047, p 38). Furthermore, the *Winterwerp* criteria were set out in Mental Health Unit policy documents examined during my research. Nevertheless, the executive's interpretation of these criteria routinely deprioritized them against the overwhelming focus on public protection. However much scholars, practitioners and advocates might have challenged those priorities, the executive maintained them as defensible within the interpretation it applied to its mandate for public protection.

The construction of human rights is not inherently straightforward. On the contrary, many scholars have pointed to the continuing tension between the application of individual and collective rights (see, for example, Zagor 2006). That is a debate we can see reflected in the evaluation of restricted patients' rights and the public's safety. By considering the construction of human rights in the restricted patient system, I do not mean to suggest that these conceptions were uniquely problematic there. Nor do I suggest that human rights should necessarily be superior to other interests. Such personal beliefs are beside the point. In England and Wales, the fact was that human rights were legislated as a fundamental structure within which law and public policy was required to operate. This created a challenge for the executive's role in the restricted patient system, where public protection was not just a focus but was given exclusive priority. While the language and obligations of human rights were part of the decision frame for those exercising the executive's discretion, they were applied within an interpretive framework constructing subjects in particular ways. For instance, the language of human rights had the potential to offer an alternative construction to the dominant notion of restricted patients as 'risky individuals'. Yet for officials struggling with the political pressures of public safety, human rights became another basis upon which to forge the dichotomy between public protection and the interests of individual patients.

Practicing a rights-based approach

The views of other actors within the system varied significantly from those of the Mental Health Unit, not just in terms of the construction of rights, but in how they perceived the effect of those constructions on decision-making about restricted patients. As discussed in previous chapters, there was considerable sympathy from practitioners and non-government organizations for the Secretary of State's role in protecting the public. Yet that consensus did not mask striking differences between the conceptions of various actors about human rights within the system. For some, the notion of 'public protection' clearly extended to the protection of patients. For others, the public protection agenda was synonymous with, not contradictory to, the rights of patients. Finally, there were those who claimed that the Home Office's approach to rights was unnecessarily narrow, ignoring the fundamental principles at the heart of both mental healthcare and law. In this section I shall explore each of these perspectives in turn.

Penal communications

A growing body of literature has challenged criminology to recognize the 'changes in the structure and parameters of penal communications' (Pratt, Brown *et al.* 2005: xv). The notion of 'penal communication' conveys the sense that the expansion of penality has been so great as to constitute its own context, its own process of communication, quite apart from how it is applied in criminal justice policy or considered within criminological inquiry. Penal policy is designed and shaped not just in government departments but by non-government organizations, academics and other research environments, the media and public opinion. Similarly, the implementation of contemporary penal policies is taking place not just in detention facilities but in an ever-expanding range of community-based initiatives. By extension, progressive penal politics, and criminology's engagement with those politics, need to engage with the changing nature of the public's interest in and effect on the policies and practices of penality (Garland 1990; Brown 2005; Ryan 2005).

The work of the Mental Health Unit was directly situated within these growing demands on both government and bureaucratic approaches to penality. The level of public pressure and expectation on the Home Office had increased significantly in recent years. One example of this was a furore that erupted during my research over the release into the community of prisoners who, under government policy at the time, should have been deported (see, for example, Weaver 2005). The outcry included a prolonged attack challenging the competency of the Home Office. The then Home Secretary Charles Clarke was eventually forced out of the ministry. The next Home Secretary, John Reid, introduced himself to his new portfolio by stating that the Home Office was 'not fit for purpose', thereby bringing the department into another round of public criticism and media condemnation (Richards 2006).

Ministers can be slow to defend their departments and civil servants working in such environments may be mindful of the risk to their own jobs. Their commitment to a particular philosophy about how the system should operate may be metered by these preoccupations. Additionally, the bureaucracy is ever mindful of scandal and policy changes can be wrought by attempts to avoid it (Pratt 2005). Consequently, the prioritization of public protection in the approach of caseworkers was in all likelihood a political necessity. Moreover, it is not for civil servants to determine which policies they do and do not support. The requirements of human rights instruments and domestic laws cannot be ignored but, by defining patients in opposition to the public and through groups like victims, the officials were able to construct a rationale for asserting the executive's mandate of public protection above the promotion of patients' rights. It could do this without breaching human rights law because, as caseworkers repeatedly pointed out, the Secretary of State rested safe in the knowledge that the Tribunal was there to protect the rights of restricted patients.

Impeding patients' therapeutic progress

By contrast, lawyers who represented restricted patients argued that the executive's approach to public protection impeded the therapeutic progress of patients through the system because the executive's processes were neither methodical nor constructive in their decisions about patient applications. One lawyer interviewed stated:

> it seems to me that what they're doing is wrong because they are impeding people's progress, and that's one thing, but they are also, as a result of that, preventing other people who are seriously in need of treatment, from getting into hospital.

In her view it was the exclusion of patients from the executive's conception of 'the public' that caused the central problem with human rights protection in the system:

> Whatever the Home Office may say about the public interest ... the law relating to detention and transfer ... is perfectly clear. People should be treated in the least restrictive alternative possible; people should only be detained in the interests of their own health and safety or [for] the protection of others.

For this practitioner, the human rights framework was intended to ensure adequate care of patients through the system in their progress towards release. Therefore, she argued, even if the Home Office was acting *lawfully* it was not operating in the interests of either human rights or mental health. Several practitioners concurred that this rigid interpretation of public policy on human rights conflicted with the broad range of rights that some groups were entitled to, including mentally disordered offenders.

Responses to the human rights framework

Some practitioners spoke of examples where the Mental Health Unit had been amenable to submissions challenging its original decision and had even reversed decisions following communication from practitioners in the case. A number of lawyers attributed this to a cultural shift that had taken place at the Mental Health Unit in response to the human rights framework, suggesting that the Unit was clearly concerned not to make decisions that might infringe a patient's human rights. Others took a more cynical view that the increased receptiveness to correspondence challenging Unit decisions was motivated more by a desire to avoid judicial review than by a genuine concern to promote the rights of restricted patients.

One example discussed by several practitioners was the extensive delay in decision-making in the system. While delays were more common at the Tribunal than with the Secretary of State, there were still delays experienced in the Unit's response to some applications. Lawyers I interviewed argued that the failure to review someone's detention could prolong a period of detention whose lawfulness was yet to be determined. Of course, tensions between legal practitioners and a decision-making body are not in themselves remarkable. Accusations that the executive was acting in bad faith could simply have been a strategy deployed by lawyers who were seeking a more favourable review of their client's detention. Yet it was the view of more than one practitioner interviewed that the human rights framework had provided no more protection for patients than had existed prior to the Mental Health Act 1983.

Opinions of psychiatrists about human rights in the system differed subtly from those of lawyers. Psychiatrists practising in forensic mental health are often extremely well apprised of its socio-legal dimensions and some of the most important sociological and socio-legal scholarship in the area has been written or contributed to by psychiatrists (see, for example, Eastman and Peay 1999; Buchanan 2002; Mullen 2002). Many of the psychiatrists interviewed for this research had pursued legal or criminological studies and had published widely on the social, legal and clinical aspects of risk assessment and management of forensic patients. Thus their analysis of human rights was often informed by a combination of clinical experience and knowledge of the law. As such their views provided an interesting counterpoint to the legal standpoint of lawyers and the administrative approach of the Mental Health Unit. For instance, one psychiatrist found the Home Office assertion that the restricted patient system was among the most 'human rights friendly' to be 'disingenuous'. In his view, the same system that enabled a hospital order to divert a person convicted of manslaughter also facilitated preventive detention through indeterminate detention 'well beyond what would have been the tariff in the original offence, in a homicide'. He argued:

> you have to look at the reality of how it operates, not just the formality of the law. And it then depends on how mental health processes function, tribunals function, and also how the Home Office functions in terms of exercising its discretion ... because if they don't properly exercise discretion but rather they see this as a tug of war between them and the Tribunal, um, well, if they think it's a human rights-friendly system it doesn't look as if their heart's in the right place with regards to the human rights of those that they're [targeting].

In rejecting the 'formality of the law', these comments supported those of the practitioner above the principles of human rights as well as their procedures. Even then, this practitioner noted, 'the European Convention isn't very good at protecting the rights of the mentally disordered'. That view was widely supported in the literature. Richardson has noted that the European Court of Human Rights 'has made a significant contribution to improving the procedural safeguards available to detained patients in England and Wales, but has played little part in questioning any more substantive aspects of our mental health law' (Richardson 2005: 129). In other words, protecting the human rights of patients required more than the mere existence of institutions like the Tribunal, even if its role was to safeguard patient rights. It followed that considering the intention and outcome of a decision was as important as its process.

In introducing the Human Rights Bill into the House of Lords, the then Lord Chancellor had said, 'our courts will develop human rights throughout society. A culture of awareness of human rights will develop' (Hansard 1997). Analyzing the effect of the Human Rights Act 1998 on the Home Office, Rock describes how the Act was 'intended by the Government to lend authority to a renewed discourse of rights and citizenship which had hitherto been somewhat alien to the British constitution' (Rock 2004: 218). Rock shows that this legislative intention was mirrored by a cultural shift from ministers down through their departments, as the basic framework through which they viewed their work and responsibilities shifted in the direction of human rights (*ibid*).

The idea that human rights shaped the culture of the system in which decisions were made resonated in the restricted patient system. One person whom I interviewed had extensive experience in policy and lobbying work for non-government organizations in the sector. In her opinion, the European human rights framework had 'made a huge difference'. However, she said, this was particularly on issues relating to the correlation between a patient's capacity to consent to treatment because of their mental disorder and the particular process applied to detain them in hospital. In her view, case law on these issues had produced a shift in the executive's approach to preventive detention, as it was now greatly concerned about how and when detention could be used appropriately. She viewed these as positive changes to the culture of the system, affecting approaches and behaviour generally, as well as in individual cases. Her assessment reflected the concerns outlined by Mental Health Unit caseworkers earlier, who had spoken of the challenge that human rights had brought to their decision-making.

The perception that human rights made a difference in the system was articulated by a psychiatrist I spoke to who had extensive clinical experience in a number of countries. He had practised in the restricted patient system, with its backdrop of both domestic and European human rights law; and also in New South Wales (NSW), Australia, where there was no equivalent domestic human rights instrument. He felt strongly that the effect of human rights law in England made a significant difference to the culture of the restricted patient system there, as well as its legal parameters. By way of example he discussed the case of a forensic patient in NSW who had escaped from hospital, had been recaptured and had been detained subsequently in a maximum security prison because the Commissioner of prisons had assessed him to be a security risk on the basis of his escape. The Commissioner had insisted on keeping the patient detained in prison, despite the fact that as a forensic patient he was legally required to be detained in a hospital. The NSW Mental Health Review Tribunal had advised the Minister for Health, in whom the formal authority over forensic patients was vested, that the patient should be transferred from prison to hospital. Indeed, legal advice from the Commissioner's own Department had advised that the patient's ongoing detention in prison was unlawful. Yet no action was taken to transfer the patient from prison to a secure hospital.

This participant commented that, had this incident happened in England, the human rights framework would have provided a clear and direct route of appeal on the part of the patient. In his words, the lawyers who represented restricted patients in the UK 'would have been on to that like nobody's business'. By contrast, he commented, there was no such appeal to human rights in Australian practice.

> I don't think lawyers have that sense of the human rights issues. And I think that's due to the fact that [then Prime Minister] John Howard says it doesn't matter but I believe it does, that there is no superior court to Australia, where there is in England. What you do is you go to Europe.

Moreover, he believed, the mere threat of taking a case 'to Europe' affected the culture of decision-making in England and Wales so much that a similar situation would be unlikely to arise there in the first place. The absence of any such framework in Australia meant that the executive was not held to account with respect to principles of human rights in its decision-making about forensic patients. Consequently, he concluded, the presence of a human rights framework in England provided essential parameters to the exercise of executive discretion over restricted patients.

Such comparisons were repeated by a number of participants throughout this research, including caseworkers at the Home Office. There was a general awareness that alternative jurisdictions were not bound by human rights in the way the English system was and that was evident in the different processes and outcomes of each system. Indeed the comparison between jurisdictions was particularly revealing about the perception of human rights. In Australia, mental health law was the fundamental framework through which the rights of patients were enshrined (even if they were not always upheld). In England and Wales, both practitioners and administrators perceived that traditional principles of mental health law were interpreted within the over-arching framework of human rights, through both domestic and international instruments. Yet that perception flew in the face of the priority placed on the public protection agenda by the executive and those administering its discretion.

Throughout this book I have argued that symbolic politics were an important aspect of the executive's function in public protection. In a similar way, symbolic politics were evident in the way that human rights operated throughout the system. In other words, the perception of human rights in the restricted patient system might vary depending on one's standpoint within it. In the concluding discussion of this chapter, I consider further the extent to which human rights operated at the level of symbolic politics in the restricted patient system.

The symbolic value of human rights

Previously I have contrasted the health system's model of individual patient need with the legal principle of procedural fairness that underpins much criminal procedure. Within the health system, one of the ways the individual needs approach took shape was through the adoption of a particular language that attempted to subvert the stigma often experienced by mental health patients. In the English and Welsh mental health systems, patients' groups often refer to themselves as 'service users'. Those who lobby in the interests of people with mental disorder are often termed 'consumer advocates'. In Australia, terms like 'stakeholder' or 'mental health consumer' serve the same purpose. This nomenclature establishes a framework in which patients claim legitimacy in the eyes of the public and those to whom their advocacy is directed, such as politicians, by asserting a form of citizenship based on their health needs. The articulation of that health citizenship speaks to presumptions about a set of rights, entitlements and responsibilities.

Service providers and service users

The terms 'service provider' and 'service user' imply a certain type of relationship between doctors or other health staff and their patients. The implications are that the service is of a known quantity; that it is a service that was sought by the consumer; and that the provider has the skills, expertise and resources to provide their 'service' to a particular standard. It is a language that suggests choice on the part of the consumer. Alongside the claim to certain entitlements or rights, the construction of people as 'consumers' rather than 'patients' is an attempt to resist various power hierarchies that exist between professionals and their subjects. Importantly, in the context of mental health treatment, it also seeks to resist the stigma associated with compulsory mental health treatment.

However, a number of scholars have argued that stigma is structurally unavoidable within the mental health system because its laws provide a framework for compulsory treatment of patients even when they have the capacity to consent to that treatment but choose not to (see, for example, Richardson 2007). They argue that, while one might agree with the principle that therapeutic need outweighs individual autonomy in some cases, it is still an inherently discriminatory practice, particularly as it is applied to cases of mental but not physical disorder (*ibid*, see also Dawson and Szmukler 2006; Thornicroft 2006).

In different terms Goffman also talked about these issues as they underpinned the tensions between patients and their psychiatrists.

> In many psychiatric settings, one can witness what seems to be the same central encounter between a patient and a psychiatrist: the psychiatrist begins the exchange by proffering the patient the civil regard that is owed a client, receives a response that cannot be integrated into a continuation of the conventional service interaction, and then, even while attempting to sustain some of the outward forms of server-client relations, must twist and squirm his way out of the predicament. (Goffman 1961: 320)

As Goffman's analysis shows, terms like service 'provider' and 'receiver' ignore the coercive power in the hands of those administering compulsory treatment under mental health law. While coercive treatment is not an inevitable outcome of mental disorder, its possibility is a significant factor in shaping the relationships between psychiatrists or other actors in the system and patients detained in hospital. Empowering language has little hope of challenging the underlying, structural disadvantage faced by mental health patients detained within such a system.

Restriction order

Challenging the structural discrimination against mental health patients was even harder for those under a restriction order. Restricted patients had been convicted of a criminal offence which, while not necessarily violent or dangerous, was serious enough to have been prosecuted in a higher court. Their detention in hospital was likely to constitute a diversion from prison rather than liberty (such as *via* a suspended sentence). Even in hospital, the extent of a restricted patient's health citizenship was likely to be complicated by problems such as the availability and consistency of specialist forensic treatment. For these reasons, the potential of autonomy as a 'service user' was significantly reduced in the context of restricted patients.

The symbolism of the language of human rights operated in a similar way to that of health citizenship. The framework of rights constructed its subjects through symbolic notions such as individual agency and entitlement. This was part of a much wider shift in government and management-speak, evidenced, for example, in passengers, students and others becoming customers. Yet the significance of this language was particularly marked when applied to people receiving treatment coercively. While the *Winterwerp* criteria had set out the parameters within which people could be detained for compulsory treatment under mental health law, restricted patients were the subjects of a discretionary power that placed priority on the protection of the public over their own rights. As such, they were rarely in a position to claim their rights as health citizens.

> Patients generally have no right to a particular form of treatment, but equally health care professionals have an ethical and legal duty to provide care of a particular standard. The relationship is perhaps best conceived as an axis of entitlement and duty. However, the situation is further complicated by the way in which mental health law sustains the anomalous position whereby patients with mental health problems who retain their capacity (but who are not subject to the Mental Health Act 1983) have an absolute right to refuse treatment but those suffering with similar problems who are subject to the 1983 Act have no right to refuse treatment for their mental disorders even if they retain all of the elements required to satisfy the notion of legal capacity. Yet those very same people will enjoy an absolute right to refuse treatment for their physical disorders. (Peay 2003: 139)

Contractual arrangement

In health care, the notion of a contractual arrangement between a service user and a service provider speaks to certain expectations about the quality of service that should be expected. It assumes a regulatory framework to ensure that level of service is maintained and often includes independent mechanisms for complaint or review in the event of dissatisfaction by consumers. Yet, as Carlin *et al.* argue:

> the concept of the user as a 'consumer' and evaluator rather than passive recipient of [National Health Service] services is more readily accepted in some areas of medical service provision,

such as primary care, than in psychiatric services, in which less emphasis has been placed on surveying user opinion. (Carlin, Gudjonsson *et al.* 2005: 715)

Their study found that involuntary patients were less likely to report satisfaction with services than voluntary patients (Carlin, Gudjonsson *et al.* 2005). Other research indicates that restricted patients suffer more stigma than other mental health patients. Examples include negative media attention (Ardron 2007); and fears and experiences of victimization in the community peculiar to their status as restricted patients (Colombo 2007).

Stigma in relation to restricted patients

Decisions to discharge high-risk offenders are necessarily difficult and there is a fine line between thorough questioning and invasive inquiry. Nonetheless stigma manifested itself in relation to restricted patients even where the process was designed to safeguard patients' rights. For instance, even hearings of the Mental Health Review Tribunal were not immune to the stigmatizing effects of the criminal histories that lay behind many restriction orders. Observing Tribunal members in their preliminary discussion and post-hearing deliberations provided a unique insight into the impact of those histories on the attitudes of Tribunal members towards patients. In one particular hearing, the panel appeared ill-disposed towards the patient, which was evident in the tenor and content of their pre-hearing discussion. When the hearing commenced, the presiding judicial member opened proceedings by commenting, 'it's a chequered history this' and subsequently observed that the patient's '18-year-old daughter has produced a child!' Although completely unrelated to the patient's mental state, these comments indicated judgments panel members had made about the patient's suitability for release and that the panel was inclined to reject the application from the outset of the hearing. The treating clinician gave evidence that the patient no longer met the criteria for detention under the Act. However, the panel focused continually on the patient's history of drug use while living in the community. They maintained this focus even after the patient's lawyer had made a submission that no correlation had been found between the patient's drug use and his mental disorder. Unsurprisingly, the panel rejected the application for conditional discharge.

What was notable about these proceedings was the way the panel – in particular the presiding member – set out a picture of the patient as undeserving of discharge. Through comments about the patient's family, his experience having worked for an escort agency and above all his history of drug use, the panel constructed an image of the patient as unworthy of being at liberty in the community. Interestingly, the matter seemed to be one of moral entitlement and there was little consideration paid to his mental state or whether it met the terms of compulsory treatment in hospital. It was a good example of what Padfield *et al.* describe as the 'ordinary problems of living' (Padfield, Liebling *et al.* 2003: 104). It was also an important insight into how stigma associated with a person's life circumstances could influence the process of decision-making, even for decisions by the body held up as the safeguard of patients' rights.

The point here is not that restricted patients were deliberately or directly denied their human rights. It was a far more complex situation. The tension between the human rights of patients and the protection of the public was a problem rooted in the intersection of two different authorities, alternative frameworks of law and the systems that supported them. There was no easy way of reconciling the public protection agenda with an individual's right to compulsory treatment in the least restrictive environment.

Patient care versus treatment and rehabilitation

Mental health policy has been much criticized for being rhetorically focused on patient care without achieving the objectives of treatment or rehabilitation. These criticisms have tended to focus on issues such as care in the community, or mental health service consumer empowerment (see, for example, Chapman, Goodwin *et al.* 1991; Pilgrim 1991). In the restricted system, the notion of human rights for patients was another example of a principle with rhetorical value that was difficult to sustain in practice. Patients' rights were acknowledged in law; accepted in the narratives told by officials and practitioners; and even protected, in theory, through the safeguard of Tribunal decision-making. But in practice, patients' rights were overshadowed by the routine priority placed on the public protection agenda in the exercise of executive discretion. In other words, the value of human rights as a mechanism available to restricted patients was largely symbolic.

To summarize, the Tribunal obtained the power to discharge restricted patients in order to meet the European Convention on Human Rights' requirement of an independent mechanism to review detention. Critics of executive discretion claimed that this would increase the rate of discharge for a section of the patient population who no longer met the criteria for detention under the 1983 Act but were unable to obtain their discharge from the executive because of concerns about public protection. Yet, as the data presented here indicate, no such increase in discharges occurred.

Meanwhile, the executive had interpreted the framework required by European human rights law as excusing the Home Secretary from the protection of patients' rights. Officials repeatedly acknowledged the relevance of human rights to restricted patients but simultaneously conferred the responsibility for their protection on the Tribunal. The relegation of that responsibility was a consequence of the executive's prioritization of the public protection agenda, conforming to its legislated mandate under the Mental Health Act 1983. Yet it involved a fundamental shift in the conceptualization of human rights by the executive, specifically what those rights were and whose responsibility it was to uphold them. In this shift, empowering the Tribunal to discharge restricted patients was perceived to entail a handover of responsibility for those rights entirely from the executive, under the authority of the Home Office, to the Tribunal. This was despite evidence of some significant concerns about the Tribunal's effectiveness in protecting the rights of restricted patients.

The ability to separate so completely the protection of patient rights from the public protection agenda was a further consequence of the executive's construction of the public as exclusive of patients. Other actors in the system did not see the public protection agenda and the human rights of patients as mutually exclusive. For example, practitioners generally saw the question of human rights as broader than the specific instruments available in law. They believed patients' rights to be a central tenet of mental health law, arguing that intention and outcome were as integral as process in safeguarding these rights.

Consequently, there were two alternative constructions of human rights in play in the restricted patient system. The first was essentially an administrative interpretation of human rights by decision-makers acting on behalf of the executive, in which rights were accorded through adherence to case law in the establishment of particular procedures. The second view constructed human rights as a framework of principles that encompassed all aspects of decision-making, even that in pursuit of the public protection agenda.

Herein lay the fundamental conflict. While the responsibility for public protection was enshrined in statute, the meaning and practices ascribed to protecting the public were very much a matter of interpretation by the various actors operating in the restricted patient system. It was the prerogative of the executive in whose authority and responsibility the discretion to protect the public lay, to determine who was protected, and how. Yet other actors were also required to consider the safety of the public. Clinicians spoke clearly of their consideration of public protection in the care and treatment of patients. Meanwhile the Tribunal was cautious to the point of refusing to discharge patients on the evidence of any risk, as inevitable as such risk might be.

Both the Tribunal and the Secretary of State operated decision-making powers under the Mental Health Act 1983. The authority of both was exercised over a population who were subject to criteria for detention clearly set out by that Act; and both placed significant emphasis on public protection in their decision-making. Within that context, the human rights of restricted patients could only operate at a symbolic level. Indeed the limitation to symbolic value was inevitable when patients' human rights were constructed in opposition to the public protection agenda. As long as the decision-making power to discharge patients was vested in competing bodies of executive authority and the Mental Health Tribunal, it was a tension that might never be resolved.

Notes

1 *Winterwerp v Netherlands* 6301/73 (1979) ECHR 4.
2 *X v United Kingdom* (1981) 4 EHRR 181.

Chapter 7

Patient rights and public protection

Control through containment

In recent years a range of detention regimes have relied upon discretionary authority as the mechanism for determining where and for how long certain people are detained. Examples include detention regimes for refugees and asylum seekers; detention without charge of terrorism suspects; and control orders which, in the UK, can entail constant surveillance and limits on movement of an individual suspected of certain activities. Many of these regimes have been a response to problems that fall beyond the traditional scope of criminal justice, particularly in terms of potential, rather than demonstrated, dangerousness. Notably, none of them has seen detention as a response to a criminal conviction. In each case, the use of detention has been justified on the basis of protecting the public.

The restricted patient system was another example of the phenomenon of discretionary authority over detention in the interests of public protection. It was particularly noteworthy because of its legacy in a monarchic system where royal sovereignty extended to individual decisions about punishing or pardoning offenders. In that sense, restriction orders have their legacy in an element of criminal law that has long since been surpassed by the separation of powers between law and government and the rise of judicial authority within contemporary criminal justice systems. Yet the executive's role in the modern restricted patient system remains highly analogous to that of old: its mandated responsibility is to provide the public with protection.

Public protection agenda

The way different actors conceptualized the public protection agenda was an important area of contention between executive and non-government actors. Some practitioners (and one or two Mental Health Unit officials) expressed the view that protecting the public was best achieved through ensuring the therapeutic progress of patients. In that sense, they argued, the interests of patients were central to the public protection agenda. Others argued that restricted patients constituted members of the public themselves. That standpoint often produced the most vehement criticism of the government's approach to public protection and was an attempt to resist the patient/public binary implicit in the executive's approach.

The construction of restricted patients as dangerous reflected another particular logic underpinning the executive's mandate for public protection. This is not to suggest that risk was irrelevant to restricted patients. The very nature of their restriction order derived from an assessment that they posed particular risks to the public. However, the representation of restricted patients as uniquely risky was also a product of the political climate at the time, in which the government was trying to tackle the fear of crime and its effect on public perceptions of law and order (Reiner 2007). Within such pervasive constructions of risk and dangerousness, any notion of the rights of restricted patients was more a symbolic than a realized consideration. At best, it was secondary to the executive's primary objective of providing public protection.

When the media or politicians talk about 'public protection', they often imply a clear, unambiguous concept of safety and an equally explicit mechanism for ensuring it. Yet closer inspection reveals a discourse that relies upon a highly subjective interpretation of key concepts such as who is included within 'the public'; what the public is being protected from; and how that protection is achieved. In essence, the meanings of each of these concepts vary depending upon who is speaking and from what perspective.

In the restricted patient system of England and Wales, the executive defined its discretion solely on the basis of protecting the public. That approach resulted in a prioritization of public safety above all other objectives of the system, including those that were therapeutic. This did not mean that the executive was unconcerned about care and treatment. On the contrary, for many of those in the Mental Health Unit whose role was the exercise of executive discretion, treatment and rehabilitation were understood as the best mechanisms of public protection. Nevertheless, care and treatment were secondary objectives, at best, to that of protecting the public.

Moreover, the actors responsible for exercising the executive's discretion perceived their preoccupation with public protection to be exceptional within the restricted patient system. Protecting the public was seen as an objective that was the paramount and unique contribution of the executive within the system. Yet, as we have seen, the Mental Health Act 1983 did not limit public protection to the executive's mandate alone. Regard for public safety was a responsibility that was shared by at least one other statutory authority, namely the Mental Health Review Tribunal. In addition, psychiatrists and lawyers all spoke of their professional responsibilities to ensure that the public was not unduly placed at risk by the interaction of restricted patients with the community.

Most importantly, the construction of 'the public' was open to starkly divergent interpretation across the system. The mandate enshrined in the Mental Health Act 1983 vested in the executive the discretion to conceive the public protection agenda as it saw fit. For Mental Health Unit officials and politicians alike, the conception of the public who were the focus of the executive's mandate seemed to operate to the exclusion of patients themselves. This is not to say that the rights of patients were deliberately ignored or undermined in the interests of the public. But the way that the public protection agenda was conceptualized by the executive and its delegates forged a distinction between public safety and patient therapy that effectively rendered the interests of one as exclusive of the other. This construction of the public and patients in such stark contrast was a logical consequence of the system's structure, particularly given the presence of two alternative authorities with the executive and the Mental Health Review Tribunal. However, that construction was also a product of the law and order politics that marked public policy at the time (Garland 2001; O'Malley 2004b; Lacey 2007; Reiner 2007). There was a political tension between protecting the public and promoting the rights of patients. Yet the system could be interpreted as providing a balance through the sum of its various parts, thereby relieving the pressure on the executive to ensure that patient rights were preserved within its own function specifically.

By contrast, other actors rejected the notion that public safety was separate to patient interests and argued that the executive's priority on public protection undermined the successful treatment and rehabilitation of patients. These actors perceived the Mental Health Act 1983 as requiring a balance between public protection and patient rights at every step of the process, including the exercise of executive discretion.

Patients' rights versus public protection

The question of where the balance lay between patients' rights and public protection was a central concern of actors throughout the system. Yet I argue that the balance struck was largely symbolic. It was spoken of frequently by decision-makers representing the executive and was central to the decision frames described by government, practitioner and non-government participants in the research. But when it came to decisions about leave or discharge by the executive, the interests of individual patients were continually subsumed within the dominance of the public protection agenda. In practice, the nature of the executive's discretionary powers, coupled with the executive's mandate for public protection, produced an imperative to control patients through the mechanisms available. Under the Mental Health Act 1983, the key mechanism was that of preventive detention. Unsurprisingly, therefore, the executive's decision-making resulted in the routine prioritization of preventive detention in the interests of public protection over clinical recommendations for less secure detention or discharge. This was one example of how the notion of balance operated symbolically. It featured in how executive decision-makers legitimized the system rather than in the individual decisions that they made.

As such, the preoccupation with control over care was a key marker of the symbolic politics in the restricted patient system. Practitioners suggested that the rejection of leave and discharge applications in the interests of protecting the public was short-sighted, because it resulted in the stalling of patient treatment and rehabilitation; a consequence that practitioners believed was counter to effective public protection in the long term. Moreover, practitioners suggested that the preoccupation with public protection sometimes resulted in patients not being treated in the least restrictive environment possible, which was a key principle of mental health law. For example, applications for leave or discharge were often granted with an accompanying measure that restricted the clinical regime being proposed in order to facilitate closer monitoring by the Home Office of the patient's behaviour in the community. Conditions might be attached to those discharge orders as an attempt at managing risk factors for the patients' behaviour. Yet we have seen how conditions did not stand up to direct challenge or there was little recourse for action by caseworkers when patients ignored them. Consequently, much of their power was coercive, such as when they were raised as a threat to curtail certain patient behaviour (Dell and Grounds 1995). However, conditions of discharge also operated as an important mechanism of public reassurance. Victims could be counselled that conditions on a patient's discharge meant they would be unlikely to encounter the restricted patient in public. These conditions carried little practical weight. Nonetheless they were important symbolically as evidence of the executive's responsiveness to the concerns of victims of restricted patients.

In talking about the symbolic politics at play in the exercise of executive discretion, I do not mean to suggest that the public protection agenda or efforts to implement it were *merely* symbolic. There were clear indications of direct action taken by the Secretary of State in the interests of protecting the public. These included maintaining certain levels of security in detention facilities and recalling patients on conditional discharge if their mental state deteriorated. In one sense the symbolic politics of the system were complementary to these operational decisions. They were an element of decision-making that served to reassure the public, the media, and politicians that decision-making was taking place in the interests of public protection. Nevertheless, symbolism was as important as action in this decision-making process. In particular, it played a vital role in maintaining and *being seen* to maintain the public protection agenda.

The patient/public divide

I have argued that the various and competing constructions of 'the public' were a central element of the symbolic politics of the restricted patient system. At one level, the public involved anyone who might come into contact with restricted patients. For those concerned about protecting the public, this was particularly important once patients had leave or discharge in the community. However, it also related to the other patients and staff whom restricted patients might come into contact with while detained in hospitals.

At another level, there were certain groups that came to figure prominently in the mental pictures through which decision-makers constructed themselves in relation to the world. Chief among these groups was the victims of restricted patients. Victims featured prominently in the explanations and examples given by Mental

Health Unit caseworkers as they described executive decision-making. In many ways, caseworkers drew on the experiences of victims as the embodiment of 'the public' that needed and expected the protection of the executive. Within the restricted patient system this focus on victims was specific to the function of the executive and was notable for its absence in the decisions frames of other actors. The increasing centrality of victims to the executive's decision frame was in turn a response to the broader shift regarding the role of victims within criminal justice policy.

The executive's approach to victims in the restricted patient system took two forms. In the first place, it was an attempt to acknowledge the harm that had been done to victims. It also reflected attempts within the criminal justice system to direct services and systems to meet victims' needs. In the restricted patient system, as in some areas of criminal justice more broadly, these shifts had forced a dichotomy between victims and offenders, constructing them as opposing categories. As victim status was consequent upon the actions of restricted patients, so too their need for attention within decision-making operated to the disadvantage of restricted patients. This was evident in the unlikelihood of patient applications for leave or discharge being granted where there was strong opposition from victims.

Such constructions fly in the face of a well-established literature indicating the common overlap in experiences and needs of victims and offenders. That evidence was borne out in the restricted patient system, where there was significant overlap between the experiences of victims and those of families of restricted patients, particularly for a family member who had been victimized by a restricted patient. Consequently, some victims were motivated by the best therapeutic outcomes for a patient, even as they expressed concerns for their own safety.

Interestingly, the overlap between victims and family members of restricted patients represented an opportunity for advocates and lawyers seeking to cast restricted patients in a non-punitive light. For instance, it could have been used to provide an alternative image of restricted patients to the construction of them as dangerous which was consistently presented in popular and political accounts. Yet my research revealed that the prominence of victims within the executive's decision frame had gone relatively unnoticed by other actors in the restricted patient system. Moreover, those who were aware of the growing involvement of victims were often lawyers seeking to minimize their impact upon decisions. The increasing involvement of victims in the executive's decision-making was not mirrored by any significant engagement with this development among other actors in the system.

Beyond the direct interest that some victims had in the therapeutic outcomes of patients, there were other factors that could have mediated against the construction of patients as inherently risky individuals. Prime among these was the government's recidivism data showing a disproportionately low reconviction rate among restricted patients compared with other offender populations. These data could have been used to argue that many restricted patients were being detained unnecessarily under executive discretion. Instead, patient advocates chose to try and distance forensic patients from the vast majority of people covered by mental health law. While understandable, that strategy meant that the government's critics never wholly engaged with the political preoccupation with dangerousness. Moreover, the opposition between patients and the public was further reinforced through the construction of patients as dangerous and risky.

The exercise of discretion

Perhaps the most surprising finding of this research was the widespread acceptance throughout the restricted patient system of the executive's mandate for public protection. No participant in the research contested that mandate. Moreover many, such as members of care teams, believed strongly that professionals engaged in the system should not be held responsible for making decisions in the interests of public protection. Their role was the provision of information or advice but it was others who ought to make the ultimate decision.

Those decision-makers were either elected representatives or judicial officers appointed by government. It was, essentially, an argument about democracy. While executive discretion was a legacy of detention at the mercy of the monarch, its exercise in the interests of public protection had become a matter of democratic accountability. Medical practitioners were capable of providing the care, treatment and supervision required to meet the legal and health objectives of the system. But where the decision about release turned on matters of public protection, practitioners were incapable of shouldering this responsibility. They wanted to give advice and were confident of their capacity in that regard. But that advice had to be weighed up against other considerations such as public confidence in the system. Participants in this research were unanimous in their agreement that these were matters of public accountability. As such, they argued, decisions about discharge should be made by those who are democratically accountable to the people. Importantly, this was not an unequivocal endorsement of executive discretion, as most participants included the Mental Health Review Tribunal in their notion of systemic accountability. But it was a revealing testament to the complexities of practice in a system where there were many interests at stake and not all of them were compatible with each other.

The widespread acknowledgement of the executive's mandate for public protection also provided a strong contrast with much of the scholarship to date. There, executive discretion has been roundly criticized for undermining the separation of powers and allowing politics to dictate a level of caution in decision-making that was not merited by individual cases. Certainly, participants in this research were concerned about over-cautious decision-making in the exercise of executive discretion. But that concern did not constitute a threat to the legitimacy of executive discretion *per se*.

The argument against executive discretion on the grounds of excessive caution also fails to acknowledge the conservatism of judicial and quasi-judicial structures when they share the same authority. There is considerable evidence that tribunals and parole boards are similarly cautious when it comes to determining discharge or release in the face of potential risk. Even when the drafting of legislation places a presumption on discharge, the reality of decision-making illustrates that any element of risk can be taken to justify a decision not to release someone. That process is consistent across decision-making environments, from judicial and quasi-judicial structures to those under executive authority.

Criticisms of executive discretion

Analyzing the symbolic politics of public protection provided a way of making sense of these issues by examining their symbolic rather than their structural value. Criticism of how the executive exercised its discretion consistently focused upon the balance between patients' interests and public protection. As long as patients and the public were seen as binary opposites, the political agenda of the executive and the health agenda of practitioners might never be reconciled. Yet one practitioner argued that the tendency of the Secretary of State to reject applications for leave or discharge indicated a failure to exercise the executive's discretion. His comment alluded to an alternative conception of the function of executive discretion, wherein the public protection agenda could be met through the rehabilitation of patients in the community, instead of through prolonged detention. That possibility supported the comments of some Home Office officials who suggested that patient progress in treatment was in the interests of public protection. However, that view was held only by a minority of officials. Moreover, it did not sit easily within a framework of public protection that involved reassuring victims and communities that they were being protected from danger, through the prolonged containment and conditions on the liberty of mentally disordered offenders.

This was the cornerstone of the symbolic politics of public protection: the extent to which executive decision-making sought to assuage public fears. Yet, if public protection was actually about managing public fear, then the interests of patients and the interests of the public could have been constructed in much closer alignment. A number of examples illustrated how victims' fears were exacerbated by their lack of knowledge about the progress of treatment for restricted patients. Those fears – and their consequent opposition to patient applications – dissipated in the face of clear information about the processes of the restricted patient system and the progress patients made in it.

Some of these examples invoked the principles of restorative justice through strategies such as victim-offender conferencing to address victims' opposition to patient progress. Yet it would be unwise to assume that increased access to information or contact between victims and restricted patients offers a 'quick fix' to tensions in the restricted patient system. Moreover, great caution should be exercised in assuming that policies such as restorative justice between offenders and their victims can be transferred to the context of forensic mental health. In the first place, restorative justice for offenders often requires a clear admission of guilt by the offender. The question of criminal liability in the context of mental disorder is highly contentious, particularly where psychosis or a similar disorder has undermined the capacity for moral responsibility for one's actions. This is particularly apposite in forensic mental health where 'offenders' might have been acquitted on the grounds of mental illness or insanity; a finding which accepts that they committed the act in question but are incapable of being found guilty for it. While successful insanity pleas were fairly rare in England and Wales, the ambiguity of the classification of someone as a mentally disordered offender was discussed in Chapter 1 and has been well established.

The successful interventions with victims discussed in Chapter 5 lend further support to an alternative conception of executive discretion, wherein the objectives of patient rehabilitation and public protection might be constructed in harmony with each other, rather than in opposition. In those examples all participants saw the merit in explaining the purpose and effects of the forensic mental health system to victims once a restriction order was made. Such an approach might also provide an opportunity to feed into the system any useful information held by victims. But the symbolic value of presenting victim and offender interests as oppositional continued to dominate the constructions of the public protection agenda and how that agenda was met.

Rights versus protection

Throughout this book I have talked about the various 'interests' that were present in the restricted patient system. Examples include victims seeking access to information about their offenders, or patients seeking leave to test their ability to live safely in the community. Nowhere were specific interests more evident than in the question of human rights as it pertained to the restricted patient system. Since the 1970s a growing body of European human rights case law had shaped the procedural requirements of the system and both the European Convention on Human Rights and the Human Rights Act 1998 compelled the administration of the restricted patient system in certain directions that it might not otherwise have gone. As we saw in Chapter 6, Mental Health Unit officials believed that 'everything we do is ECHR-sensitive'.

The study of executive discretion revealed an interesting effect of European human rights law on the restricted patient system. For the Home Office, compliance with human rights law was achieved when decision-making authority was extended to the Mental Health Review Tribunal. This was more than just a proceduralist approach to human rights. It indicated a decisive abrogation of the state's direct responsibility for the protection and promotion of human rights, on the grounds that a statutory authority had been established with this purpose. Consequently, Home Office decision-makers perceived that they were no longer responsible for the protection of patients' human rights, which was something they had already been finding hard to balance with the public protection agenda. Yet, as the discussion in Chapter 6 showed, there was considerable evidence that the Tribunal was itself an inadequate safeguard for the rights of patients. Even if the *structure* of the system met the formal requirements for the protection of patient rights, its *realities* raised serious doubts about whether those rights could be preserved alongside the policy priority on public protection. This was another illustration of the symbolic politics of the system, wherein the discourse of human rights masked the reality of a population who had very little resource or recourse to access them.

Once again, to say that human rights operated at a symbolic level in the restricted patient system is not to suggest that they had no practical value. As well as extending the authority to discharge restricted patients to the Mental Health Review Tribunal, the framework of human rights had been instructive in the daily processes of decision-making by Mental Health Unit officials. Moreover, as the evidence of practitioners with international experience attested, comparable systems that operated in the absence of a human rights framework were far less aware of and less able to protect the rights of patients. Yet not even the presence of a legal framework of human rights could shift the policy priority that was placed on public protection, at least by those exercising discretion on behalf of the executive.

Of course, the protection of human rights was not confined to restricted patients. Victims also had been demanding that their rights in criminal trials and parole board hearings to give and receive information be extended to the restricted patient system. While the Home Office had conceded these rights, first in policy and then through legislative change, legal and clinical practitioners appeared to have little knowledge of or interest in the extent to which victim involvement was shaping executive decision-making.

The point was not that victim involvement in the restricted patient system was necessarily a cause for concern. These developments were entirely in keeping with policy shifts across criminal justice broadly. Additionally, their exclusion would have rendered victims of restricted patients at a significant disadvantage from those of offenders who were detained in prison or were on probation or parole. However, the potential outcomes of victim involvement in the restricted patient system were different simply because of the function of executive discretion in that system. As already discussed, the legitimacy of the executive's authority turned on notions of democratic accountability. By that same reasoning, the executive was sensitive to the mechanisms of such accountability that included elections, lobbying and media or other public attention. The mental pictures of 'the public' that influenced the executive's decision frame were informed very much by such mechanisms. Yet there were other, equally important, aspects of public policy that had less impact upon the decision frame of officials exercising executive discretion. As we have seen, notions of procedural fairness and human rights for restricted patients simply did not feature as prominently as those of distraught victims or vengeful communities. Practitioners and advocates who ignored or underestimated the importance of victim involvement in criminal justice broadly did so at the expense of their own interests in the progress of restricted patients through the system.

Conclusion

Although reliant upon preventive detention, the restricted patient system was not designed to be punitive. Decisions about leave and discharge were predominantly made on the criterion of preventing risk of harm to others. However, because the focus was on preventing *risk* rather than preventing *harm*, the inevitable operational effect of that criterion was the control of offenders through prolonged and indefinite containment, albeit under the guise of treatment and rehabilitation (Hillyard 2004). While executive authority derived from the Mental Health Act 1983, the application of that authority prioritized public protection over all other principles. Yet there were a number of other principles that could have operated in parallel with the executive's objectives of public protection. Traditionally, mental health law comprised the dual objectives of compulsory treatment in the least restrictive circumstances alongside the protection of the patient and the public. The exercise of executive discretion could have approached those principles as coterminous with the discharge of patients to test their readiness for the community constructed as a central component of public safety. Such dual considerations had informed the executive's decision frame in the past.

Even before the 1983 Act, if patients were *not* suffering, there would have been no basis for continuing detention even if they remained a risk to the public. However, where in the Home Secretary's opinion, such a risk to the public existed, the view was repeatedly taken that the absence of the disorder had to be established *beyond all doubt* before patients would be discharged. Thus ... the conflict between individual and societal rights was resolved, in practice, by Home Secretaries adopting, on the one hand, a narrow view of individual rights and, on the other, a broad interpretation of what society should rightfully be protected from. (Peay 1989: 12)

Instead, periods of leave or discharge were seen as challenges to the protection of the public. By 2005, the application of the criteria for detention under the Mental Health Act 1983 had been completely subordinated to the executive's preoccupation with public protection. Despite attempts at reconciling private rights with public benefit, in practice the Home Office conceptualized the public in a way that underlined its opposition to patients. This necessarily subsumed patients' rights within the interests of public protection. As a result, any balancing of patients' rights and public protection was largely symbolic. In reality, criminal justice policy was underpinned by a heightened fear of crime and public perceptions of risk. Political responsiveness required the public protection agenda to assuage those fears as much as possible.

References

Advisory Council on the Treatment of Offenders (1963) *Preventive Detention*, Secondary Advisory Council on the Treatment of Offenders.

Ardron, C. (2007) *In the public interest? The impact of the media on patients in a medium secure unit*, British Society of Criminology annual conference, 19 September, London School of Economics.

Ashworth, A. (1983) *Sentencing and Penal Policy*. London: Weidenfeld and Nicolson.

BBC (2001) 'Yorkshire Ripper jailed for life,' 22 May. Retrieved 12 October 2007, from: http://news.bbc.co.uk/onthisday/hi/dates/stories/may/22/newsid_2504000/2504409.stm.

BBC (2006) 'Mental care of killer condemned,' 16 November. Retrieved 15 October 2007, from: http://news.bbc.co.uk/1/hi/england/london/6153592.stm.

Bianchi, H. (1994) *Justice as Sanctuary: Toward a New System of Crime Control*. Bloomington and Indianapolis: Indiana University Press.

Bittner, E. (1963) 'Radicalism and the Organization of Radical Movements', *American Sociological Review*, 28: 928–40.

Blom-Cooper, L., Grounds, A. *et al.* (1996) *The Case of Jason Mitchell: Report of the Independent Panel of Inquiry*. London: Duckworth.

Brown, D. (2005) 'Continuity, rupture, or just more of the "volatile and contradictory"? Glimpses of New South Wales' penal practice behind and through the discursive', in *The New Punitiveness: Theories, Trends, Perspectives*, J. Pratt, D. Brown, M. Brown, S. Hallsworth and W. Morrison. Cullompton: Willan Publishing.

Buchanan, A. (2002) *Care of the Mentally Disordered Offender in the Community*. Oxford: Oxford University Press.

Carlin, P., Gudjonsson, G. *et al.* (2005) 'Patient satisfaction with service in medium secure units,' *The Journal of Forensic Psychiatry & Psychology*, 16(4): 714–28.

Chakrabarty, S. (2007) 'Where next for criminal justice policy?' British Society of Criminology Annual Conference, 19 September, London School of Economics.

Chapman, T., Goodwin, S. *et al.* (1991) 'A new deal for the mentally ill: progress or propaganda?,' *Critical Social Policy*, 11(32): 5–20.

Christie, N. (1986) 'The ideal victim', in *From Crime Policy to Victim Policy: Reorienting the Justice System*, E. Fattah. London: Macmillan.

Clarke, J. (2008) 'Clarke Inquiry into the case of Dr Mohamed Haneef', 24 November. Retrieved 17 May 2009 from http://www.haneefcaseinquiry.gov.au/.

Colombo, T. (2007) 'Violent victimisation: understanding why people with Schizophrenia often feel scared in the community', British Society of Criminology annual conference, 19 September, London School of Economics.

Condry, R. (2007) *Families Shamed: The Consequences of Crime for Relatives of Serious Offenders*. Cullompton: Willan Publishing.

Cunneen, C. (2001) *Conflict, Politics and Crime*. Sydney: Allen & Unwin.

Daruwala, M. and Boyd-Caine, T. (2007) *Stamping Out Rights: The Impact of Anti-terrorism Laws on Civilian Policing*. New Delhi: Commonwealth Human Rights Initiative.

Davies, P., Francis, P. *et al.* (1996) 'Understanding victimology: theory, method and practice', in *Understanding Victimisation*, P. Davies, P. Francis and V. Jupp. Gateshead: Northumbria Social Science Press.

Dawson, J. and Szmukler, G. (2006) 'Fusion of mental health and incapacity legislation', *British Journal of Psychiatry*, 188: 504–09.

de Sola Pool, I. and Shulman, I. (1959) 'Newsmen's fantasies, audiences, and newswriting', *The Public Opinion Quarterly*, 23(2): 145–58.

Dell, S. and Grounds, A. (1995) *The Discharge and Supervision of Restricted Patients*, Cambridge: Institute of Criminology, University of Cambridge.

Department of Constitutional Affairs (2006) 'Hearing the relatives of murder and manslaughter victims'. Retrieved 11 November 2009, from: http://www.dca.gov.uk/consult/manslaughter/manslaughter.htm.

Department of Health (2001) *Safety First: Five-year Report of the National Confidential Inquiry into Suicide and Homicide by People with Mental Illness*. London: Department of Health.

DiMaggio, P. and Powell, W. (1983) '"The iron cage revisited" institutional isomorphism and collective rationality in organizational fields', *American Sociological Review*, 48: 147–60.

Douglas, J.D. (1967) *The Social Meanings of Suicide*. Princeton: Princeton University Press.

Douglas, M. (1992) *Risk and Blame: Essays in Cultural Theory*. London: Routledge.

Downes, D. and Morgan, R. (2002) 'The skeletons in the cupboard: The politics of law and order at the turn of the millennium', in *The Oxford Handbook of Criminology*, M. Maguire, R. Morgan and R. Reiner. Oxford: Oxford University Press.

Downes, D. and Rock, P. (1979) *Deviant Interpretations*. New York: Barnes & Noble.

Eastman, N. and Peay, J. (1999) 'Law without Enforcement: theory and practice', in *Law Without Enforcement: Integrating Mental Health and Justice*, N. Eastman and J. Peay. Oxford: Hart Publishing.

Edelman, M. (1964) *The Symbolic Uses of Politics*. Urbana: University of Illinois Press.

Ericson, R.V. and Haggerty. K.D. (1997) *Policing the Risk Society*. Toronto: University of Toronto Press.

Fattah, E. (1986) *From Crime Policy to Victim Policy*. London: Macmillan.

Fennell, P. and Yeates, V. (2002) '"To serve which master?" – criminal justice policy, community care and the mentally disordered offender', in *Care of the Mentally Disordered Offender in the Community*, A. Buchanan. Oxford: Oxford University Press.

Freiberg, A. and Gelb, K. (eds) (2008) *Penal Populism, Sentencing Councils and Sentencing Policy*. Sydney: Hawkins Press.

Gardiner, J.A. (1970) *The Politics of Corruption: Organized Crime in an American City*. New York: Russell Sage Foundation.

Garland, D. (1990) *Punishment and Modern Society: A Study in Social Theory*. Oxford: Clarendon Press.

Garland, D. (2001) *The Culture of Control: Crime and Social Order in Contemporary Society*. Oxford: Oxford University Press.

Gelsthorpe, L. and Padfield, N. (2003) 'Introduction', in *Exercising Discretion: Decision-making in the Criminal Justice System and Beyond*, L. Gelsthorpe and N. Padfield. Cullompton: Willan Publishing.

Genders, E. and Player, E. (1995) *Grendon: A Study of a Therapeutic Prison*. Oxford: Clarendon Press.

Gibney, M. J. (2004) *The Ethics and Politics of Asylum: Liberal Democracy and the Response to Refugees*. Cambridge: Cambridge University Press.

Giddens, A. (1991) *Modernity and Self-Identity: Self and Society in the Late Modern Age*. Cambridge: Polity Press.

Gigerenzer, G. (2003) *Reckoning with Risk: Learning to Live with Uncertainty*. London: Penguin.

Goffman, E. (1961) *Asylums: Essays on the Social Situation of Mental Patients and Other Inmates*. London: Penguin Books.

Gouldner, A. (1960) 'The norm of reciprocity: a preliminary statement,' *American Sociology Review*, 25: 161–78.

Hansard (2007) 'Lord Irvine introducing the Human Rights Bill', (3 November 2007, 3.14pm), Column 1228.

Hawkins, K. (1986) 'On legal decision-making,' *Washington and Lee Law Review*, 43 (4): 1161–1311.

Hawkins, K. (1992) *The Uses of Discretion*. Oxford: Clarendon Press.

Hawkins, K. (2003) 'Order, rationality and silence: some reflections on criminal justice decision-making', in *Exercising Discretion: Decision-making in the Criminal Justice System and Beyond*, L. Gelsthorpe and N. Padfield. Cullompton: Willan Publishing.

Hayward, K. and Young, J. (2004) 'Cultural criminology: some notes on the script', *Theoretical Criminology*, 8 (3): 259–73.

Henham, R. (2003) 'The policy and practice of protective sentencing,' *Criminal Justice*, 3 (1): 57–82.

Hillyard, P. (ed) (2004) *Beyond Criminology: Taking Harm Seriously*. London: Pluto Press.

Hillyard, P., Sim, J., Tombs, S. and Whyte, D. (2004b) 'Leaving a "stain upon the silence": Contemporary criminology and the politics of dissent', *British Journal of Criminology*, 44: 369–90.

Holloway, K. and Grounds, A. (2003) 'Discretion and the release of mentally disordered offenders', in *Exercising Discretion: Decision-making in the Criminal Justice System and Beyond*, L. Gelsthorpe and N. Padfield. Cullompton: Willan Publishing.

Home Office (1982) *British Crime Survey*. London: Home Office Research and Planning Unit.

Home Office (2001) 'Making a victim personal statement', 9 August. Retrieved 9 November 2007, from: http://www.homeoffice.gov.uk/documents/victimstate.pdf?view=Binary.

Home Office (2006) 'Rebalancing the criminal justice system in favour of the law-abiding majority: Cutting crime, reducing reoffending and protecting the public'. Retrieved 12 October 2007, from: www.crimereduction.homeoffice.gov.uk/criminaljusticesystem19.htm.

Home Office (2006b) 'Home Office targets autumn performance report'. Retrieved 1 November 2007, from: http://www.homeoffice.gov.uk/documents/ho-targets-autumn-report-06?view=Binary.

Home Office (undated) 'Objectives, aims and values'. Retrieved 19 July 2009, from: http://www.homeoffice.gov.uk/about-us/purpose-and-aims/.

Home Office (undated) 'Victims' rights'. Retrieved 22 January 2009, from: http://www.homeoffice.gov.uk/crime-victims/victims/Victims-rights/.

Hope, T. (2005) 'Things can only get better', *Criminal Justice Matters*, 62 (Autumn): 4–5.

Hope, T. and Sparks, R. (2000) 'Introduction', in *Crime, Risk and Insecurity*, T. Hope and R. Sparks. London: Routledge.

Hough, M. and Roberts, J. (1998) *Attitudes to Punishment: Findings from the British Crime Survey*. London: Home Office.

Howarth, G. and Rock, P. (2002) 'Aftermath and the construction of victimisation: "The other victims of crime"', *Howard Journal of Criminal Justice*, 39 (1): 28–77.

HREOC (2004) *A last resort? National Inquiry into Children in Immigration Detention.* Sydney: HREOC.

Jacobs, J.B. and Potter, K. (1998) *Hate Crimes: Criminal Law and Identity Politics.* New York: Oxford University Press.

James, D., Farnham, F., Mooney, H., Lloyd, H., Hill, K., Blizard, R. and Barnes, T.R.E. (2002) *Outcome of Psychiatric Admissions through the Courts.* London: Home Office Research, Development & Statistics Directorate.

Jay, A. and agencies (2005) 'Home Office defends Yorkshire Ripper's day visit', 20 January, Guardian Unlimited. Retrieved 9 October 2007, from: http://politics.guardian.co.uk/homeaffairs/story/0,11026,1394696,00. html#article_continue.

Johnson, S. and Taylor, R. (2002) *Statistics of Mentally Disordered Offenders 2001.* London: Research and Development Statistics Directorate, Home Office.

Johnston, P. (2005) 'Sutcliffe's day trip to the Lake District condemned by families', 21 January, Daily Telegraph. Retrieved 12 October 2007, from: http://www.telegraph.co.uk/news/main.jhtml?xml=/news/2005/01/21/ nripr21.xml.

Jones, R. (2004) *Mental Health Act Manual.* London: Thomson.

Kendall, K. (2005) 'Beyond reason: social constructions of mentally disordered female offenders', in *Women, Madness and the Law*, W. Chan, D. Chunn and R. Menzies. London: Glasshouse Press.

Kitsuse, J.I. and. Cicourel, A.V. (1963) 'A note on the use of official statistics', *Social Problems*, 11: 131–8.

Lacey, N. (2007) *Escaping the Prisoner's Dilemma*, Hamlyn Lecture, London School of Economics.

Law Council of Australia (2008) *Policing in the Shadow of Australia's Anti-Terror Laws: Law Council Presentation to Clarke Inquiry Public Forum*, Secondary Law Council of Australia. Accessed 24 February 2010, at: http://www. haneefcaseinquiry.gov.au/www/inquiry/rwpattach.nsf/VAP/

Lippmann, W. (1922) *Public Opinion.* New York: Harcourt, Brace and Company.

Loader, I. (2006) 'Fall of the "Platonic Guardians"', *British Journal of Criminology*, 46(4): 561–86.

Loughnan, A. (2005) 'The role of lay understanding of mental illness in mental incapacity defences', *Criminal Justice Matters* 61 (Mental Health): 36–7.

Ly, L. and Howard, D. (2004) *Statistics of Mentally Disordered Offenders 2003.* London: Home Office Research Development Statistics.

Maden, A. (2007) *Treating Violence: A Guide to Risk Management in Mental Health.* Oxford: Oxford University Press.

Maguire, M. and Kynch, J. (2000) *Public Perceptions and Victims' Experiences of Victim Support: Findings from the 1998 British Crime Survey.* London: Home Office Research Development Statistics.

Manderson, D. (2008) 'Not Yet: Aboriginal People and the Deferral of the Rule of Law', *Arena* 30(29).

Mason, T. and Mercer, D. (1999) *A Sociology of the Mentally Disordered Offender.* Essex: Pearson Education Limited.

Mawby, R. and Walklate, S. (1994) *Critical Victimology: International Perspectives.* London: Sage Publications.

Mead, G.H. (1918) 'The Psychology of Punitive Justice,' *American Journal of Sociology,* 23(5).

Mead, G.H. (1934) *Mind, Self, and Society: From the Standpoint of a Social Behaviorist.* Chicago: The University of Chicago Press.

Mental Health Review Tribunal (undated) 'Practice Direction – Mental Health Cases'. Retrieved 11 September 2009, from: http://www.mhrt. org.uk/Documents/3nov08/TribunalJudiciaryPracticeDirectionHealth EducationandSocialCareChamberMentalHealthCases.pdf

Ministry of Justice (2009) 'Sara Payne appointed independent Victims' Champion,' Retrieved 27 September, 2009, from http://www.justice.gov. uk/news/newsrelease260109a.htm.

Mohan, D., Murray, K. *et al.* (1998) 'Mental health review tribunal decisions in restricted hospital order cases at one medium secure unit, 1992–1996,' *Criminal Behaviour and Mental Health* 8: 57–65.

Monahan, J. (2004) 'The Future of Violence Risk Management' in *The Future of Imprisonment*, M. Tonry. Oxford: Oxford University Press.

Monahan, J. and H. Steadman, (eds) (1994) 'Violence and Mental Disorder: Developments in Risk Assessment' in *The John D. and Catherine T. MacArthur Foundation Series on Mental Health and Development*, Chicago: University of Chicago Press.

Monahan, J., Steadman, H.J. *et al.* (2001) *Rethinking Risk Assessment: The MacArthur Study of Mental Disorder and Violence*, Oxford: Oxford University Press.

Morgan, R. and A. Sanders (1999) *The Uses of Victim Statements.* London: Home Office Research Development and Statistics Directorate.

Mullen, P. (2002) 'Introduction' in *Care of the Mentally Disordered Offender in the Community*, A. Buchanan. Oxford: Oxford University Press.

Nacro (2007) *Black Communities, Mental Health and the Criminal Justice System,* London: Nacro.

Newburn, T. (2002) 'Atlantic crossings: "Policy transfer" and crime control in the USA and Britain,' *Punishment and Society* 4(2): 165–94.

Newburn, T. and Jones, T. (2005) 'Symbolic politics and penal populism: the long shadow of Willie Horton,' *Crime Media Culture* 1(1): 72–87.

Newburn, T. and Merry, S. (1990) *Keeping in Touch: Police-Victim Communication in Two Areas*. London: Home Office, p. 59.

Newburn, T. and Stanko, E. (1994) *Just Boys Doing Business*. London: Routledge.

O'Malley, P. (1999) 'Volatile and contradictory punishment,' *Theoretical Criminology* 3(2): 175–96.

O'Malley, P. (2004b) 'Globalising Risk? Distinguishing Style of "Neoliberal" Criminal Justice in Australia and the USA' in *Criminal Justice and Political Cultures: National and International Dimensions of Crime Control*, T. Newburn and R. Sparks. Cullompton: Willan Publishing.

Oliver, W. and Marion, N. (2008) 'Political Party Platforms: Symbolic Politics and Criminal Justice Policy,' *Criminal Justice Policy Review* 19(4): 397–413.

Padfield, N. (2002) *Beyond the Tariff: Human Rights and the Release of Life Sentence Prisoners*, Cullompton: Willan Publishing.

Padfield, N., Liebling, A. and Arnold, H. (2003) 'Discretion and the release of life sentence prisoners' in *Exercising Discretion: Decision-making in the Criminal Justice System and Beyond*, L. Gelsthorpe and N. Padfield. Cullompton: Willan Publishing.

Peay, J. (1989) *Tribunals on Trial: A Study of Decision-making under the Mental Health Act 1983*. Oxford: Clarendon.

Peay, J. (1993) 'A criminological perspective – the influence of fashion and theory on practice and disposal: life chances in the criminological tombola' in *Mentally Disordered Offenders in the Era of Community Care*, W. Watson and A. Grounds. Cambridge: Cambridge University Press.

Peay, J. (2002) 'Mentally Disordered Offenders, Mental Health, and Crime' in *The Oxford Handbook of Criminology*, M. Maguire, R. Morgan and R. Reiner. Oxford: Oxford University Press.

Peay, J. (2003) *Decisions and Dilemmas: Working with Mental Health Law*. Oxford: Hart Publishing.

Peay, J. (2004) *Submission to Joint Scrutiny Committee into the Draft Mental Health Bill 2004*, DMH 407, Ev 1161.

Perkins, E. (2003) *Decision-Making in Mental Health Review Tribunals*. London: Policy Studies Institute.

Pezzani, R. (2007) 'The Re-call of Conditionally Discharged Patients – the breadth of the Secretary of State's discretion,' *Journal of Mental Health Law* (November).

Pilgrim, D. (1991) 'Rhetoric and nihilism in mental health policy: a reply to Chapman *et al* CSP Issue 32,' (34): 106–13.

Potts, J. (1995) 'Risk Assessment and Management: A Home Office Perspective' in *Psychiatric Patient Violence: Risk & Response*, J. Crichton. London: Duckworth.

Power, M. (1999) *The Audit Society: Rituals of Verification*. Oxford: Oxford University Press.

Pratt, J. (2005) 'Elias, punishment and decivilization' in *The New Punitiveness: Trends, Theories, Perspectives*, J. Pratt, D. Brown, M. Brown, S. Hallsworth and W. Morrison. Cullompton: Willan Publishing.

Pratt, J., Brown, D. *et al.* (2005) 'Introduction' in *The New Punitiveness: Trends, theories, perspectives*, J. Pratt, D. Brown, M. Brown, S. Hallsworth and W. Morrison. Cullompton: Willan Publishing.

Prins, H. (1993) 'Offender-patients: the people nobody owns' in *The Mentally Disordered Offender in an Era of Community Care*, W. Watson and A. Grounds. Cambridge: Cambridge University Press.

Public Administration Select Committee (2007) *Politics and Administration: Ministers and Civil Servants*. London: Public Administration Select Committee.

Reiner, R. (2007) *Law and Order: An Honest Citizen's Guide to Crime and Control*. Cambridge: Polity Press.

Richards, S. (2006) 'Here we go again – but why does a Labour government fuel this hysteria over crime?', *The Independent*, 20 June 2006.

Richardson, E. and Freiberg, A. (2004) 'Protecting dangerous offenders from the community: the application of protective sentencing laws in Victoria', *Criminal Justice* 4(1): 81–102.

Richardson, G. (1993) *Law, process and custody: prisoners and patients*. London: Weidenfeld & Nicholson.

Richardson, G. (1999) *Review of the Mental Health Act 1983: Report of the Expert Committee*. London: Department of Health.

Richardson, G. (2005) 'The European convention and mental health law in England and Wales: Moving beyond process?,' *International Journal of Law & Psychiatry* 28: 127–39.

Richardson, G. (2007) 'Balancing autonomy and risk: A failure of nerve in England and Wales?,' *International Journal of Law & Psychiatry* 30(1): 71–80.

Richardson, G. and Thorold, O. (1999) 'Law as a Rights Protector: Assessing the Mental Health Act 1983' in *Law Without Enforcement: Integrating Mental Health and Justice*, N. Eastman and J. Peay. Oxford: Hart Publishing.

Robinson, R. and Scott-Moncrieff, L. (2005) 'Making Sense of Bournewood', *Journal of Mental Health Law*.

Rock, P. (1986) *A View from the Shadows: The Ministry of the Solicitor General of Canada and the Making of the Justice for Victims of Crime Initiative*. Oxford: Clarendon Press.

Rock, P. (1996) 'The Inquiry and Victims' Families' in *Inquiries After Homicide*, J. Peay. London: Gerald Duckworth & Co, pp. 101–19.

Rock, P. (2002) 'On Becoming a Victim' in *New Visions of Crime Victims*, C. Hoyle and R. Young. Oxford: Hart Publishing.

Rock, P. (2004) *Constructing Victims' Rights: The Home Office, New Labour, and Victims*. Oxford: Oxford University Press.

Rock, P. (2004b) 'Victims, Prosecutors and the State in Nineteenth Century England and Wales,' *Criminal Justice* 4(4): 331–54.

Rock, P. (2008) 'The Treatment of Victims in England and Wales', *Policing* 2: 110–19.

Rose, N. (2000) 'Government and Control,' *British Journal of Criminology*, 40: 321–39.

Rose, N. (2002) 'Society, Madness and Control' in *Care of the Mentally Disordered Offender in the Community*, A. Buchanan. Oxford: Oxford University Press.

Rose, N. (2002b) 'At Risk of Madness' in *Embracing Risk: the changing culture of insurance and responsibility*, T. B. J. Simon. Chicago: The University of Chicago Press.

Rose, N. (2004) *Society, Madness and Control*, Paper at a conference of the Department of Forensic Mental Health, Institute of Psychiatry.

Ryan, M. (2005) 'Engaging with punitive attitudes towards crime and punishment: some strategic lessons from England and Wales' in *The New Punitiveness: Trends, theories, perspectives*, J. Pratt, D. Brown, M. Brown, S. Hallsworth and W. Morrison. Cullompton: Willan Publishing.

Sanderson, N. (2009) 'Making sense of new sentences', *Prison Service News (Magazine)*: Her Majesty's Prison Service.

Schoenholtz, A.I. and Hojaiban, J. (2008) *International Migration and Anti-Terrorism Laws and Policies: Balancing Security and Refugee Protection*, Volume 4. Washington D.C.: Institute for the Study of International Migration, Walsh School of Foreign Service, Georgetown University.

Scott, M.B. and Lyman, S. (1968) 'Accounts,' *American Sociological Review* 33(1): 46–62.

Seddon, T. (2007) *Punishment and Madness: Governing prisoners with mental health problems*. London: Routledge-Cavendish.

Shapland, J., Willmore, J. and Duff, P. (1985) *Victims in the Criminal Justice System*. Aldershot: Gower.

Shea, P. (2003) *Risk Assessment*, Mental Health Review Tribunal of NSW: unpublished.

Shultz, A. (1967) *The Phenomenology of the Social World*. Evanston: Northwestern University Press.

Simon, J. (2007) *Implications of the War on Crime*, British Society of Criminology Annual Conference, London School of Economics.

Simon, J. and Feeley, M. (1995) 'The New Penology and Public Discourse on Crime' in *Punishment and Social Control*, T. Blomberg and S. Cohen. New York: Aldine de Gruyter.

Simpson, A., McKenna, B., Moskowitz, A., Skipworth, J. and Barry-Walsh, J. (2003) *Myth and Reality: the Relationship between Mental Illness and Homicide in New Zealand*. Auckland: Health Research Council of New Zealand.

Solomon, E. (2005) 'Editorial', *Criminal Justice Matters* 61 (Mental Health): 3.

South, N., Smith, R. *et al*. (2005) 'Mental health, social order, system disorder', *Criminal Justice Matters* 61 (Mental Health): 4–5.

Sparks, R. (2000) 'Risk and blame in criminal justice controversies: British press coverage and official discourse on prison security (1993–6)' in

Dangerous Offenders: Punishment and Social Order, M. Brown and J. Pratt. London: Sage.

Stanko, E. (2000) 'Victims R Us: The life history of "fear of crime" and the politicisation of violence', in *Crime, Risk and Insecurity*, T. Hope and R. Sparks. London: Routledge.

Stenson, K. and Edwards, A. (2004) "Policy transfer in local crime control: beyond naïve emulation" in *Criminal Justice and Political Cultures: National and international dimensions of crime control*, T. Newburn and R. Sparks. Cullompton: Willan Publishing.

Strange, C. and Bashford, A. (eds) (2003) *Isolation: Places and Practices of Exclusion*. London: Routledge.

Strauss, A.L. (1963) 'The hospital and its negotiated order' in *The Hospital in Modern Society*, E. Freidson. New York: Free Press of Glencoe.

Street, R. (1998) *The Restricted Hospital Order: From Court to Community*. London: Research and Statistics Directorate, Home Office.

Stubbs, J. and Tolmie, J. (2005) 'Defending Battered Women on Charges of Homicide' in *Women, Madness and the Law*, W. Chan, D. Chunn and R. Menzies. London: Glasshouse Press.

Szasz, T.S. (1974) *The Myth of Mental Illness: Foundations of a Theory of Personal Conduct*. New York: Harper & Row.

Szmukler, G. (2005) "Book review of *Release decision making: Assessing violence risk in mental health, forensic, and correctional settings*, by Webster & Hucker, Hamilton, ON.,' *The Journal of Forensic Psychiatry and Psychology* 16(4): 774–76.

Tait, L. and Lester, H. (2005) 'Encouraging user involvement in mental health services,' *Advances in Psychiatric Treatment* 11: 168–75.

Taylor, P. and Gunn, J. (1999) 'Homicides by people with mental illness: myth and reality,' *British Journal of Psychiatry* 174: 9–14.

The Zito Trust (2006) 'About the Zito Trust', 1 April. Retrieved 15 October 2007, from http://www.zitotrust.co.uk/.

Thomas, D. (2003) 'Judicial discretion in sentencing' in *Exercising Discretion: Decision-making in the Criminal Justice System and Beyond*, L. Gelsthorpe and N. Padfield. Cullompton: Willan Publishing.

Thomas, J.M. (1986) 'The Interpretive Method in the Study of Legal Decision-Making,' *Washington and Lee Law Review* 43(4): 1267–91.

Thornicroft, G. (2006) *Shunned*. Oxford: Oxford University Press.

Verdun-Jones, S.N. (1989) 'Sentencing the Partly Mad and the Partly Bad: the Case of the Hospital Order in England & Wales,' *International Journal of Law & Psychiatry*, 12: 1–27.

Von Hentig, H. (1940) 'Remarks on the interaction of perpetrator and victim', *Journal of Criminal Law and Criminology*, 31: 303–9.

Walklate, S. (2007) *Imagining the Victim of Crime*. Maidenhead: Open University Press.

Walters, R. (2005) 'Boycott, resistance and the role of the deviant voice,' *Criminal Justice Matters* 62 (Winter): 6–7.

Weaver, M. (2005) 'Freed foreign prisoner committed murder', *The Guardian*, 29 June.

Wolpert, J. and Wolpert, E. (1976) 'The relocation of released mental patients into residential communities', *Policy Sciences*, 7: 31–51.

Young, J. (2007) *The Vertigo of Late Modernity*. London: Sage.

Zagor, M. (2006) 'Uncertainty and Exclusion: Detention of Aliens and the High Court,' *Federal Law Review*, 34: 127–60.

Zedner, L. (2002) 'Victims' in *The Oxford Handbook of Criminology*, M. Maguire, R. Morgan and R. Reiner. Oxford: Oxford University Press.

Index

accountability
  democracy and 176–7, 180–1
  internal processes 45
  Mental Health Unit 48–54
  overview 44–5
  public perception of 22, 67
  recall 64
  Tribunal 54–6, 84
  uncertainty and 15
actuarial justice 13–14
actuarial risk assessment 51
adjournments 55
alcohol use 66
Anti-Terrorism, Crime and Security
  Act 2001 3
Ashworth 46
asylum seekers 3, 5, 170
Australia
  executive discretion 81
  forensic psychiatry 10–14
  human rights 161–2
  Migration Act 1958 3, 4
  terrorism 3–4
away days 86

behavioural changes 49–50
Blunkett, David 139
Broadmoor 46

burden of proof 145

cabinet ministers 2
care in the community 167
Carlin, P. 165–6
case law 61
Caseworker Manual 68–9
cautiousness
  executive discretion 74–5, 79, 84,
    97–101
  Tribunal 147–9
Christie, N. 18
Clarke, Charles 157
clinical decisions
  basis for 132
  detention criteria 61, 144, 155
  executive discretion and 85–9
  forensic psychiatry 10–14
  'Guidance for Responsible
    Medical Officers' 58
  interpretation 50
  overruled 64, 66, 69–70, 88
  recall 61–2, 153
  role of 94–7
Clunis, Christopher 96
Colombo, T. 132–3
Commonwealth of Nations 1–2
compulsory treatment

Mental Health Act 1983 46
    purpose of 64
    vs patient care 167–9
conditional release
    determinations 59
    licences 6–7
    monitoring 48–9
    numbers of 46
    recall 60–7
    supervision 52
contractual arrangements 165–6
control orders 170
counter-hegemonic research 36
Criminal Justice Act 1948 6
criminal justice decision making 2,
    30–2

dangerous offenders 6–7, 10–14, 16,
    171
de Sola Pool, I. 106
decision frame 31, 34
decision-making 30–2, 106–7
delays 154, 159
Dell, S. 32, 48, 61, 64, 71, 84, 90–1,
    154
detention criteria
    burden of proof 145
    cautiousness 74–5, 79, 84, 97–101,
        147–9
    determinations 58–60
    differences in 84–5
    Mental Health Act 1983 83, 146
    MM case 61–3
    overview 182
    unequal rates of discharge 55–6
    Winterwerp criteria 61, 144, 155
deterrence 77
diplomatic relations 137–8
discharge applications 47–8, 91–2
    determinations 58–60
discretion *see also* executive
    discretion
    concept of 79
    importance of 5, 80
discretionary life sentences 6, 8, 83

Discretionary Lifer Panels 53
documentary evidence 38
Domestic Violence (Crime and
    Victims) Act 2004 113, 123, 124
double jeopardy 80
Douglas, M. 15, 16
drug use 66–7

Edelman, M. 72–3
European Convention on Human
    Rights 1, 25, 143–4, 160
European Court of Human Rights
    160
    Winterwerp criteria 61, 144, 155
    X v UK 1 25
executive discretion
    alternatives to 81
    attitudes to 89–92
    clinical decisions and 85–9
    criticisms of 79–80, 177–9
    not absolute 9–10
    operational differences 4–8
    other actors and 85–9
    overview 176–7, 181–2
    practice 32–5
    public policy 2–4
    public protection agenda 171–3
    restriction orders 26
    structural advantage 84–5

fair hearings 1
families of restricted patients 117–18,
    132–3, 175–6
fear of crime 72, 131
fear of patients 133–4
Feeley, M. 13
flexibility 34
forensic psychiatry 10–14

Gardiner, J.A. 73
Garland, D. 69, 77
Gelsthorpe, L. 79
Genders, E. 37, 40, 41
Gibney, M.J. 3
Giddens, A. 14–15

Goffman, E. 15, 26–7, 164
Gouldner, A. 41
Grounds, A. 32, 48, 61, 64, 71, 84, 90–1, 154
group behaviour 73
'Guidance for Responsible Medical Officers' 58
Gunn, J. 16, 131

Haneef, Mohammed 3–4
hate crime laws 18
Hawkins, K. 30, 33, 34, 53
Home Office Research and Statistics Directorate 80
Home Secretary, see Secretary of State
homicides 16
hospital security levels 46–7
human rights
    external pressures 156–63
    impeding progress 158
    legal and procedural obligations 151–2
    Mental Health Act 1983 167–9
    overview 143–4
    patient care vs treatment 167–9
    patients' rights 149–50
    prior to 1983 145–6
    prior to 1998 3
    vs public protection 173–4
    public protection agenda 10
    responses to 159–63
    responsibility for 155–6
    role of 179–81
    safeguards 144–5, 146–7
    stigma 166–7
    symbolic value 163–9
    theory and practice 150–1
    treatment and 164–5
Human Rights Act 1998 10, 79, 160–1

ideal victim 18–19, 109, 123, 132
Immigration, Asylum and Nationality Act 2006 3

indefinite detention 5, 6–7, 145, 181
independence 1–2
indeterminate sentences 6–7
insider experience 40–2
institutionalization 100
International Convention on Civil and Political Rights 1
interviews 38–9

Jacobs, J.B. 18
Jones, R. 73–4
justifiable risk 68–9

K v United Kingdom (1998) 40 BMLR 20 61, 153

leaked information 52–3
leave applications
    determinations 58–60
    performance indicators 47
    recall 60–7
legal decision-making 2, 30–2
legitimacy
    Australia 4
    as essential element 107–8
    legalization 97–101
    MM case 61–3
    political interest 22, 96, 180
Liberty 109
licences 6–7
Liebling, A. 83
Lippmann, W. 106, 135
London bomb attacks 2005 5

Mason, T. 101
Mead, G.H. 73, 77
media attention 76–7, 106, 115–17
    adverse publicity 138–41
medication, risk and 71
Mental Health Act 1959 25, 69–70, 144
Mental Health Act 1983
    civil provisions 9
    compulsory treatment 46
    detention criteria 83, 146

human rights 167–9
recall 60–1
risk assessment 103, 148, 149
Secretary of State powers 44
Mental Health Act 2007 113
Mental Health Alliance 122
Mental Health Review Tribunal
    cautiousness 147–9
    delays 154
    discharge numbers 46, 146–7
    independence 33–4, 56
    Mental Health Unit and 82–4,
        99–100
    monitoring 54–6
    powers of 8, 9–10, 25–6, 143–6
    prior to 1983 145–6, 181–2
    recall 60
    research 32, 35
    transfer decisions 80
    victim involvement 125, 126–7,
        128–30
Mental Health Unit
    Caseworker Manual 68–9
    confidence in 44
    delays 159
    dual responsibilities 44–5
    Mental Health Review Tribunal
        and 82–4, 99–100
    Ministry of Justice 28–9
    professional expertise 31–2
Mental Health Unit Casework
    Guide 33, 87
mental hospitals 26–7
mentally disordered offenders
    contested category 28
    terminology 23
Mercer, D. 101
methodology 37–43
ministerial protection 137–8
Ministry of Justice 28–9
MM case 61–3
modernity thesis 14–15
Mohan, D. 86
Monahan, J. 12
monarchy 2

monitoring
    internal processes 45
    of Mental Health Review
        Tribunal 54–6
    by Mental Health Unit 48–54
Mullen, P. 13

New South Wales (NSW) 10–14, 161–2
Newburn, T. 73–4

offending history 50
open hospitals 46
organizational contingencies 48

Padfield, N. 28, 79, 83, 149
Parole Board 7, 83, 149
patients
    care vs treatment 167–9, 171–3
    confidentiality 111–12, 113, 114,
        121–2
    families 117–18, 132–3, 175–6
    monitoring 48–54
    patient/public divide 132–6,
        174–6
    population 44, 45–8
    progress 33, 145, 158
    psychiatrists and 27
    public protection 27–8
    rights 173–4
    risk to 132–3
    terminology 23–4
    victimization 132–3
    welfare 134–5
Peay, J 15, 32, 165, 181–2
penal communications 157–8
performance indicators 47–8
Perkins, E. 148
phenomenology 31
Player, E. 37, 40, 41
policy
    penal communications 157–8
    politicization 74, 92, 107–8, 136
    rule of law 2–4
    symbolic politics 72–8, 163–9,
        173–4, 178

victim involvement 16–17, 21–3, 108–10
policy-relevant research 36–7
Potter, K. 18
preventive detention 6
Probation Service 111–12, 113, 114–15, 124
proportionality 7–8
psychiatric evidence
 see clinical decisions
the public
 adverse publicity 138–41
 concept of 115–17
 demands of 136–7
 explanation of 35
 interpretation 172
 overview 105, 141–2
 patient/public divide 132–6, 174–6
 patient welfare and 134–5
 public interest, definition 106–8
 social rules 135–6
 victim status 120–5
 victims 118–20
public perception
 confidence 53, 77
 media attention 76–7, 116–17
 surveys 21
 symbolic politics 31, 72–8, 163–9, 173–4, 178
public policy 2–4
public protection agenda 56–7, 171–3
punitiveness 130–2

qualifications 57
quality of service 165–6

R (on the application of MM) v Secretary of State for the Home Dept and Five Boroughs NHS Trust [2007] EWCA (iv 687) 61–3
Rampton 46
recall
 accountability 64
 case law 61–3
 clinical decisions 61–2, 64, 69–70, 153
 conditional release 60–7
 as failure 83–4
 increase in 63
 justification for 64–6, 153
 leave applications 60–7
 Mental Health Act 1983 60–1
 Mental Health Review Tribunal 60
 power to 60–1
 procedural safeguards 154–5
 Secretary of State powers 60–7
reciprocity 41–3
reconvictions 101–2
refugees 3, 5, 170
rehabilitation 6, 69, 167–9, 172–3
Reid, John 157
Reiner, R. 7, 72
reintegration 7
relapse indicators 70
restorative justice 178
restricted patients
 see patients
restriction orders 25–7, 164–5
Richardson, G. 146, 160
risk
 concept of 14–16
 terminology 15
risk assessment
 approaches to 101–2
 clinical decisions 94–7
 determining risk 58–60, 67–72
 interpretation 50–1
 legality 97–101
 limitations of 12–13, 93
 Mental Health Act 1983 103, 148, 149
 subjective assessments 56–7
risk management 14
risk, to patients 132–3
Rock, P. 19, 20, 21, 27, 122–3, 160–1
Rose, N. 8, 12, 13, 16, 71

Sanderson, N. 6–7
secondary victimization 117–18
Secretary of State
  David Blunkett 139
  Charles Clarke 157
  John Reid 157
  protection of 136–8
  statements 48
Secretary of State powers
  discharge applications 91–2
  human rights 168
  Mental Health Act 1983 44
  mental health offenders 8
  public protection mandate 29
  recall 60–7
  terrorism 3
  Tribunal and 144–5
Seddon, T. 13–14
sensitive cases 136–41
sentencing laws, reform of 6–7
separation of powers 1, 9–10, 81,
  170, 177
serious harm 68–9
service providers/users 163–4
Shulman, I. 106
Simon, J. 13, 72
social behaviour 73
social values, medical processes and
  26
stigma 19–20, 163–4, 166–7
Street, R. 32
subjective assessments 8, 14–15,
  56–7, 88
suicide 16
surround concept 34
surveys 21
Sutcliffe, Peter 138–9, 140
symbolic interactionists 31
symbolic politics 72–8, 163–9, 173–4,
  178
Szasz, T.S. 26
Szmuckler, G. 13

Taylor, P. 16, 131
terminology 15, 23–4, 163–4

terrorism 3, 5, 170
therapeutic intervention 8
Thomas, J.M. 107
transfer decisions 55, 80, 97–8
  determinations 58–60
treatment, purpose of 62, 64
treatment vs patient care 167–9,
  171–3
trust 52, 88

unlawful detention 1
USA, hate crime laws 18

vengeance 122–3
victim involvement
  limiting 128–30
  overview 178–9
  policy 16–17, 108–10
  political interest 21–3
  punitive effect 130–2
  resistance to 126–8
  Tribunal 125, 126–7, 129–30
  views on 125–6
Victim Personal Statements 130
victimization 132–3
victims
  criminal justice role 16–17,
    108–10
  families of restricted patients
    117–18, 175–6
  fear of patients 133–4
  human rights 180
  ideal victim 18–19, 109, 123,
    132
  peace of mind 110–12
  political interest 21–3
  proportionality of the choice of
    harm 113–15
  the public 118–20, 175
  stigma 19–20
  surveys 21
  victim contact 76, 112–13, 124–5
  victim status 120–5
Victims Liaison Officers 124–5
voluntary readmission 61

Walklate, S. 109
Winterwerp v. Netherlands 6301/73
  (1979) ECHR 4 61, 144,
  155
women, as victims 18
Woolf, Lord 94

X v United Kingdom (1981) 4 EHRR
  181 25, 144
Yorkshire Ripper 138–9, 140

Zedner, L. 20
Zito Trust 96, 120–1, 122, 126, 130–1